THE LIBRARY
ST. MARY'S COLLEGE OF MARYLAND
ST. MARY'S CITY, MARYLAND 20686

D0918545

DIVINE EMPTINESS
AND
HISTORICAL FULLNESS

A BUDDHIST-JEWISH-CHRISTIAN CONVERSATION
WITH
MASAO ABE

DIVINE EMPTINESS

AND

HISTORICAL FULLNESS

Edited by
CHRISTOPHER IVES

TRINITY PRESS INTERNATIONAL
Valley Forge, Pennsylvania

First Edition 1995
Trinity Press International
P.O. Box 851
Valley Forge, PA 19482-0851

All rights reserved. No part of this publication may be reproduced, stored in a retrieval system, or transmitted in any form or by any means, electronic, mechanical, photocopying, recording, or otherwise, without the prior permission of the publisher, Trinity Press International.

© 1995 Trinity Press International

Where noted, Scripture quotations are from the King James Version of the Bible and from the Revised Standard Version of the Bible, copyrighted 1946, 1952, © 1971, 1973, by the Division of Christian Education of the National Council of the Churches of Christ in the U.S.A., used by permission.

The section on pages 210–12 entitled "From Modern Nihilism to Postmodern Belief in God" is from *Does God Exist? An Answer for Today* by Hans Küng (New York: Doubleday, 1980) and is used by permission of Bantam Doubleday Publishing Group, Inc.

"Kenotic God and Dynamic Sunyata" by Masao Abe originally appeared in *The Emptying God: A Buddhist-Jewish-Christian Conversation*, ed. John B. Cobb, Jr. and Christopher Ives (Maryknoll, N.Y.: Orbis Books, 1990) and is used here by permission.

Cover design by Jim Gerhard

Library of Congress Cataloging-in-Publication Data

Abe, Masao, 1915–
    Divine emptiness and historical fullness : a Buddhist-Jewish-Christian conversation with Masao Abe / edited by Christopher Ives.
        p. cm.
    Includes bibliographical references and index.
    ISBN 1-56338-122-2
    1. Abe, Masao, 1915– . 2. Christianity and other religions—Buddhism.
3. Buddhism—Relations—Christianity. 4. Judaism—Relations—Buddhism.
5. Buddhism—Relations—Judaism. 6. Sunyata. 7. Incarnation. 8. Holocaust
(Jewish theology) I. Ives, Christopher, 1954– . II. Title.
BR128.B8A24   1995
291.1'72—dc20   95-13764
                                                                    CIP

Printed in the United States of America on acid-free paper
95 96 97 98 99 00 6 5 4 3 2 1

CONTENTS

II. RESPONSES TO MASAO ABE

III. A REJOINDER
Masao Abe

God and History
Sunyata, Trinity, and Community
Karl Rahner in Dialogue
Sunyata and Ethics
The Reversibility of Time

IV. FURTHER DIALOGUE WITH HANS KÜNG AND WOLFHART PANNENBERG

A NOTE ON ORTHOGRAPHY

With the general English reader in mind, the editor and publisher decided not to use diacritical marks for foreign technical terms in this volume. Scholars familiar with the original terms in Sanskrit and Japanese will know the proper diacritical marks, and those who are unfamiliar with these languages will in all likelihood find diacritics a distraction. The editor and publisher realize that eliminating diacritics takes away from the distinctiveness and specificity of the Sanskrit and Japanese terms and might displease those who are from cultures in which these languages have central linguistic and religious importance.

EDITOR'S PREFACE

This book parallels in large part the format of *The Emptying God: A Buddhist-Jewish-Christian Conversation* (Maryknoll, N.Y.: Orbis Books, 1990), which consisted of Masao Abe's "Kenotic God and Dynamic Sunyata," responses by seven theologians (Thomas Altizer, Eugene Borowitz, John B. Cobb, Jr., Catherine Keller, Jürgen Moltmann, Schubert Ogden, and David Tracy), and Abe's rejoinder. *The Emptying God* generated enthusiastic responses from its audience and contributed significantly to ongoing Buddhist-Christian dialogue.

The discussions initiated by that volume have continued in two arenas. First, essays by four of the seven original theologians (Thomas Altizer, Eugene Borowitz, John Cobb, and Catherine Keller) in response to Abe's rejoinder in *The Emptying God* were published in the 1993 issue (Volume 13) of *Buddhist-Christian Studies* together with another, final rejoinder by Abe and an "Editor's Note" by David W. Chappell. Second, for this follow-up volume to *The Emptying God*, Christopher Ives, Sandra B. Lubarsky, Heinrich Ott, Richard L. Rubenstein, Marjorie Hewitt Suchocki, and Hans Waldenfels agreed to serve as new respondents to the original essay, "Kenotic God and Dynamic Sunyata." Their responses, together with Abe's rejoinder, constitute the middle section of this book. The final section of the book consists of responses by and rejoinders to Hans Küng and Wolfhart Pannenberg, both of whom had taken up Abe's essay in other contexts.

The responses by Richard Rubenstein and Wolfhart Pannenberg and Abe's responses to them were first presented in the Purdue University

Interfaith Dialogue Series. The Rubenstein-Abe dialogue took place on November 11, 1992, at Indiana University–Purdue University at Indianapolis. The Pannenberg-Abe dialogue took place on April 23, 1992, at Earlham College. This dialogue series was directed by Donald W. Mitchell of Purdue University and was funded by the Lilly Endowment, Inc.

Hans Küng's response was first published in *Buddhist Emptiness and Christian Trinity*, ed. Roger Corless and Paul F. Knitter (New York: Paulist Press, 1990). The essay was translated by Farrell D. Graves, Jr., and the section entitled "From Modern Nihilism to Postmodern Belief in God" has been excerpted from *Does God Exist?* Heinrich Ott's response was translated by Armin Münch and Nancy Bedford in Germany. David Cockerham revised the first draft of "Beyond Buddhism and Christianity: 'Dazzling Darkness.'" Professor Gishin Tokiwa of Hanazono College provided assistance in tracking down bibliographical information for several of the citations in Abe's essay.

John Cobb of the School of Theology at Claremont provided important guidance in the early stages of this project, and Paul Knitter of Xavier University was instrumental in securing the publisher's interest.

Carol Avery at the University of Puget Sound typed Abe's rejoinder and several other sections of the book and provided editorial assistance. Her contribution was made possible by a grant from the University of Puget Sound.

At Trinity International, Hal Rast, Publisher, and Laura G. Barrett, Managing Editor, shepherded this volume along with highly appreciated professionalism and warmth.

Christopher Ives

Introduction

DAVID W. CHAPPELL

As the foremost contemporary representative of the Kyoto School of philosophy, Masao Abe is both a major Japanese Buddhist critic of Western philosophy and religion, and a leading dialogue partner. Although his professional career in Japan was spent teaching Western philosophy to Japanese students (1946–1980), he is even more famous in the West where he has often lived, first as a student at Columbia University (1955–1957) and later as a visiting professor at ten different American universities.[1] What began as an occasional teaching semester in America in the mid-1960s turned into a two-year appointment at Princeton (1977–1979). Shortly thereafter Abe retired from his main academic position at Nara University of Education (1952–1980) and moved to America in order to be a "visiting" professor full-time. Accordingly, unlike his contemporary Japanese colleagues in the Kyoto School, Abe is unique in his constant journeys to America and Europe to challenge Christian and Jewish thinkers in their own language and on their home turf.

Abe's "second career" of studying and teaching in the West includes approximately two decades of living in America during the past forty years, and can be compared only with D. T. Suzuki in its biculturalism and impact. Not only has Abe's presence in the West provided a chance for living interchange, but he has attracted Western thinkers by his effort to deepen and correct their views by applying Buddhist insights and values to Western concepts and symbols. It is now thirty years since Abe provoked public dialogue with his English essay on "Buddhism and Christianity as a Problem of Today," yet Abe is still on center stage as the major Buddhist leader in Buddhist-Christian dialogue. More recently, because of his reflections on the Holocaust he has also been at the forefront of Buddhist-Jewish interchange.

Although D. T. Suzuki was a more prolific writer than Abe, Suzuki's writings dealt almost entirely with Buddhism. Abe's uniqueness rests not primarily in being a Buddhist thinker nor in bringing the message of Buddhism to the West, but in applying the insights and practices of Buddhism in a critical and constructive way to the philosophical and religious traditions of the West. Far more than Suzuki, Abe has assimilated the Western religious and philosophical traditions and can use the West's technical vocabulary and major principles to engage and challenge its contemporary thinkers. In a modern twist on the Socratic method, Abe has absorbed the language and ideas of the West and then has turned Westerners back to reflect on themselves by asking Buddhist questions of Western materials. This is an astonishing intellectual feat, as this collection of essays shows. Accordingly, Abe stands almost alone as a Buddhist thinker who is able to enter into Western discussions on the West's own terms and, rather than simply rejecting Western ideas or merely replacing them with Buddhist ones, to clothe Buddhist insights in Western garb in order to enliven Western thought to new possibilities in its own tradition.

The intellectual and physical effort and skill that Abe has spent in journeying so frequently to the West has been deeply appreciated by many theologians who welcomed his fresh challenges at a time when their discipline has often been characterized by redundancy. Accordingly, Abe has become a model of intellectual biculturalism, as he has constructively challenged Western thought to discover universal truths cherished in Asia, and has thereby stimulated, deepened, and enlarged Western sensibilities.

This volume consists of four parts. Part I is a reprint of Abe's major theological statement, "Kenotic God and Dynamic Sunyata." Part II contains articles by six distinguished Jewish, Christian, and Buddhist thinkers—Richard L. Rubenstein, Sandra B. Lubarsky, Heinrich Ott, Marjorie Hewitt Suchocki, Hans Waldenfels, and Christopher Ives. Part III presents Abe's collective response to those writers. Part IV contains articles by Hans Küng and Wolfhart Pannenberg, whose articles are followed by separate responses by Abe. I will briefly highlight some of the distinctive arguments of each contribution and will conclude with some reflections on the project as a whole.

JEWISH-BUDDHIST DIALOGUE

Abe's theological essay has been circulated and enlarged over the last decade, and since 1990 has included an important statement on the Holocaust. This initiated a dialogue with Eugene Borowitz that continued in a variety of formats.[2] In this volume the Jewish dialogue partners are Sandra B. Lubarsky and Richard L. Rubenstein. Both Borowitz and Rubenstein, who have written extensively about the significance of the Holocaust for Jewish life, appreciate how Abe approaches the Holocaust by agreeing with the horror and shared responsibility for its occurrence. However, when Abe revealed in his "Rejoinder" to Borowitz how the Buddhist doctrine of karma implicates all people in the Holocaust,[3] both Borowitz and Rubenstein came to share John Cobb's critique that it is not enough to accept general responsibility by saying we also embody the universal ignorance and hatred that led to the Holocaust. Rather, each individual has to ask about the specific causes that led to the Holocaust and to trace one's individual path for responding. For example, in this volume Rubenstein shows an example of an individual response by giving a summary of how Japan acted positively in refusing to copy Germany's extermination policy.

In his Rejoinder to Borowitz, Abe had asserted that there can be no resolution of the Holocaust dilemma within history at the level of ethics and desire, and to attain peace we must go beyond the horizontal dichotomy between good and evil and return to the vertical level of Sunyata, or emptiness, where such distinctions are transcended. Indeed, Abe posits a discontinuity between ethics and enlightenment: "In Buddhism ethics and religion are dialectically connected through mutual negation."[4] In this dialogue it becomes clear how different Abe's view of Buddhism is from the Judaism of Borowitz, because for Borowitz ethics and religion are deeply connected in Judaism: "Because God is holy/good, Jews are to be holy/good."[5] Abe also observed that Christians also differ from his Buddhist view by having "a continuous path from religion to ethics (God's commandments constitute the basis of ethics)," although Christians agree with his view in other respects, for "there is no continuous path from ethics to religion (before God 'there is none righteous, no, not one')."[6]

RICHARD RUBENSTEIN

In this volume, Richard Rubenstein offers a very helpful outline of the various Jewish responses to the Holocaust: (1) as punishment by God for disobedience by the Jews, (2) as birth pangs for the future arrival of the Messiah, or (3) as an event beyond human comprehension that still leaves Jews with the option of returning to the daily goodness of the God of the covenant. Rubenstein himself rejects these views, as well as the view that this was (4) an isolated event or (5) the expression of absolute evil. Instead, he finds that "there is no way to affirm the traditional God of covenant and election without affirming that God as the ultimate

Author of Auschwitz" (p. 109). Accordingly, Rubenstein concludes that after the Holocaust Jews can no longer affirm the goodness of God, and the biblical God of Judaism is dead. In great sympathy with Abe, he finds that for him there is now a discontinuity between Jewish ethical distinctions and ultimate reality, and he affirms the identity between ultimate reality and Sunyata.

Even though Sunyata brings resolution of conflicts at the ultimate level, Rubenstein still finds Abe's treatment of the Holocaust to be a "meaningless abstraction," and he awaits Abe's advice on "how solidarity could actually be achieved in the concrete, historical instance of Nazis and Jews" (p. 105). However, Abe responds in his Rejoinder by arguing that the religious level is not to be separated from the search for concrete reconciliation, but must be present as "the only legitimate *basis*" (p. 180)[7] for a solution at the time when a historical solution is being worked out. Awakening to Sunyata may not be a sufficient cause, but it is a necessary cause, for a satisfactory historical solution. Otherwise the separation at the historical level will be absolutized.

A point of frequent fascination and contention is Abe's emphasis on Christ's self-emptying based on the kenosis hymn in Philippians, because the discussion sometimes takes a metaphysical twist, and at other times it remains in the mythological mode of Father and Son. Finally, in response to Rubenstein's inquiry about how kenosis operates within the covenantal relationship, Abe admits that "Christ's kenosis and vicarious atonement should not be taken objectively as nonexistential events, but subjectively and existentially in relation to our own self-negation" (p. 177). Only through "the complete negation of the self on the human side of the relationship" (p. 178) can the kenosis of God and Christ effectively restore the covenant, no matter how one is conceptualizing it. This existential realization seems to be Abe's main goal.

The most poignant and vital interchange between Rubenstein and Abe, however, takes place at the painful point where Rubenstein seems to abandon the covenant based on the failure of God to protect his people from the Holocaust. In his Rejoinder, Abe goes to some lengths (pp. 180–82) to outline Rubenstein's rejection of the God of Sinai and his acceptance of God as the "Holy Nothingness." Although agreeing that Rubenstein is moving toward the Buddhist experience of Sunyata, Abe then takes an important turn by affirming the positive dimension of Sunyata for Buddhists. Accordingly, given the failure of the traditional understanding of God in the face of the Holocaust, Abe questions the uniqueness of the Holocaust and asks Rubenstein now to reconstruct a view of history, of the covenant, of God, and of the peoplehood of Israel that can be meaningful and that can benefit the world (p. 183).

SANDRA B. LUBARSKY

Sandra B. Lubarsky also takes up Abe's invocation of Sunyata and praises it as a useful concept to prevent Judaism from making an idol out of its own community or its own history, and to de-absolutize even the Holocaust. On the other hand, in a way parallel to that of Rubenstein, she feels that Abe eloquently advocates Sunyata while neglecting history. In particular, Lubarsky questions Abe's apparent dualism between the historical realm of "time, distinctions, particularity, and ethics" and a religious realm of "nontemporality, nondiscrimination, universality, and equality" (p. 118). Indeed, she feels as if Abe is proposing a cosmic dualism between the vertical dimension of Sunyata and the horizontal dimension of history, and asks how Judaism may contribute to Abe's appropriation of history. In his Rejoinder, Abe reiterates his fundamental point that for a religious person every act at every moment is worked out at the intersection of the horizontal and vertical. Accordingly, he feels that the charge of dualism is based on a misunderstanding of his views.

What is not addressed by Abe is Lubarsky's surprise at how confidently Abe asserts that the self-awakening of Zen can be achieved by people,[8] whereas Judaism attacks such claims as arrogant. Later she asks, "How much self-transcendence is possible?" It is interesting that Abe does not discuss the practice of Buddhism by citing the familiar trio of morality, meditation, and wisdom as the sum of a Buddhist's life. Instead, Abe asserts the Mahayana identification of samsara and nirvana (pp. 187–88, while making the vertical dimension of Sunyata more primary than distinctions between good and evil or any mundane conditioned practice. Indeed, in his Rejoinder to Lubarsky Abe worries about Jewish self-confidence in being able to be obedient to God's commands, because in his view, "humans can enter the religious realm only by overcoming—by negating—the ethical, sociohistorical dimension; that is, by realizing the limitation of the ethical dimension" (p. 188). To some degree this disagreement echoes the medieval Chinese debate about enlightenment, with Abe advocating a Zen position of sudden enlightenment after seeing "the endlessness of samsara" followed by Bodhisattva practice (p. 188), whereas Lubarsky seems to support the view of gradual practice and gradual enlightenment based on the assurance of being in God's image (= having Buddha nature?). Abe misses the "negation of holiness understood as the negation of dailiness" (p. 189), but this is a problem from his standpoint, not from hers.

5

HEINRICH OTT

The starting points of the various Christian respondents are very different from each other. Heinrich Ott begins his remarks by accepting Abe's view that religion is being threatened by modern science and nihilism, and applauds Abe's insistence that interfaith dialogue is the best method for religion to find its deepest strength to resist these threats. Ott supports this claim by defining religion as "the deepest possible experience of reality" and individual religions as "specific ways of achieving this deepest experience of reality" (p. 129). Accordingly, by focusing on the existential level Ott proposes that Christian-Buddhist dialogue should not focus on religious doctrines, but seek "a similar movement" between them at the psychological level. Contrary to Hans Küng, Ott says that it is counterproductive to argue whether or not the kenosis hymn of Philippians is the core of Christianity. "The dogmatic question, to what extent one can think of the kenosis of the Son of God (a mythological notion) as a kenosis in the being of God himself, should be left to the search for agreement within Christianity" (p. 129).

Having defined religion at the experiential level, Ott identifies the "ceaseless emptying movement of Sunyata" as the core inner event for Abe (p. 52), and affirms that in Christian faith-consciousness it is possible to find something of this "dynamic movement" of Sunyata (p. 51). Agreeing with Waldenfels, Ott emphasizes that Abe's use of the word "emptiness" is not nihilistic, but implies an openness like the brightness of the sky that "comprises and surpasses all known possibilities" (p. 130). Ott agrees that this view reflects Martin Heidegger's thought, as Abe has suggested (p. 50), and Ott argues that our encounter with the ineffable concreteness of experience in the interpersonal, ethical, esthetic, and religious realms is not adequately expressed by Western notions of inherent existence, substances, attributes, and so forth. Because the "realities" that we encounter in these areas are not substantial, Ott finds that Abe's emphasis on the experience of suchness is an important corrective to the mindset of traditional philosophy and modern technology. After mentioning various paintings and poems as examples, Ott selects the Christian teaching of the "forgiveness of sins" as an experience that moves beyond concepts of substance or their absence. Ott proposes that Christians "may indeed come across problems that we can solve more easily from the perspective of Sunyata, of kenosis . . . than by using the thought patterns characteristic of Western metaphysics and Christian dogmatics" (p. 130). Hence, Ott is grateful to Abe for offering a means for affirming basic Christian experiences of reality expressed mythologically by showing that these have more in common with the emptying movement of Sunyata than with the substantive view of objectivity implied in science and nihilism. These remarks by Ott are a great tribute to Abe and touch the core of his thought (pp. 183–85), so that future dialogue would do well to start from this basis.

MARJORIE HEWITT SUCHOCKI

The broadest Christian perspective is provided by Marjorie Hewitt Suchocki, who gives an overview of Western interreligious encounter as a background to the discussion. After recalling the negativity with which medieval Christians treated Judaism and Islam, she reminds us how *piety* and *morality* became the two bases for common ground proposed by enlightenment thinkers to rationalize the existence of other religions reported by voyagers in the sixteenth and seventeenth centuries. This led to other efforts to find a common ground in more recent centuries, such as *subjective awe* (Rudolph Otto), *metaphysics* (Arthur Schopenhauer), or *transcendent deity* (Friedrich Schelling), but always with the assumption that Christianity was supreme. More recently, phenomenologists sought *common structures and functions* among all religions, whereas historical research finally convinced Ernst Troeltsch that Christianity was as *culture-bound* as other religions.

After reviewing the past, Suchocki summarizes the writings of the earlier respondents to Abe printed in *The Emptying God* and wonders if they really represent "dialogue," for all except Altizer work from the normativity of their own religion and translate Abe's ideas into their own categories. As a result, they judge Abe's ideas by their own norms and otherwise hardly seem open or changed by Abe. For example, Moltmann likes the fact that Abe finds new reasons for affirming the mutuality of each person of the Trinity, but doesn't like his sense of justice and eschatology to be undermined by Sunyata. Ogden finds that Abe doesn't fit his own categories, so finds little common ground. Eugene Borowitz appreciates Abe's sense of responsibility for the Holocaust, but finds that his ideas do not support Jewish covenantal responsibilities. Catherine Keller finds the "selfless self" at odds with the needs of feminine spiritual growth, whereas Cobb finds common ground not with Abe, but with the Sambhogakaya idea. Tracy rejects Abe's view of the Trinity, but finds a Christian basis for Buddhist wisdom and compassion. Altizer, on the other hand, simply agrees with Abe as affirming Altizer's own idea that God is now emptied into the world.

In contrast to the effort to interpret other religions in Christian categories, Suchocki sees Abe's proposals as an effort to interpret Christianity in Buddhist terms, and agrees with Hans Küng that this risks

7

"remaining monological rather than dialogical." As Hans Küng writes: "Nothing personal is at stake because, even in foreign raiment, one finds only one's own world again" (p. 215). Suchocki asks: "Is it not better to find ways within our own traditions to affirm the integrity of our differences" (p. 144) and thereby be as open as possible to the full otherness of people of other faiths in their fullness and uniqueness? Accordingly, we should seek to become "conversational partners after the manner of friends. In such a fashion, we might transform the world into a community of communities, each with its own distinctiveness and richness" (p. 144).

In place of Sunyata as a model, Suchocki turns to the Trinity as inspiration and justification for dialogue activity. Because the Trinity affirms that God's very nature involves enduring differences and relationships, and a unity through irreducible diversity, it implies unceasing dialogue and communion. Because each member of the Trinity necessarily reaches beyond itself in union with the other members, so the church as bearing the image of God "cannot be content with a fullness of love within its own borders" (p. 146). The Christian community, therefore, "like the God it serves . . . must reach beyond its own borders in love" (p. 146) and embrace diversity through dialogue, diplomacy, and a commitment to mutual well-being. Abe in his Rejoinder is attracted to this use of the Trinity and attempts to clarify how his views can deepen the meaning of the Trinity.

HANS WALDENFELS

In contrast to how Suchocki broadens the discussion with a sense of history and the need to affirm diversity in dialogue, Hans Waldenfels deepens our understanding of Abe by tracing his ideas back to his earlier writings and to the influential pioneer Keiji Nishitani (1900–1990). In addition, he makes at least three critical but constructive comments. Whereas Abe had thought that Karl Rahner's ideas were somewhat abstract, Waldenfels shows the experiential basis of Karl Rahner's thought and the need to understand him from this basis. Nevertheless, Abe in his Rejoinder feels his original questions still remain.

Second, Waldenfels argues that Nishitani's discussion of Sunyata and kenosis had a stronger connection between insight and ethics. For example, the intellectual idea of *not-self* also includes the ethics of *selflessness*, so that *not-self* is better translated as *nonego* in order to contain both dimensions. This contrasts with Abe's claim that ethics is dualistic and is left behind in Sunyata. Although Waldenfels shows how Abe has pointed to the need for ethical considerations from the beginning,

Waldenfels feels he has not developed this area. In particular, when Abe divides the world into three realms—(1) the natural realm, (2) the human, historical realm, and (3) the transhuman, fundamental dimension—Waldenfels objects to limiting ethical concerns only to the historical realm. He notes that most of the world religions do not separate faith from ethics (the third realm), nor should we separate science from ethics after the experience of Hiroshima (the first realm). In his Rejoinder Abe again feels that his view of each moment as the intersection of the vertical and horizontal dimensions is not fully appreciated (pp. 193–194).

In his conclusion, Waldenfels agrees with Abe that self-emptying is the highest form of self-realization, but urges that this self-emptying is not to be done in isolation or just between dialogue partners as an in-group or escape, but should be done inside "the uncountable amounts of need, distress, anguish, and despair among the peoples of the world" (p. 161), and therefore will involve ethical dilemmas.

CHRISTOPHER IVES

Christopher Ives returns to the issue raised by Borowitz, Rubenstein, and Cobb by claiming that the distinction between a Jewish infant and a Nazi guard at Auschwitz is undermined when Abe uses the concept of collective karma to claim that all of us are responsible for the Holocaust. Instead, Ives wants to preserve "the distinction between those who are related to an event and those who caused it and hence must take ethical responsibility for it" (p. 167). Second, Ives asks why and how an awareness of emptiness and suchness (beyond the distinctions of good and evil) "must" prompt and guide ethical action in the world. Did not Zen leaders fail to resist government aggression during the war? Third, he notes that Abe seems to be confusing the categories of religion and ethics. Fourth, Ives speaks for many Western readers when he questions what Abe means when he claims that history is reversible from a Zen viewpoint. Finally, Ives briefly raises issues dealing with the question of justice, the status of the saving work of Amida Buddha, and the relation between Sunyata and a personal deity (pp. 170–71).

Because the second, third, and fourth issues touch on the core of his religious life, Abe responds to these but has to bypass the others. Abe admits that the Bodhisattva activity in history "does not directly issue forth from the vertical dimension," which is "a necessary—but not sufficient—condition for the generation of an active, engaged response to specific social ills" (p. 196). Nevertheless, wanting to affirm the inseparability of religious realization and ethical action, Abe quotes the

Four Major Bodhisattva Vows, listing the first as concerned with others, and the second, third, and fourth as pointing to one's own awakening.[9] Also, he refers to his teacher, Shin'ichi Hisamatsu, who tried to implement his ethical concerns based on their inseparability from Sunyata by forming the FAS Society. Abe wants to affirm "dynamic Sunyata" by claiming that somehow the religious realization of emptiness inherently or spontaneously results in "vow and act" in an existential way, but is not based on a logical or linear necessity. Accordingly, Abe clarifies and reiterates his own position, but does not provide any guidelines for distinguishing the Jewish infant from the Nazi guard, nor does he explain the failure of his Zen teachers to protest the war.

Abe rejects the suggestion that ethical and religious criteria function on two separate levels: even though there is not direct transference of religious realization into ethical norms, "ethical value judgment is embraced and reappraised by nondiscriminating love or compassion" (p. 199). For Abe, this is not the difference between two categories, ethics and religion, but between two approaches to life: one caught in the unresolvable dualistic conflict of ethics, and the other returning to the true ground of Sunyata. Abe feels that Ives "absolutizes ethical judgment somewhat apart from" the religious dimension (p. 203), and insists that a person is always living at the intersection of the vertical and horizontal dimensions. Nevertheless, Abe still maintains the primacy and finality of religious experience as transcending the dualism of the distinction between good and bad. Although ethics is illuminated by emptiness, ethics remains at the secondary, historical, and horizontal level.

Abe does clarify the "reversibility of history" by rejecting a mechanical or mythological meaning, and by affirming that it is "existential through the realization of the Great Death, the death of the beginningless and endless process of living-dying" (p. 201). Whereas Abe often writes as if he is speaking metaphysically, his reply to Ives is very helpful in locating the reversibility of time in our inner personal experience, not as an external and public event. Accordingly, Abe warns us not to grasp time from the outside, "but existentially from within" so that we can realize "the discontinuity of time at each moment" (p. 202). Nevertheless, it is still hard to understand how this insight allows or leads to the "repeatability and reversibility" of time except in one's mind. Yet Abe still seems to resist saying that it is just a psychological wiping away of the past, or a reinterpretation of the past, by pointing to the death of the ego-self that implies moving beyond subjectivity and revealing true reality. Although not responding to the Christian analogy of repentance and the forgiveness of sins raised by Ott and Ives, Abe does demonstrate that he is referring to our false sense of external or objective history and its replacement by a truer awareness of the discontinuity and continuity of time. However, Abe's choice of language is still troublesome, for returning to the "root-source of time and history in the vertical dimension" is not to repeat or reverse the sequence of public, historical events, but to deepen, transform, and renew *our experience* of history.

HANS KÜNG

Included in this volume is a very important reply by Abe to questions raised by Hans Küng in an earlier article in *Buddhist Emptiness and Christian Trinity*[10] that is reprinted in this volume. For example, Küng made the same charge as Marjorie Suchocki that Abe is reinterpreting Christianity in terms of his own categories and therefore is not engaged in dialogue, for he is only finding his own world in Christianity. But Abe responds that his essay is an effort to deepen Christianity from within; he asks that it not be judged on Buddhist terms, but on "whether or not it is in accord with Christian spirituality" (p. 225).

In using Christian criteria to evaluate Abe's proposals, Küng finds Abe's focus on the kenosis passage of the Epistle to the Philippians as selective and reductive (p. 215). However, Abe responds by quoting a New Testament scholar, Jennings Reid, who holds that the kenosis theme pervades the New Testament. Küng then presents an argument later stated by Wolfhart Pannenberg that the New Testament is unanimous in saying that it was Christ who emptied himself, not God. If God was emptied on the cross, who would have raised Jesus from the dead? Abe replies by quoting Moltmann and Rahner to argue for God's active self-emptying as a new awareness in response to the Holocaust and that a loving God must be a self-emptying God: "If God is really an all-loving God, he is not self-affirmative, but self-negating, not self-assertive, but self-emptying" (p. 226). In addition, Abe rejects the question "Who would raise Jesus if God was emptied?" for the emptying and filling are not sequential, not a cause and effect series of events, but at that very moment, God's self-emptying is the manifestation of his fullness (pleroma).

In a very perceptive section, Küng argues that Abe's description of absolute Sunyata sounds parallel to Hegel's dialectical description of Being and Nothing. Abe tries to slip away from this parallel by suggesting that Being is always prior to Nothing in Hegel, but the reverse is true for Buddhism. This seems to be a weak response, for Abe had just negated the importance of sequence in the experience of emptiness-fullness. Furthermore, Abe's contrast of Hegel's synthesis with Buddhism's interdependence and nonduality still does not alter Küng's point, but demonstrates that Abe is arguing metaphysically in the same manner as Hegel.

Based on his knowledge of the diversity of Buddhism, Küng then questions the primacy of Sunyata for all Buddhists. Abe acknowledges Küng's point and admits that he did not pay due attention to other schools of Buddhism when he discussed Sunyata as ultimate reality in Buddhism. Nevertheless, Abe then argues for the shared ground of Sunyata for Madhyamika and Yogacara, although he does not attempt to argue against the secondary role of Sunyata in early Buddhism or in the *Uttaratantra-ratnagotravibhaga Sutra*, which has a positive view of Buddha-nature. Accordingly, Küng has helped to clarify the position of Abe by locating it within a particular Buddhist line of thought found in the Perfection of Wisdom scriptures, Nagarjuna, and recent Japanese Zen philosophy.

Küng feels an obligation in dialogue to sharpen the points of agreement or difference, and concludes his response by boldly asking whether what Christians call "God" is present in Buddhism under very different names, such as nirvana, dharma, emptiness, or the primal Buddha. In a very significant answer, Abe offers no objection: "I fully admit that 'what Christians call "God" is present, under very different names, in Buddhism.'" Abe does object to Küng's and Pannenberg's description of God as "the one infinite reality," however, because Buddhism is neither monistic nor monotheistic, but affirms dependent co-origination, anatman, and nonduality.

To describe the Buddhist understanding of reality that is called God by Christians, Abe accepts the term "panentheism," which means that "immanence and transcendence are identical through the negation of negation, that is, the negation of immanence and the negation of transcendence." Although this statement reaffirms the "boundless openness" advocated by Abe, his language becomes extreme:

> Ultimate Reality relates to itself through the bottomless ground of its own ultimacy or unconditionality by negating itself from within itself, by emptying itself of its own infinite unrelatedness and embracing the form of its own self-negation (p. 239).

In this passage Abe shows one of the major problems of his rhetoric when he argues that reality empties itself of "its own infinite relatedness." Because Buddhism is based on the central insight of dependent co-origination (*pratitya-samutpada*), how could Abe make such a statement? Is Abe a victim of his own logic of "inverse correspondence"? Abe explains this logic as a "functionalist ontology" of reality that takes its full meaning only alongside of the notion of the principle of self-transcendence via internal self-negation, or self-affirmation through self-negation, of the unobjectifiable Whole itself. This is what is meant as *dynamic* Sunyata (p. 240).

In this description Abe changes the use of Sunyata from being a Buddhist *critique of mental categories*, such as denying the ultimacy or permanency of our notions of things and their relationships, into the use of Sunyata as a metaphysical *description of reality*. Abe's description echoes the common but confusing rhetoric often found in the Perfection of Wisdom scriptures like the *Diamond Sutra*, which moves from a conventional use of language ("How many beings were saved?") to a critique of mental categories ("No beings were saved.") without telling the reader that this transition is being made. A similar shift in the use of language is often used in Zen koans ("Does a dog have a Buddha nature?" "No.") to test a student's freedom from attachment to mental categories and language and to show the student's continual awareness of boundless and unobjectifiable reality. However, it may be asked whether this kind of rhetorical shift is appropriate in dialogue without giving your partner some warning.

WOLFHART PANNENBERG

Wolfhart Pannenberg echoes some of the questions of Küng and sharpens others. For example, regarding a Buddhist equivalent to God, Pannenberg incisively asks Abe "whether beyond the finite things and processes and beyond their universal interrelatedness there is an ultimate reality distinct though not separate from the fleeting world of finite phenomena" (p. 245). It is important that Abe answers by discussing the concept of nirvana, which is generally considered to be the human experience of what is unconditioned and beyond finitude: it is the *experience* of "ultimate reality," but not ultimate reality itself. In fact, the word is a negative term, meaning a "blowing out," or elimination, of ignorance, hatred, and attachment. By implication, nirvana is the peace, bliss, and "reality" that is experienced after these defilements are eliminated. It would seem that nirvana is much closer to the Christian experience of the Holy Spirit that is received as an indication of salvation (see Acts 8:15–22; 10:44–48) instead of being an equivalent to the ultimate reality that Pannenberg is asking about.

Abe continues in his response to Pannenberg by asking whether or not transcendence has a priority over immanence. In Buddhist use of the concept of the two truths, *paramartha* (ultimate and saving truth) originally had priority over *samvriti* (conventional wisdom).[11] However, Professor Abe's logic reflects later Mahayana use whereby the two truths are completely reversible, unless one conceives of *paramartha* as embracing and being beyond binaries instead of being one part of a dialectic. A main thrust of Professor Abe's argument, accordingly, seems to be to push Christians to see God as embracing and being beyond the dialectic, rather than describing God as one part of a dialectic.

Professor Abe has differed with Küng and Pannenberg because of their affirmation of monotheism, which he feels is a false oneness. Instead, he urges them to understand the kenotic God, the "empty God," as a "common ground with Buddhism by overcoming Christianity's monotheistic character, the absolute oneness of God" (p. 258). However, Pannenberg has a similar problem with Abe's own writings and challenges Abe to clarify his frequent use of self-referential language in describing Sunyata when he says that "Sunyata is not self-affirmative, but thoroughly self-negative." Pannenberg asks Abe, "What is the self" used in these phrases, but receives no reply. Nevertheless, by calling attention to the linguistic habit of capitalizing "emptiness" and treating it as an active agent that can be "self-negative," Pannenberg raises an important issue both for Abe and for the Perfection of Wisdom scriptures where this practice originates. In these scriptures and in the writings of Abe, priority often seems to be given to emptiness (both metaphysically and experientially), and this move needs further discussion.

SUNYATA AND ETHICS:
CAN THERE BE DIFFERENT ULTIMATES?

Many discussants have challenged the priority that Abe has given to Sunyata, and have questioned the adequacy of the experience of Sunyata to prompt and guide ethical responsibility in history. Before grappling with Abe's ideas, however, it is important to appreciate the fact that Abe engages in dialogue based on his own religious experience, not primarily on an inherited set of dogmatic or institutionalized positions. This personal approach to dialogue both enlivens and limits the views that Abe offers to us. Specifically, from Abe's religious biography as outlined by Ives in his Introduction to *The Emptying God*, it is clear that ethical contradictions were Abe's greatest religious challenge, and that the resolution came under the influence of Hisamatsu's Zen and is epitomized by the experience of Sunyata. As Abe himself recalls:

> In my personal experience the more seriously I tried to do good and to avoid evil, the more clearly I realized myself to be far away from good and

to be involved in evil. The realization of the radical evil at the bottom of the struggle between good and evil, and the realization of my fundamental ignorance of ultimate truth were the outcome of my ethical life. In short, this realization in its ultimate form was nothing other than a realization of the death of the ego-self. Through this realization of the ego's death, however, the "holy" was opened up in me. It is not, however, God as the absolute good but God as the absolute nothingness that is neither good nor evil and yet both good and evil dynamically. To me, this realization of absolute nothingness is the basis of my life and the source of my activity.[12]

When we ask what experience Abe is using as the source of his ethics, we find him saying that the "realization of absolute nothingness is the basis of my life and the source of my activity." It seems clear that Abe is transferring this emptiness experience into a metaphysics and creatively expressing it through Western images and ideas, as well as generalizing this experience as the ground for dialogue and the basis for all other profound religious experiences.

What is at stake in this volume of essays, therefore, is not Buddhism versus Judaism or Christianity. Rather, it is the Buddhist Sunyata experience of Abe in comparison to the experience of others, both Buddhists and non-Buddhists. It seems clear that the ethical issue has been raised so often because, contrary to Abe's experience, ultimacy and transcendence have been experienced by many discussants precisely in the midst of relationships and ethical issues, not by going beyond them to "absolute nothingness." Given the differences among the dialogue partners, must we conclude that only one way is correct, or can there be a diversity of ways to experiencing transcendence?

Although the ethical conflicts inherent in life were resolved for Abe by his Sunyata experience, this collection of essays has repeatedly shown a tension between Sunyata and ethics. However, in the classic Hindu tradition, Sunyata and ethics were not seen in competition, but as two legitimate alternative ways of experiencing ultimacy within a fourfold scheme: karma-yoga, dhyana-yoga, jnana-yoga, and bhakti-yoga. Ethical imperatives fit into karma-yoga, whereas Abe's Sunyata experience seems to fit best under jnana-yoga. More recently, Seiichi Yagi has proposed that his Buddhist-Christian dialogue partners in Japan can be placed into three groups: (1) those (like Nishida) who emphasize pure experience, (2) those who (like many Christians) emphasize the I-Thou relationship, and (3) those (like Hisamatsu) who emphasize the formless self.[13] Abe fits into the third group, but is being challenged in this volume by thinkers for whom ethics and the "I-thou" experience are primary. For example, we can see how he approaches the Holocaust issue:

> To me, the realization of the spiritual death of the ego is essential for a new religious life. It is the radical realization of our finitude in both the ethical and the ontological senses. It is not a pessimistic but a highly realistic event, which provides us with a basis for a resurrected, creative life. From this point of view the Holocaust is not the responsibility of the holy/good God but our responsibility, to be realized through the death of the ego in the bottomless depths of our existence.[14]

Although Abe's approach to the Holocaust is profound and consequential, will he consider an "I-Thou" approach also to provide a transcendent (vertical) framework as a basis for resolution?

At the end of his response to Christopher Ives, Abe offers two possibilities why Ives does not find Abe's method of subordinating ethics to Sunyata as adequate: either Ives is lacking the realization of the ego's death (the Great Death) or he has "absolutized ethical judgment somewhat apart from the dialectical character of the human self working at the intersection of the horizontal, ethical dimension and the vertical, religious dimension" (p. 203). In either case, Abe rejects the objections of Ives by implying that his own religious life is not adequately developed. Certainly Abe may feel free to make this response to Ives as his former student on the assumption that Ives is dedicated to realizing the same path as Abe. However, Ives can appeal to the larger Jewish and Christian communities, for Abe appears to be rejecting much of their experience. Is Abe also judging them as not fully developed? Although they may be absolutizing the ethical experience, is not Abe in turn absolutizing his own Sunyata experience as normative and failing to see the truth that Ives is affirming? Do we find here two different and competing absolutes, one based on the truth of Sunyata and the other based on the truth of relationships?

Zen masters have not been shy about criticizing other Buddhists who have lived a life different from their ideal of enlightenment. On the other hand, other Buddhists have in turn been critical of Zen. Hans Küng has made the point that within the Buddhist tradition, Abe as a Zen teacher does not represent all, or even most, Buddhists.[15] As was mentioned earlier, the contrasting positions of Lubarsky and Abe strongly echo the issues debated in Chinese Buddhism between the gradual and the sudden path. I might add that the classic defining action for becoming a Buddhist has not been taking refuge in Sunyata, but in the Three Jewels of the Buddha, the Dharma, and the Sangha, and ethics has always been inherently present in the Buddhist dharma.[16] According to the Tibetan tradition, Zen teachers were defeated in debate in Lhasa in the eighth century by Kamalasila, who taught that compassion took priority over emptiness in the Buddhist life. Zen was rejected in Tibet for denying the primacy of ethics and compassion, and instead elevated the experience of Sunyata and sudden enlightenment as supreme.[17] There are many other Buddhists for whom morality continues to take precedence over Sunyata, such as vinaya masters, Theravadin monks, and Nichiren Buddhists. Even though they might agree with Abe about the theory of Sunyata, they do not want to subordinate or negate the practical primacy of most Buddhist scriptures, rules, obligations, and relationships as guides for the religious life.

In East Asia the T'ien-t'ai tradition is another example of Buddhists who affirm the importance of Sunyata, both as an experience and as a doctrine, but then qualify it and subordinate it within the fuller dharma of the Three Truths. This doctrine gives equal emphasis to the partial and the temporary by returning from emptiness to realize the importance and necessity of the temporary distinctions of the mundane world. T'ien-t'ai endeavors to establish religious life in that balance that incorporates both emptiness and mundane distinctions as equally valuable, calling this position the "threefold truth" of emptiness, temporary existence, and the middle that embraces the other two. This position rejects Abe's view that gives special weight to emptiness, emphasizing instead the middle path and Buddha nature.[18] The priority given to the Sunyata religious experience as the vertical dimension of life is emphasized within Zen circles, but is at odds with other, very important Buddhist traditions.

In contemporary American studies of moral development, Abe's view can find strong support in the research of Lawrence Kohlberg, former Director of the Center for Moral Development at Harvard University. From his research Kohlberg concluded that at a certain stage morality comes to be seen as relative and arbitrary, and the universal moral principles that are articulated in maturity are evolved in the light of this discovery of the emptiness of moral rules.[19] On the other hand, Abe might be opposed by Carol Gilligan, who argues that the male separation from mother and the quest for an independent source of strength such as provided by definitive rules are characteristic of male life cycles. However, this male experience differs from that of women, who maintain continuity with their mothers who are of the same sex. Because women's ultimate values are more marked by an emphasis on connectedness rather than distinctions, on relationships rather than rights, they are less prone to see morality in terms of the failed ultimacy of ethical distinctions between good and evil.[20]

Gilligan's book offers the important consideration that the differences between Sandra Lubarsky and Masao Abe may not just be the difference between Judaism and Zen, or between gradual and sudden enlightenment, but between the life experience of women and men. Accordingly, before Abe and others become too firm in their theories that true religion must pass through emptiness, or that the discontinuity of morality and religion is in contrast to "a continuous path from the human to the divine" (p. 188), it may also be important to take gender issues into account. John Cobb has long proposed that different religious people may affirm different ultimates: different religions are not only different paths up the same mountain, but different paths up different mountains. Is the discussion about Sunyata and ethics a discussion about two different ways of being human, and two equally legitimate ways of being religious?

It is this appeal to the importance of distinctions that is mentioned by Catherine Keller when she questioned Abe's "revision" of Buddhism, because the "particularity of individuals, groups, and historical moments" seems lost in an overemphasis on experiencing these particulars in their suchness where the bite of their differences is lost in nondifferentiation. Abe seems to think that he grasps her point by emphasizing the ultimate importance of each particular moment when he says "the whole beginningless and endless process is concentrated *in this moment.*" However, he again has removed the differences from each moment by emphasizing what is common to all moments, namely, their embodiment of "the beginninglessness and endlessness of the process."[21]

Abe has maintained that meaningful dialogue must be grounded in one's own religious experience; this is a legacy of Abe's teacher, Shin'ichi Hisamatsu, who insisted that Abe first practice zazen before beginning to discuss Zen philosophy. One of Abe's dialogue contributions, accordingly, is his rejection of a literal, external reading of religious statements and his insistence on grounding them in his own life. Nevertheless, one of the problems that dialogue partners have is that in much of his writing Abe *moves beyond this experiential basis* to make *metaphysical and normative generalizations.* Rather than writing autobiographically, Abe piles up normative adjectives: "the *pure* activity of *absolute* emptying is *true* Sunyata" (emphasis added) (p. 51). Indeed, as we have seen above, one of the most illuminating responses to Abe has been by Hans Küng, who compared the dialectical description of Being by Hegel with Abe's method of writing about Sunyata in his essay on "Dynamic Sunyata."[22]

I deeply appreciate Abe's energy in applying his emptiness experience to all other realms and religions, especially because it challenges other religious thinkers to delve into their own deepest levels in order to respond. Perhaps because of his background in philosophy, and also because there is a need to critique other philosophies, Abe often expresses his religious experience in a metaphysical language that seems to make *ontological* claims that become *totalistic*. In a revealing remark to Ives, however, Abe says that his use of the word "must" was not based on logic or sequence, but on existential experience. This seems to imply that Abe sublimates the intensity and profundity of his personal Sunyata experience into his metaphysical arguments so that it emerges as the *logic of necessity*. Abe repeatedly argues by saying "only" such-and-such or that we "must" conceive of God in this way or that. Because this way of writing leaves description and becomes prescription, Abe's urgent personal message when transformed into philosophical writing sometimes seems totalistic, and Sunyata becomes the answer for everything. Accordingly, the very virtues of Abe's life, which is dedicated to constructively engaging the thought of others, sometimes leads him into linguistic and conceptual patterns of expression that may move him or his readers from an experiential ground. Moreover, Abe's metaphysical generalizations, his shorthand technical vocabulary, his tendency to use totalistic and paradoxical language,[23] unfortunately can also lead to misunderstanding.

One area of misunderstanding that is crucial for all of Abe's writings is the subject of Sunyata. Perhaps because of Abe's writing style, such prominent Western thinkers as John Cobb and, in this volume, Richard Rubenstein have assumed that "ultimate reality for Buddhists is emptiness." Taken in isolation, this statement is simply not true for most Buddhists who do not hold that emptiness is ultimate reality, but that all our ideas and all things are empty (of permanency, of "inherent self-nature"). When Buddhists say that ultimate reality is empty, it is only an abbreviation, a shorthand way of saying that for Buddhists all reality bears the mark or characteristic of emptiness, namely, that all things are interdependent and in flux without the capacity for isolated and unchanging self-existence. This characteristic of things can then be seen in a totalistic vision where everything at once, including ourselves, is seen as empty (of permanence), which in one moment unifies everything as well as frees everything from a false rigidity, isolation, and formalism. By being empty of permanence, everything can then develop novelty and fullness. This is a long-winded way of saying what I think Abe means when he uses phrases like "absolute emptiness and absolute fullness" or "dynamic Sunyata." On the other hand, maybe I am wrong and Abe does not share the majority view of Buddhism about the meaning of Sunyata.

Because the experience of Sunyata was foundational to Abe's religious life, it is natural for him to propose this as the inner nature of God and Christ. For example, Abe suggests that the self-emptying love of Christ originated in the love of God, and because "kenosis is implied in the original nature of God," the notion of a "crucified God" is essential: "Without the self-emptying of God 'the Father,' the self-emptying of the Son of God is inconceivable" (p. 37). Contrary to Abe, however, it is perfectly conceivable for Jesus to be self-emptying, but not necessarily God, for the New Testament never mentions God's self-emptying. Although we appreciate the truth of Abe's creative proposal, does he not overstate his case by rejecting other approaches as "inconceivable"?

Beginning in 1963 and continuing in his latest essays, Professor Abe has worked within a framework of the common threat to all religious traditions posed by nihilism. Although this was a pressing concern in the 1950s and 1960s, it seems less relevant in the 1990s when the major threat is not nihilism but religious fundamentalism and fanaticism. We seem surrounded by religion, and in America, the Middle East, India, and Southeast Asia, politics is being dominated by religious right-wing reactionaries. Accordingly, for many people the question of the 1990s is not whether religion is possible, but what kind of religion.

Given Abe's lifelong role in sponsoring interreligious dialogue, it may be his actions more than his words, his lifetime of reaching across boundaries rather than his insistence on Sunyata, that is his greatest gift. On the other hand, because we are indebted to him for showing in his career how the experience of Sunyata can result in helping others live more collaboratively, more deeply, and more fully, his own life may be the most persuasive argument of all for the religious significance of Sunyata.

NOTES

1. For an illuminating intellectual biography of Abe, see the Introduction by Christopher Ives in John B. Cobb, Jr., and Christopher Ives, eds., *The Emptying God: A Buddhist-Jewish-Christian Conversation* (Maryknoll, N.Y.: Orbis Books, 1990), pp. xiii–xix.

2. See Eugene B. Borowitz, "Dynamic Sunyata and the God Whose Glory Fills the Universe," with Abe's rejoinder, "The Problem of the Holocaust: The Relationship Between Ethics and Religion," in Cobb and Ives, eds., *The Emptying God*, pp. 79–90, 180–84; Eugene B. Borowitz, "Buddhism and Judaism: Some Further Considerations," with "A Response to Eugene B. Borowitz" by Masao Abe, *Buddhist-Christian Studies* 13 (1993): 223–31; and a concluding reflection by Eugene B. Borowitz, "When Theologians Engage in Inter-faith Dialogue," printed together with the previous articles in a booklet published by *Sh'ma*, Inc., Indianapolis, n.d.

3. Cobb and Ives, eds., *The Emptying God*, p. 186.

4. Ibid., p. 185.

5. Ibid., p. 82.

6. Ibid., p. 185.

7. Page numbers in parentheses refer to page numbers within this volume.

8. Lubarsky refers to Masao Abe's book *Zen and Western Thought* (London and Honolulu: Macmillan and University of Hawaii Press, 1985), p. 21.

9. It is interesting that T'ien-t'ai Chih-i, who first formulated these four vows, considered the third vow as also concerned with saving others, for it involved learning methods for helping them. See Neal Donner and Daniel Stevenson, *Great Calming and Concentration* (Honolulu: University of Hawaii Press, 1993).

10. Hans Küng, "God's Self-Renunciation and Buddhist Emptiness: A Christian Response to Masao Abe," in Roger Corless and Paul F. Knitter, eds., *Buddhist Emptiness and Christian Trinity* (New York: Paulist Press, 1990), pp. 26–43.

11. See Gadjin Nagao's brief but brilliant review of the history of these terms in his article on "Samvrti," in the *Silver Jubilee Volume of the Jinbun-kagaku Kenkyusho* (Kyoto: Jinbunkagaku Kenkyusho, 1954).

12. Cobb and Ives, eds., *The Emptying God*, p. 188.

13. Seiichi Yagi, "Buddhist-Christian Dialogue in Japan: Varieties of Immediate Experience," *Buddhist-Christian Studies* 14 (1994), pp. 11–22.

14. Cobb and Ives, eds., *The Emptying God*, p. 188.

15. Abe sometimes writes as an intellectual historian by presenting various Buddhist doctrines in agreement with his own, but omitting those that disagree, such as the idea of gradual enlightenment, partial emptiness, transcendent dharma that is not beyond ethical demands, and so forth (see pp. 57–70, 84–86). By writing on behalf of Buddhism, rather than on the basis of his experience, he steps beyond the authority of his own experience and is making historical claims that are open to criticism, because, as we have just seen, his own experience does not represent the full range of Buddhism. Accordingly, Abe's metaphysical generalizations become further misleading when he claims that they represent all of Buddhism.

16. See the writings of John Ross Carter on dharma in early Buddhism.

17. See the essay by Luis Gomez, "Purifying Gold: The Metaphor of Effort and Intuition in Buddhist Thought and Practice," in Peter N. Gregory, ed., *Sudden and Gradual: Approaches to Enlightenment in Chinese Thought* (Honolulu: University of Hawaii Press, 1987), esp. pp. 96–120.

18. See Paul Swanson, *Foundations of T'ien-t'ai Philosophy* (Berkeley: Asian Humanities Press, 1989), and Ng Yu-kwan, *T'ien-t'ai Buddhism and Early Madhyamika* (Honolulu: Buddhist Studies Program, University of Hawaii, 1993).

19. The stage wherein all moral distinctions are seen as arbitrary and lacking final guiding principles is identified as a transition period from Stage 4 (the stage of conventional morality) to Stage 5 (involving individual choice), according to Lawrence Kohlberg. See his *The Philosophy of Moral Development* (San Francisco: Harper & Row, 1981).

20. See Carol Gilligan, *In a Different Voice* (Cambridge: Harvard University Press, 1982).

21. Cobb and Ives, eds., *The Emptying God*, pp. 110, 200.

22. Hans Küng, "God's Self-Renunciation and Buddhist Emptiness," in Corless and Knitter, eds., *Buddhist Emptiness and Christian Trinity*, pp. 35–36.

23. I have written more about this tendency of Abe in an article entitled "Mr. Dialogue: A Tribute to Masao Abe," in a forthcoming collection of essays edited by Donald Mitchell.

PART I

KENOTIC GOD AND DYNAMIC SUNYATA

Kenotic God and Dynamic Sunyata

MASAO ABE

INTRODUCTION

Interfaith Dialogue and Antireligious Ideologies

Over the past few decades the dialogue between Buddhism and Christianity has evolved considerably. It has gone beyond the stage of promoting mutual understanding between the two religions, and is now entering a new stage in which the mutual transformation of Buddhism and Christianity is being seriously explored.[1] This development concerns not only theology or doctrinal understanding but also spirituality. This tendency, I hope, will continue to accelerate in the future.

The dialogue between Buddhism and Christianity should not, however, be regarded simply as an interfaith dialogue, for it must be engaged in with awareness of a wider sociohistorical context. In particular, although interfaith dialogue presupposes the validity and significance of religion, many persons in our present secularized world do not. They ask, "Why is religion necessary?" and "What meaning does religion have for us today?" They think they can live without religion and thus are quite skeptical about or indifferent to religion. Moreover, ideologies that negate religion prevail in our society. Scientism, Marxism, traditional Freudian psychoanalytic thought, and nihilism in the Nietzschean sense all deny the *raison d'être* of religion, not merely on emotional grounds but on various rational or theoretical grounds. Not stopping with criticism of particular religions, these ideologies negate the very being of religion itself.

The most crucial task of any religion in our time is to respond to these antireligious forces by elucidating the authentic meaning of religious faith. This is why, as early as 1963, in a paper entitled "Buddhism and Christianity as a Problem of Today," I emphasized:

> Apart from the context of the issue between religion and irreligion there wouldn't be much sense in taking up the problem of Buddhism and Christianity. If a discussion of the theme should not throw any light on our search for the being of religion itself which can overpower all negation, then it would be indeed futile to engage in it. It is precisely at the meeting point of the two problems, namely, the interreligious problem of Buddhism and Christianity on the one hand, and the problem of religion and irreligion on the other, that the most serious question for modern man, the question of his self-estrangement, should be asked; and it is precisely there that we may expect to find an answer to it.[2]

The necessity of considering Buddhist-Christian dialogue not merely as interfaith dialogue but as an inseparable part of the wider, sociocultural problem of religion versus irreligion has become increasingly evident in the past few decades. To use the terminology of Thomas S. Kuhn and Hans Küng, both Buddhism and Christianity are now facing "a transitional period of uncertainty" or "crisis" in which continuous "organic development" or the usual cumulative process of "normal science" is no longer appropriate.[3] Both religions must fundamentally transform themselves such that their prevailing basic assumptions are drastically changed and a new paradigm, or model, of understanding can emerge. This might involve a revolutionary reinterpretation of the concept of God in Christianity and the concept of emptiness in Buddhism.

Insofar as Buddhist-Christian dialogue is undertaken as an interfaith dialogue in which the validity and significance of religion are taken for granted, it will fail to reach the core of the present crisis all religions are now facing, and will not lead to a much-needed search for a new paradigm. Only when Buddhist-Christian dialogue is pursued with an appreciation of the wider context of the contemporary confrontation of religion and irreligion will it be able to open up a deeper religious dimension in which Buddhist and Christian truth can be fully realized in a new paradigm beyond the religion-negating principles of scientism, Marxism, traditional Freudian psychoanalytic thought, and nihilism in the Nietzschean sense.

Scientism and Religion

I will confine my discussion of religion-negating ideologies to scientism and nihilism in the Nietzschean sense.[4]

We should not confuse the basis of science with the basis of scientism. The standpoint of science does not necessarily contradict that of religion. Of course, science and religion exhibit points of essential difference, but they do not always mutually exclude each other, and are at least potentially compatible. The standpoint of scientism, however, can never be compatible with that of religion. By making the standpoint of science absolute, scientism claims that the "scientific" method constitutes the *one* and *only* criterion of truth. Anything nonscientific is false. Religion, being nonscientific, is thus considered false. Because science has made remarkable advances in modern times and scientific laws are subject to widely accepted forms of experimental demonstration, scientific truth has impressed many as the absolute truth, even though it is only one kind of truth. Although eminent scientists rarely espouse scientism, there are many scientists and nonscientists who judge everything in a scientistic way. And if "scientific" truth is taken as the only criterion of truth, the dismissal of religion inevitably follows.

Proponents of scientism maintain that religion still exists today only because the scientific way of thinking has not yet sufficiently permeated the masses. Scientism believes that religion will naturally disappear once science has progressed to the extent that the scientific way of thinking is embraced by all. For scientism, the continued existence of religion has nothing to do with the nature or essence of religion but merely reflects slowness in an inevitable demise in history. Thus, religion is dismissed in principle by scientism.

Given this situation, we must ask the question, "What is the 'scientific' method?" Classical physics was based on mathematical rationality and viewed humans and nature mechanistically. In contrast to this view, contemporary physics, with Einstein's theory of relativity and Heisenberg's uncertainty principle, does not consider its method and perceived truth absolute. As Hans Küng expresses it:

> Hence today, in physics, chemistry, biology and other natural sciences, it is customary to speak not of universally valid truths copying reality but of hypothetically valid "projects" and "patterns" that hold only in virtue of certain conditions and within certain limits, while fully permitting the coexistence of other projects and patterns. . . . An absolutely objective truth is not envisaged but only one that is relatively objective. In perspectivity and variability, any number of methods and aspects, projects and patterns, are possible in regard to the one reality, which itself always remains infinitely richer and more complex than all the statements—even the most exact—about it.[5]

The mechanistic and strictly objective view of nature in classical physics has been jettisoned by contemporary physics with its relativistic and more process-oriented paradigm of nature. Consequently, the "scientific" way of thinking and the "scientific" picture of the world now are certainly less mechanical and consequently less incompatible with religion than earlier in the history of modern science.

This does not mean, however, that contemporary science no longer challenges religion. However relativistic the contemporary scientific view may be, if its perspective is dogmatized or taken ideologically, it turns into a form of scientism. In this regard, I agree with Hans Küng when he says:

> The idea of critical rationality must be entirely approved; but the ideology of a critical rationalism, absolutizing and mysticizing the rational factor, must be rejected. . . . Rationalistic ideology is characterized by rationalistic dogmatism and rationalistic intolerance.[6]

Hans Küng also reminds us that in the sixteenth and seventeenth centuries, because of their failure to become allies with the new science and new philosophical and social-political development, Christian theology and the church contributed substantially to the rise of both scientific and political atheism. But Küng insists:

> There was, however, no necessity in principle for autonomous reason, for modern natural science, increasingly so, to generalize their conclusions as to leave no place for a belief in God and in practice largely to substitute belief in science for belief in God.[7]

While I have no real objection to this statement, I am tempted to ask how belief in God can embrace autonomous reason without marring it. It is clear that, as Küng emphasizes, "the God of the Bible is not identical with the God of the ancient world picture or with the God of Greek philosophy." God in the Bible is "one who faces me, whom I can address," and is "subject and not predicate: it is not that love is God, but that God is love." Precisely in this sense, God in the Bible is "a thou who may be called person and personal or even suprapersonal and transpersonal." If, as Küng rightly suggests, we must entirely approve the idea of critical rationality and autonomous reason,[8] what is the ground on which critical rationality, autonomous reason, and God as thou, not only are compatible but also work positively together without detracting from one another? To this serious challenge of contemporary science, Christianity must respond.

This challenge of modern science is much less serious for Buddhism, because its basis is not faith in a God who faces us and can be addressed as a thou, but awakening to the Dharma (truth) that is termed "suchness" or "emptiness." Even Pure Land Buddhism, which, like Christianity, emphasizes faith (though in Amida Buddha), takes suchness or emptiness as the basic Reality (*Dharmakaya*). Nevertheless, Buddhism must still address the issue of how the Buddhist notion of suchness or emptiness can embrace critical rationality while still allowing reason to function autonomously. An important task for contemporary Buddhist thinkers is to demonstrate the religious significance of Buddhist truth in relation to scientific truth.

Nihilism in the Nietzschean Sense and Religion[9]

The problem of nihilism *for us today* is neither an emotional problem masquerading as an intellectual one, nor a recurrence of the age-old issue of nihilistic feeling found in both the East and the West. Since the writings of Friedrich Nietzsche, nihilism is no longer an emotional and timeless theme universally seen in human history; it has become an acute issue that, through a discerning historical awareness of human destiny, demands the modern person to rethink the foundation of cultural and religious life. Indeed, Nietzsche's nihilism is an existential realization clearly based on a philosophy of history. This is, I understand, why Heidegger says, "Nietzsche thinks of nihilism as the 'inner logics' of occidental history." Elucidating Nietzsche's phrase, "God is dead," Heidegger says, "The names of God and Christian God in Nietzsche's thought are used as the designation for the supersensible world in general," and "the phrase 'God is dead' means: the supersensible world is without active power. It dispenses no life."[10] Nietzsche's nihilism is an acute realization, through the history of European nations, that "the highest values are 'depreciated' (*sich entwerten*),[11] entirely deprived of meaning," the highest values here being the supersensible world established by Platonism and Christianity.

In *Beyond Good and Evil*, Nietzsche presents his unique idea of the three stages of human history:

> Once on a time men sacrificed human beings to their God, and perhaps just those they loved the best. . . . Then, during the moral epoch of mankind, they sacrificed to their God the strongest instincts they possessed, their "nature"; *this* festal joy shines in the cruel glances of ascetics and "anti-natural" fanatics. Finally, what still remained to be sacrificed? . . . Was it not necessary to sacrifice God himself . . . ? To sacrifice God for nothingness—this paradoxical mystery of the ultimate cruelty has been reserved for the rising generation; we all know something thereof already.[12]

To the first stage of human history Nietzsche ascribes the sacrifice of all primitive religions and also the sacrifice of the Emperor Tiberius in the Mithra Grotto on the Island of Capri. It may be said that this first stage corresponds to the time of the Old Testament that relates the stories of this kind of sacrifice in such cases as Abraham and Isaac. The second stage of human history indicates the time of the New Testament and the Christian era following it, in which the death and sacrifice of Jesus has been seen as the redemption of original sin inherent in human nature. The third historic stage, in which one does "sacrifice God for nothingness," indicates nihilism in Nietzsche's sense.

Here we see how deeply and uniquely Nietzsche's nihilism is rooted in a historical awareness of human destiny. It is noteworthy, however, that Nietzsche regards Christian morality, at least hitherto, as a "support" that preserves the integrity of human existence and as a "great antidote" for nihilism. For Christian morality, in Nietzsche's view, gave humans an absolute value to counteract the meaninglessness of life, and served as an advocate for God against suffering and evil in the world. Thus, for Nietzsche, Christianity (as well as metaphysics) has had biological utility in the sense that it was an invention useful for the preservation of human beings, an invention of the instinct for self-preservation inherent in us. Yet Nietzsche believed that in Christianity (and metaphysics) there was a latent fiction, indispensable to human life, which "deceives oneself in an effective way."[13] According to Nietzsche, though, the time when Christianity (and metaphysics) could have utility for human beings has ended. This implies the arrival of the third stage, in which one should "sacrifice God for nothingness." Upon realizing that faith in God is an unconscious fiction invented by the more basic will that is the "will to power," is it not being honest to one's life to return consciously to and ground oneself in the "will to power" as such? Nietzsche thus declares "God is dead" and thereby announces the advent of nihilism, in which one ought to endure meaninglessness—without God.

In this connection, we need to distinguish two forms of nihilism, "nihilism before religion" and "nihilism beyond religion."[14] Nihilism is often understood as a standpoint from which one recognizes the meaninglessness of human life, while denying everything, including the existence of God. It is in this naive nihilistic perception, and not through and after one's God-experience, that one opts for nihilism and insists "there is no God." This form of nihilism I call "nihilism before religion," for it is a realization of the meaninglessness of life before definitive religious experience, and it therefore may be overcome by religion when one comes to have a genuine religious experience. This "nihilism before religion" is found universally in human history and recurs as a theme in both Eastern and Western thought.

Though equally godless, Nietzsche's nihilism declares "God is dead" rather than "God is not." The statement "God is dead" can be uttered only by those for whom God *was alive*—that is, by those who have lived

religion. Nietzsche came to advocate nihilism through the clear realization of the "depreciation" (*Unwertung*) of the traditional religious values
of the past, including those of Christianity. For him, nihilism is a realization of the nothingness or meaninglessness of human life, not before,
but through and after, religion. Accordingly, his nihilism cannot be overcome by religion, at least in its traditional form. In this sense, I would
call Nietzsche's nihilism "nihilism beyond religion," in contrast to "nihilism before religion."

Unlike "nihilism before religion," which simply maintains "God is
not," Nietzsche's nihilism, declaring "God is dead," challenges the
core of traditional religion. He negates religion not simply from the outside, but from within. This is why in my paper "Buddhism and Christianity as a Problem of Today" I stated:

> Nihilism, though it may not yet be a conspicuous historic power [as scien-
> tism and Marxism], should be regarded as a sharp dagger pointed at the
> very heart of religion, because it radically negates religion, threatening to
> destroy it in its innermost core.[15]

Although Nietzsche criticizes Christianity exclusively, all religions,
including Buddhism, lie vulnerable to his attack. Now that Nietzsche's
nihilism is so influential, it is perhaps meaningless for us, without con-
fronting his nihilism, to speak of a religion as something self-evident—
as a "religion." All religions, then, must now examine whether or not
Nietzsche's nihilism is really "nihilism *beyond* religion," and assume the
burden of demonstrating, practically and theoretically, the *raison d'être*
of religion.

The problem of scientism and nihilism is thus a serious challenge to
all religions today: we should not avoid the confrontation. To become
truly significant and creative, interfaith dialogue between Buddhism
and Christianity must be set against the background of these two issues.
Bearing this in mind, let me propose how Buddhism and Christianity
can overcome these issues. And at the same time, let me also propose
how the two religions can respectively open up a deeper religious dimension in which they can collectively share a much greater religiousness.

KENOTIC GOD

The Kenosis of Christ

As a starting point for exploring Christianity, I want to quote the following passage of Paul from the Epistle to the Philippians:

Have this mind in you, which was also in Christ Jesus, who, existing in
the form of God, counted not the being on an equality with God a thing
to be grasped, but emptied himself, taking the form of a servant, being
made in the likeness of man; and being found in fashion as a man, he
humbled himself, becoming obedient *even* unto death, yea, the death of
the cross.

(Phil. 2:5–8)

To me, this is one of the most impressive and touching passages in the
Bible.

I feel this way for two reasons. First, although Christ existed in the
form of God – that is, was of the same divine nature as God – he refused
to dwell in the glory that belonged to God: instead, he abdicated his
divine rank and assumed the form of a servant. Thus, while in the form
of God, Christ emptied himself.[16] Further, according to the scripture,
"he humbled himself, becoming obedient *even* unto death, yea, the death
of the cross." This is a complete abnegation of Christ as the Son of God.

Second, this abnegation of Christ indicates the self-sacrificial love of
Christ for humankind disobedient to and rebellious against the will of
God. Through the incarnation (kenosis), death, and resurrection of the
Son of God, Christ, God reveals Godself in terms of unconditional love
beyond discriminatory justice. The unfathomable depth of God's love is
clearly realized when we come to know and believe that Christ as the
Son of God emptied himself and became obedient to the point of death
on the cross.

According to the exegesis of that passage in *The Interpreter's Bible*, at
one time – as most readers well know – there was a theological debate
"which turned largely on the question of how far Christ had ceased to
be God when he became man. Did he strip himself entirely of the
divine nature, or merely forgo certain attributes of majesty?" In my
view, however, such a theological debate misses the point. Christ's kenosis and his abnegation must be understood not as partial, but as complete and thoroughgoing. As *The Interpreter's Bible* states, "He [Paul] says
only that Christ *emptied himself*," and "emphasizes the full identity of
Christ with the race of men." Christ did not merely disguise himself as
a servant, as Docetism suggests, but in fact became a servant. Inasmuch
as the term "form" (*morphei*) in the above passage signifies not mere
shape or appearance, but substance or reality,[17] so we can say that in
Paul's understanding, the Son of God abandoned his divine substance
and took on human substance to the extreme point of becoming a servant crucified on the cross. Accordingly, Christ's kenosis signifies a
transformation not only in appearance but in substance, and implies a
radical and total self-negation of the Son of God.

Further again in my view, this doctrine of Christ's kenosis should not be understood to mean that Christ was *originally* the Son of God and *then* emptied himself and became identical with humans. Such a view in the temporal order, or the sequential order, is nothing but a conceptual and objectified understanding of the issue, not an experiential and religious understanding. Instead, we should understand the doctrine of Christ's kenosis to mean that Christ as the Son of God is *essentially* and *fundamentally self-emptying* or *self-negating* — because of this fundamental nature, the Son of God *is* Christ — that is, the Messiah. It is not that the Son of God *became* a person through the process of his self-emptying, but that fundamentally he *is* the true person and the true God at one and the same time in his dynamic work and activity of self-emptying.

This signifies that traditional understandings of incarnation, especially based on John's prologue — that is, the preexisting Logos (the Son of God) "became flesh" for us — need a new interpretation. Does John's Gospel talk about the Logos and its preexistence simply *objectively* apart from the grace of God and thereby apart from us? Who can properly and legitimately talk about the Logos and its preexistence without its revelation to the person? Is it not that only a person who receives revelation can properly speak of the Logos and its preexistence? There can be no Son of God existing merely as "the Son of God" apart from us. Without encountering it, one can talk about the preexistence of Logos only theoretically or theologically. The "preexisting" Son of God must be realized right here, right now, at the depth of our present existence, as the self-emptying Son of God. The Son of God becomes flesh simply because the Son of God is originally self-emptying.

Consequently, we may reformulate the doctrine of Christ's kenosis as follows:

> The Son of God is not the Son of God (for he is essentially and fundamentally self-emptying); precisely because he *is not* the Son of God he *is* truly the Son of God (for he originally and always works as Christ, the Messiah, in his salvational function of self-emptying).

If we speak of *homoousia* indicating an identity of the full divinity and full humanity of Jesus Christ in one person, it must not simply signify "consubstantiality" of two substances, divine and human, as understood traditionally, but rather "one function" or "nondual function" of self-emptying or self-negation. Without the deeply dynamic nondual function of self-emptying, the consubstantiality of the divinity and the humanity in Jesus Christ cannot be properly understood.

All discussion of Christ as the Son of God will be religiously meaningless if engaged in apart from the problem of human ego, our own existential problem of the self. The notion of Christ's kenosis or his self-emptying can be properly understood only through the realization of our own sinfulness and our own existential self-denying. Jesus himself emphasizes, "He that finds his life shall lose it; and he that loses his life for my sake shall find it" (Matt. 10:39). And Paul says, "Even so reckon you also yourselves to be dead unto sin, but alive unto God in Christ Jesus" (Rom. 6:11). "We are . . . always bearing about in the body the dying of Jesus, that the life of Jesus may also be manifested in our body" (2 Cor. 4:10). These words of Jesus and Paul clearly indicate that the denial of our life, or the death of our ego-self, because of our sinfulness, is necessary for our new life in Christ Jesus. This denial of our life, this death of our ego-self, should not be partial but total. Without the total negation of our life, or the complete death of our ego-self, our new life as a manifestation of the life of Jesus is impossible. There can be no continuity between the "old person" and the "new person" in the Pauline faith. If one believes the self of Christianity is somewhat continuous between the "old person" and the "new person" in terms of a responsible subject in relation to God's calling, the religious significance of the self-emptying and abnegation of Christ—that is, the death and resurrection of Jesus—is not fully grasped.

Just as the self-emptying or abnegation of the Son of God must not be partial but total and thoroughgoing for him to be Christ, the self-denial or death of the human ego-self must not be partial, but also total and complete. Only then can the new person be realized as the true and authentic self who confesses "it is no longer I that live, but Christ liveth in me; and that *life* which I now live in the flesh I live in the faith, *the faith* which is in the Son of God, who loved me, and gave himself up for me" (Gal. 2:20).

Accordingly, can we not reformulate the notion of the new person as the true self who resurrects through the death of the old person in such a way that "self is not self (for self as the old person must die on account of its sin), and precisely because it is not, self is truly self (for self is now alive as the new person, together with Christ)"? This is especially the case when we recall the following point made by Paul: "As in Adam all die, so also in Christ all shall be made alive" (1 Cor. 15:22), and "faithful is the saying: For if we died with him, we shall also live with him" (2 Tim. 2:11). Or in our faith in Jesus as Christ, we die together with Christ day by day and are revived together with Christ day by day (1 Cor. 15:1; 2 Cor. 4:16). Everyday, here and now, we die as the old person and resurrect as the new person with Christ. In this absolute present, we can properly say "self is not self; precisely because it is not, self is truly self."

Now, we have two formulations. First, in relation to the Son of God, we can say:

The Son of God is not the Son of God (for he is essentially and fundamentally self-emptying); precisely because he *is not* the Son of God he *is* truly the Son of God (for he originally and always works as Christ, the Messiah, in his salvational function of self-emptying).

Second, in relation to the human self, we can say:

Self is not self (for the old self must be crucified with Christ); precisely because it is not, self is truly self (for the new self resurrects with Christ).

The two formulations do not stand separately but signify respectively the two aspects of one and the same living reality—that is, one's faith in Jesus Christ.

The Humiliation and Exaltation of Christ

With regard to the kenosis of Christ, however, there is an important point for Christian faith that one should not overlook. Immediately after the above quotation from the Epistle to the Philippians (2:5–8), the following passage occurs:

Wherefore also God highly exalted him, and gave unto him the name which is above every name; that in the name of Jesus every knee should bow, of *things* in heaven and *things* on earth and *things* under earth, and that every tongue should confess that Jesus Christ is Lord, to the glory of God the Father.

(Phil. 2:9–11)

This is the exaltation of Christ, whereas the kenosis in the previous passage signifies the humiliation of Christ. Precisely as a result of his humiliation, Christ was raised to a place higher than before. "The way he took was that of self-denial and entire obedience, and by so acting he won his sovereignty."[18] In order to understand properly the kenosis of Christ we must clearly recognize the two states of Christ, that is, the state of humiliation and the state of exaltation. Criticizing a perceived one-sidedness in Martin Luther's *theologia crucis*, Karl Barth emphasizes that the theology of the cross is abstract without the theology of glory—that is, *theologia gloriae;* the state of humiliation and the state of exaltation must be grasped inseparably:

We cannot properly magnify the passion and death of Jesus Christ unless this magnifying includes within itself the *theologia gloriae*—the magnifying of the one who in His resurrection is the recipient of our right and life, the One who has risen again from the dead for us.[19]

Given the inseparability of the state of humiliation and the state of exaltation, my formulation of the doctrine of Christ's kenosis, which

35

reads, "The Son of God *is not* the Son of God; precisely because he is not the Son of God, he is truly the Son of God," may appear to emphasize unduly the state of humiliation or that of self-emptying in relation to the state of exaltation. This is so especially when I reject the notions of sheer "preexistence" of the Son of God and his "becoming flesh," and instead emphasize the complete self-emptying or negation of the Son of God in the absolute present.

As I suggested earlier, however, I believe that it is now necessary to take a new look at the notion of the preexistence of the Logos as the Son of God. Although this notion is essential to Christian faith, if we take current religion-negating ideologies into account, it must be reexamined or at least be demonstrated through confrontation with these ideologies. For the notion of preexistence of the Son of God is incompatible with the critical rationality and autonomous reason so important in the modern world. The notion of preexistence of the Son of God is also challenged by contemporary existentialistic atheism and active nihilism, which proclaim the death of God.

Another reason for a reexamination of the notion of the preexistence of the Son of God arises not merely from the necessity of responding to challenges posed by today's antireligious ideologies, but from within Christian faith itself. For in Christian faith, the problem of the kenosis of Christ inevitably leads us to face the problem of the kenosis of God. In other words, if Christ the Son of God empties himself, should we not consider the self-emptying of God, that is, the kenosis of the very God? We must now ask together with Jürgen Moltmann, "What does the cross of Jesus mean for God himself?"[20] This is not merely a theological question, but an existential and religious question deeply rooted in Christian faith.

The Kenosis of God

Christian theology generally states that the Son of God became a human without God ceasing to be God. In his book *Does God Exist?* Hans Küng says:

> The distinction of the Son of God from God the Father, his obedience and subordination to the Father, is of course upheld everywhere in the New Testament. The Father is "greater" than he is and there are things that are known only to the Father and not to him. Neither is there any mention anywhere in the New Testament of the incarnation of God himself.[21]

Küng also clearly says, "We should not of course speak of a 'crucified God.' That would suggest that God the Father, and not the Son, had been crucified. . . . But we can and may certainly speak of a 'hidden

God revealed in the Crucified.'"[22] As a Buddhist, however, who is concerned with promoting Buddhist-Christian dialogue to open up a new and deeper religious dimension in the contemporary context of religion versus antireligious ideologies, I realize that the kenosis of God is a crucial issue for our dialogue. Is it not that the kenosis of Christ—that is, the self-emptying of the Son of God—has its origin in God "the Father," that is, the kenosis of God? Without the self-emptying of God "the Father," the self-emptying of the Son of God is inconceivable. In the case of Christ, kenosis is realized in the fact that one who was in the form of God emptied "himself" and assumed the form of a servant. It originated in the will of God and the love of God, which is willing to forgive even the sinner who has rebelled against God. It was a deed that was accomplished on the basis of God's *will*. On the other hand, in the case of God, kenosis is implied in the original *nature* of God, that is, love.[23] In this sense, the notion of "crucified God," as discussed by Moltmann, is essential.[24]

My emphasis on the kenosis of God seems to be supported by Karl Rahner, who writes in *The Foundations of Christian Faith*:

> The primary phenomenon given by faith is precisely the self-emptying of God, his becoming, the kenosis and genesis of God himself. . . . Insofar as in his abiding and infinite fullness he empties himself, the other comes to be as God's very own reality. The phrase is already found in Augustine that God "assumes by creating" and also "creates by assuming," that is, he creates by emptying himself, and therefore, of course, he himself is in the emptying.[25]

In *Sacramentum Mundi*, under the title "Jesus' death as the death of God," Rahner emphasizes the death of Jesus as the death of God:

> Christology at the present day must reflect more closely on Jesus' death, not only in its redemptive effect, but also in itself. . . . If it is said that the incarnate Logos died only in his human reality, and if this is tacitly understood to mean that this death therefore did not affect God, only half the truth has been stated. The really Christian truth has been omitted. . . . Our "possessing" God must repeatedly pass through the deathly abandonment by God (Matt. 27:46; Mark 15:4) in which alone God ultimately comes to us, because God has given himself in love and as love, and thus is realized, and manifested in his death. Jesus' death belongs to God's self-utterance.[26]

Reading Karl Rahner more closely, however, I find an important point I cannot accept. Referring to the mystery of the incarnation, Rahner argues:

God can become something. He who is not subject to change in himself, can *himself* be subject to change *in something else.* . . . The absolute One [God] in the pure freedom of his infinite unrelatedness, which he always preserves, possesses the possibility of himself becoming the other, the finite. He possesses the possibility of *establishing* the other as his own reality by dispossessing *himself,* by giving *himself* away. . . . God goes out of himself, he himself, he as the self-giving fullness. Because he can do this, because this is his free and primary possibility, for this reason he is defined in scripture as love.[27]

Although these statements emphasize the self-emptying of God, they still leave behind traces of dualism, a dualism of God and the other, the infinite and the finite, immutability and change, within and without, and so forth. Of course, this is not a simple dualism in the ordinary sense, because God as the absolute, infinite One is understood here to possess "the possibility of becoming the other, the finite . . . by dispossessing himself." This dynamic interpretation of God, however, implies two things. First, by virtue of love, God does not remain in infinite unrelatedness but goes out of "himself" and gives "himself" away to the other. Second, even so, as the absolute One, God "always preserves" this infinite unrelatedness. This implies that God's infinite unrelatedness has priority over this relatedness with the other. Again, God's infinite fullness, being abiding, has priority over God's self-emptying. This is clearly seen in Rahner's statement "Insofar as in his abiding and infinite fullness he empties himself, the other comes to be as God's very own reality."[28]

This second point is what I referred to by speaking of "traces of dualism." Are these "traces of dualism" absolutely necessary for Christian faith in God? Do these "traces of dualism" have a positive rather than negative significance in Christianity? Rahner himself emphasizes, "The primary phenomenon given by faith is precisely the self-emptying of God, his becoming, the kenosis and genesis of God himself."[29] If this is the case, then the "traces of dualism" must be not only minimized, but also eliminated. God's self-emptying must be understood not as partial but as total to the extent that God's infinite unrelatedness has no priority over relatedness with the other and that God's self-emptying is dynamically identical with God's abiding and infinite fullness.

Inasmuch as we do not see this kind of *total* self-emptying of God in Rahner's interpretation, I cannot help but say that even for Karl Rahner, the kenosis of God, God's self-emptying, is still somewhat conceptualized or objectified. If God is really unconditional love, the self-emptying must be total, not partial. It must not be that God *becomes something else* by partial self-giving, but that in and through total self-emptying God *is* something—or more precisely, God _is_ each and every thing. This emphasis, however, should not be taken to signify pantheism (see the following section). On the contrary, only through this total kenosis and God's self-sacrificial identification with everything in the world is God truly God. Here we fully realize the reality and actuality of God, which is entirely beyond conception and objectification. This kenotic God is the ground of the kenotic Christ. The God who does not cease to be God even in the self-emptying of the Son of God, that is, the kenosis of Christ, is not the true God.

Accordingly, concerning faith in God, it must be said:

> God is not a self-affirmative God (for God is love and completely self-emptying); precisely because God is not a self-affirmative God, God is truly a God of love (for through complete self-abnegation God is totally identical with everything, including sinful humans).

This means that kenosis or emptying is not an _attribute_ (however important it may be) of God, but the fundamental _nature_ of God. God is God, not because God had the Son of God take a human form and be sacrificed while God remained God, but because God is a suffering God, a self-sacrificial God through total kenosis. The kenotic God who totally empties Godself and totally sacrifices Godself is, in my view, the true God. And it is precisely this kenotic God who thoroughly saves everything, including human beings and nature, through self-sacrificial, abnegating love.

I also believe that the notion of the kenotic God can overcome Nietzsche's nihilism, which insists upon the need to "sacrifice God for nothing," because instead of being sacrificed for nothingness by radical nihilists in the third stage of human history, the kenotic God sacrifices Godself not for relative nothingness but for _absolute_ nothingness, which is at one and the same time absolute Being.

God's total kenosis is not God's self-sacrifice for something else or God's self-negation for nihilistic nothingness, but God's self-sacrifice for absolutely "nothing" other than God's own fulfillment. Only in God's total kenosis is everything, including the unjust and sinner, natural and moral evil, forgiven, redeemed, and satisfied, and the love of God completely fulfilled. The notion of the kenotic God thus goes beyond Nietzsche's radical nihilism by deepening the religious significance of the Christian notion of the love of God.

In addition, the notion of the kenotic God opens up for Christianity a common ground with Buddhism by overcoming Christianity's monotheistic character, the absolute oneness of God, and by sharing with Buddhism the realization of absolute nothingness as the essential basis for the ultimate. This can be accomplished through the notion of the kenotic God—not through losing Christianity's self-identity, but rather through deepening its spirituality.

Furthermore, the notion of the kenotic God can also embrace the autonomous reason of modern science and the rationalistic subjectivity of the modern world because in the notion of the kenotic God, who is totally self-emptying, God's infinite unrelatedness and abiding fullness, which are incompatible with autonomous reason and modern rationalistic subjectivity, are eliminated. And yet, through total self-emptying, God is believed to reveal love most profoundly to embrace even a person's ego-self, which with its autonomous reason stands against God.

However, insofar as a person's ego-self remains with itself, the kenotic God is not really understood. Only when the ego-self negates itself completely does it come to understand who the kenotic God is and what God's total self-emptying means to the self. Accordingly, the above statement, "God is not a self-affirmative God, and precisely because God is not a self-affirmative God, God is truly God," can be properly grasped by the parallel existential realization that "self is not self, and precisely because it is not, self is truly self."

God: Each and Every Thing

In the previous section, I emphasized that in and through God's total self-emptying, God does not become something else, but *is* something or, more precisely, God *is* each and every thing. This emphasis may immediately give rise to the following two objections. First, such an emphasis leads to pantheism, which is rejected by authentic Christianity. Second, such an emphasis excludes the uniqueness of Jesus Christ as the only incarnation of the Son of God in history.

As for the first objection, I argue that the above emphasis should not be confused with pantheism. Pantheism as exemplified by Spinoza's dictum, *deus sive natura*, signifies the identity between God and empirical things in the world without a realization of God's self-negation. I am, however, discussing God's *being* each and everything through God's total kenosis, through the complete abnegation or self-emptying of God. Accordingly, my understanding of the relationship between God and nature is essentially different from that of Spinozan pantheism. Although Spinoza conceives of God as impersonal and immanent in all finite things and the individual self, God is still somewhat transcendent in that God's countless attributes remain inaccessible to us.[30]

In contrast, I am contending that through the kenosis of God, "God is truly God." This indicates a truly personal God who is identical with everything—including the sinful person—precisely because God is not a self-affirmative God (not one substance) but a completely self-emptying God. The completely kenotic God, in my view, is neither immanent nor transcendent, but thoroughly immanent and thoroughly transcendent at one and the same time. The completely kenotic God is not merely impersonal but deeply personal, in the sense that this God is self-emptying and fulfills God's unconditional love to save everything without exception, including the unjust and sinful. In the completely kenotic God, personality and impersonality are paradoxically identical.

The second possible objection concerning my emphasis that God *is* each and every thing through total kenosis demands a more detailed exploration and response. My emphasis seems to exclude the uniqueness of Jesus Christ as the only incarnation of the Son of God in history. That emphasis is, however, based on the notion that the kenotic Christ cannot be fully grasped without a realization of the total kenosis of God. Ultimately God incarnates Godself in the form of Jesus Christ not because God "can himself be subject to change in something else,"[31] but because through unconditional love God abnegates Godself so completely that God fully identifies with the crucified Christ on the cross. The resurrection of Christ should be understood precisely on this basis. If this total identity of God with the crucified Christ on the cross is a necessary premise for Christian faith, why is this total identity of God with Christ through God's kenosis not applicable to everything in the universe beyond Christ? Can we not legitimately say that each and every thing in the universe is also an incarnation of God together with Jesus Christ on the cross and his glorious resurrection?

But a further objection to this understanding might be raised by claiming that it eliminates the uniqueness of Jesus Christ in history, a concept essential to Christianity. To this objection, the following two points must be raised.

First, if Jesus Christ *is* uniquely Christ in the sense that the Son of God *became* a human through the process of self-emptying but *without a total abnegation of divinity,* his uniqueness as Christ will be destroyed or at least diminished by saying "each and every thing in the universe is also an incarnation of God together with Jesus Christ on the cross and his glorious resurrection." However, if the uniqueness of Jesus Christ is understood in the sense that the Son of God is essentially self-emptying and the crucified Christ is nothing but the revelation of this completely self-emptying Son of God *through total abnegation of his divinity,* the situation is different.

In other words, if the uniqueness of Jesus Christ is understood in the sense that the Son of God is truly the Son of God precisely because the

Son of God *is not* the Son of God, then that statement does not necessarily eliminate the uniqueness of Jesus Christ. Rather, due to his uniqueness of this kind, everything in the universe is understood to be an incarnation of God as well, for the uniqueness of Jesus Christ is here grasped in and through the total abnegation of the divinity of the Son of God.

Second, as discussed earlier, the kenosis of Christ has its origin in God, in the kenosis of God. Without the self-emptying of God, the self-emptying of the Son of God is inconceivable. In interpreting Paul, Moltmann states that just as the Son is delivered up to the death on the cross in order to become the Lord of both the dead and the living, "the Father delivers up his Son on the cross in order to be the Father of those who are delivered up." It is worth noting that Cyril of Jerusalem said, "On the cross, God stretched out his hands to embrace the ends of the earth," and "O blessed tree on which God was outstretched." On these words of Cyril, Moltmann comments:

> He [God] invites the whole earth to understand his suffering and his hopes in the outstretched arms of the crucified Jesus and therefore in God. . . . This symbol is an invitation to understand the Christ hanging on the cross as the outstretched God of the trinity.[32]

If this is the case, my understanding that each and every thing in the universe is also an incarnation of God together with Jesus on the cross and his glorious resurrection—because God is completely self-emptying—does not necessarily exclude the uniqueness of Jesus Christ, but broadens the Christian notion of an all-loving God.

Moltmann's Notion of the Crucified God

On the basis of the preceding understanding of the kenotic God, I find Jürgen Moltmann's notion of the "crucified God" extremely provocative and penetrating. In his book *The Crucified God*, Moltmann takes the event of the cross as an event of God and states that "[God] also suffers the death of his Fatherhood in the death of the Son."[33] For Moltmann, God is crucified in the crucified Christ. He emphasizes, however, that the trinitarian interpretation of the event of the cross rather than the traditional doctrine of the two natures in the person of Christ is necessary to understand properly the notion of the crucified God.

In the following I will (1) clarify why the trinitarian interpretation of the Christ event on the cross is necessary to Moltmann, (2) try to summarize his discussion of the trinitarian interpretation of the event on the cross, and (3) offer a critique of Moltmann's interpretation and thereby conclude with my own view.

Moltmann appreciates Karl Barth's position because "Barth has consistently drawn the harshness of the cross into his concept of God."[34] After quoting Barth's words in *Church Dogmatics*, "In God's eternal purpose it is God Himself who is rejected in His Son," for "God wills to lose that man may win,"[35] Moltmann states:

> Because Barth thought consistently of "God in Christ," he could think historically of God's being, speak almost in theopaschite terms of God's suffering and being involved in the cross of the Son, and finally talk of the "death of God," *de facto*, if not in those very words.[36]

Moltmann, however, criticizes Barth because Barth's approach is still too *theo*-logically oriented and is not sufficiently trinitarian. "In stressing constantly and rightly that '*God* was in Christ,' *God* humbled himself, *God* himself was on the cross, he [Barth] uses a simple concept of God which is not sufficiently developed in a trinitarian direction." For Moltmann, once one abandons the simple concept of God, there is a trinitarian solution to the paradox that God is "dead" on the cross and yet is not dead.[37]

Thus, Moltmann strongly emphasizes the necessity of the trinitarian understanding of God as the proper way to understand the significance of the death of Jesus for God:

> When one considers the significance of the death of Jesus for God himself, one must enter into the inner-trinitarian tensions and relationships of God and speak of the Father, the Son and the Spirit. But if that is the case, it is inappropriate to talk simply of "God" in connection with the Christ event. When one uses the phrase "God in Christ," does it refer only to the Father, who abandons him and gives him up, or does it also refer to the Son who is abandoned and forsaken? The more one understands the whole event of the cross as the event of God, the more any simple concept of God falls apart. In epistemological terms it takes, so to speak, trinitarian form. One moves from the exterior of the mystery which is called "God" to the interior, which is trinitarian. This is the "revolution in the concept of God" which is manifested by the crucified Christ.[38]

Thus Moltmann extensively discusses the trinitarian interpretation of the event of the crucified Christ in contrast to the traditional doctrine of two natures.

Moltmann's discussion may be summarized in the following three points. First, the doctrine of two natures understands the event of the cross statically as a reciprocal relationship between two qualitatively different natures, the divine nature, which is incapable of suffering, and the human nature, which is capable of suffering. The doctrine of kenosis, the self-emptying of God, was conceived within the framework of the distinction of the divine and the human. It has found few followers, because the framework of thought it has presented leads to difficult and impossible statements.[39] In the trinitarian interpretation, by contrast, the event of the cross is grasped as an event concerned with a relationship among the three persons: the Father, the Son, and the Spirit. The death of Jesus is not interpreted as a divine-human event, but as a trinitarian event among the Son, the Father, and the Spirit:

> What is in question in the relationship of Christ to his Father is not his divinity and humanity and their relationship to each other but the total, personal aspect of the Sonship of Jesus.[40]

> Christian theology cannot develop any bipolar theology of the reciprocal relationship between the God who calls and the man who answers: it must develop a trinitarian theology, for only in and through Christ is that dialogical relationship with God opened up.[41]

This implies that the event of the cross in God's being must be understood in both trinitarian and personal terms.[42]

Second, within the framework of the doctrine of two natures:

> One would have to say: what happened on the cross was an event between God and God. It was a deep division in God himself, in so far as God abandoned God and contradicted himself, and at the same time a unity in God, in so far as God was at one with God and corresponded to himself. In that case one would have to put the formula in a paradoxical way: God died the death of the godless on the cross and did not die. God is dead and yet is not dead. If one can only use the simple concept of God from the doctrine of two natures, one will always be inclined to restrict it to the person of the Father who abandons and accepts Jesus, delivers him and raises him up, and in so doing will "evacuate" the cross of deity.[43]

In contrast, to talk in trinitarian terms, Moltmann maintains:

> In the forsakenness of the Son the Father also forsakes himself. In the surrender of the Son the Father also surrenders himself, though not in the same way. . . . The Son suffers dying, the Father suffers the death of the Son. The grief of the Father here is just as important as the death of the Son. The Fatherlessness of the Son is matched by the sonlessness of the Father, and if God has constituted himself as the Father of Jesus Christ, then he also suffers the death of his Fatherhood in the death of the Son. Unless this were so, the doctrine of the Trinity would still have a monotheistic background.[44]

Furthermore, Moltmann emphasizes the deep community of will between Jesus and his God, which is expressed even in their deepest separation. Moltmann holds that it is through the spirit that such community and separation between Jesus and his God can go together:

> In the cross, Father and Son are most deeply separated in forsakenness and at the same time are most inwardly one in their surrender. What proceeds from this event between Father and Son is the Spirit which justifies the Godless, fills the forsaken with love and even brings the dead to life, since even the fact that they are dead cannot exclude them from this event of the cross; the death in God also includes them.[45]

Third, stating that the doctrine of the two natures in Christ began from the distinction between the immortal, unchangeable God and the mortal, corruptible human, Moltmann insists:

> The theistic concept of God according to which God cannot die, and the hope for salvation, according to which man is to be immortal, made it impossible to regard Jesus as really being God and at the same time as being forsaken by God.[46]

Moltmann maintains that the Godforsakenness of Christ is a historical event; his resurrection, however, is not a historical but an eschatological event. If both historical Godforsakenness and eschatological surrender can be seen in Christ's death on the cross, then we can realize that this event contains community between Jesus and his Father in separation, and separation in community:

> Faith understands the historical event between the Father who forsakes and the Son who is forsaken on the cross in eschatological terms as an event between the Father who loves and the Son who is loved in this present spirit of the love that creates life.[47]

Like Hegel, speaking of the life of God within the Trinity as the "history of God," Moltmann states:

> The concrete "history of God" in the death of Jesus on the cross on Golgotha therefore contains within itself all the depths and abysses of human history and therefore can be understood as the history of history. All human history, however much it may be determined by guilt and death, is taken up into this "history of God," i.e., into the trinity, and integrated into the future of the "history of God." There is no suffering which in this history of God is not God's suffering, no death which has not been God's death in the history of Golgotha. Therefore there is no life, no fortune and no joy which have not been integrated by his history into eternal life, the eternal joy of God.[48]

Precisely in this sense, Moltmann speaks of a "theology after Auschwitz" and maintains that "like the cross of Christ, even Auschwitz is in

God himself. Even Auschwitz is taken up into the grief of the Father, the surrender of the Son and the power of the Spirit."[49]

The above three points are a synopsis of Moltmann's discussion of the event of Christ on the cross in trinitarian terms. To Moltmann, the doctrine of the Trinity is not "an exorbitant and impractical speculation about God":

> [It] is nothing other than a shorter version of the passion narrative of Christ in its significance for the eschatological freedom of faith and the life of oppressed nature. It protects faith from both monotheism and theism because it keeps believers at the cross.[50]

Appreciation and Criticism of Moltmann

To me, Moltmann's interpretation of the event of Christ on the cross in trinitarian terms is quite discerning and stimulating. Moving from the traditional doctrine of two natures to the doctrine of Trinity in the understanding of the significance of the death of Jesus for God, Moltmann then moves "from the exterior of the mystery which is called 'God' to the interior, which is trinitarian," from the simple concept of God (*esse simplex*) to the intertrinitarian tensions of God.[51] I have a great sympathy and appreciation for Moltmann's approach. I have, however, two mutually related questions concerning the basic standpoint of Moltmann's trinitarian interpretation.

Moltmann presents a trinitarian interpretation of the significance of the crucified Christ for God as *the solution* to the paradox inevitable in the doctrine of two natures—that is, "God is 'dead' on the cross and yet is not dead."[52] My first question is whether the trinitarian interpretation as illustrated by Moltmann is a *real* solution of that paradoxical statement about God. And my second question, closely related to the first, is whether in Moltmann's trinitarian theology the event of the cross in God's being is, as Moltmann claims, really understood in *both* trinitarian *and* personal terms, or in *both* christocentric *and* trinitarian terms?

It is clear that by adopting the trinitarian interpretation instead of the doctrine of two natures Moltmann moves from the exterior of the mystery of God and enters into the interior. Is not this movement, however, merely one step into the interior and not a complete penetration into the depth of God's mystery? Is it not a partial solution rather than a complete solution? In order to resolve completely the paradox involved in the traditional doctrine of two natures in the person of the Christ, must one not enter into a still greater "interior" than the trinitarian position outlined by Moltmann? Is not the mystery of God found not in the interior as distinguished from the exterior, but only in the still greater interior of the interior? Cannot God's mystery and therefore the solution of the paradoxical statement "God is dead on the cross and yet is not dead" be realized only in the absolute interior which, transcending the duality between the interior and the exterior, is neither interior nor exterior in the relative sense?

These questions may be restated in the following manner. Can the doctrine of Trinity, which may be "the unity of three persons in one God or Godhead," truly resolve the paradox involved in the doctrine of two natures? In the doctrine of the Trinity, it is clear that the one God is not the fourth person or the fourth being. The one God is the common *substantia* or *essentia*, whereas the three persons are three distinct *hypostases*. Although there are clear differences and mutual relationships among the three persons, the one God is the undivided essence, indicating the unity of God. The distinction between *essentia* (which is one and unity) and *hypostasis* (which is three and trinity) is indispensable and should not be confused in the doctrine of the Trinity. If this distinction is vital, however, the one God as *essentia*, though clearly not the fourth being, is not completely independent of or free from the character of the fourth being. In my view, in order to overcome the presence of the character of the fourth being, the oneness of this one God must possess the characteristic of zero. The one God in the Trinity must be the great zero that is free even from oneness as distinguished from threeness.

This means that only when the one God is understood to have the characteristic of zero can the doctrine of Trinity be fully and dynamically realized. This is because three distinctive beings—Father, Son, and Spirit—are then clearly and thoroughly realized in their distinctiveness without any possibility of being reduced to one Godhead, and because at the same time the oneness of the one God is completely preserved from the haunting presence of the fourth being. Furthermore, only at this point (only when the one God is understood in terms of the great zero) can the doctrine of Trinity be a real solution to the paradox involved in the traditional doctrine of two natures; that is, God is dead on the cross and yet God is not dead.

What, then, is the nature of the zero that is indispensable to the one God of the Trinity? It indicates *Nichts* or *Ungrund* as the Godhead, as exemplified by Christian mystics such as Meister Eckhart and Jakob Böhme. And it is nothing other than "the still greater interior of the interior" mentioned earlier. In order for the trinitarian structure to be truly possible, the one God should not be *essentia* as distinguished from *hypostasis*, much less *substantia*, but *Nichts* or *Ungrund*. Only when the doctrine of Trinity is understood in this way are the unity and the trinity of God fully and harmoniously realized without conflict. And only then is the event of the cross in God's being, as Moltmann requires, understood in *both* trinitarian *and* personal terms, or "simultaneously in both christocentric and trinitarian terms."[53]

This last point leads us to my second question and raises the following issue. When one moves from the traditional doctrine of two natures in Christ to the trinitarian understanding of the Christ event and thus moves from the exterior of the mystery of God to the interior, one may lose direct contact with the historical event of the cross. Even in entering into the inner trinitarian tensions in God, the human hope for salvation should not be neglected. This is precisely because Moltmann emphasizes the necessity of understanding the event of the cross in God's being in both christocentric and trinitarian terms.

I do not think, however, that Moltmann's interpretation of Trinity sufficiently enables one to understand the event of the cross in God's being both in christocentric and in trinitarian terms. For by the relative movement from the exterior of God's mystery to the interior, one cannot reach the deepest depth of God's mystery, which is common ground (as *Ungrund*) for both the unity and the trinity of God. Only when one goes beyond the interior of God's mystery and enters into its still more fundamental interior, the absolute interior, can one understand the event of the cross in God's being both in christocentric and trinitarian terms. This is because the absolute interior is dynamically identical with the absolute exterior—the interior still more fundamental than the mere interior is nothing but the exterior still more fundamental than the mere exterior. In the deepest dimension of God's mystery, the absolute interior and the absolute exterior are paradoxically and dynamically identical and are beyond dualism. Right here, both the eschatological hope of salvation and the internal, undivided oneness of God are fully and thoroughly realized.

The simultaneous understanding of the event of the crucified Christ both in christocentric and trinitarian terms is possible only by penetrating into the absolute interior of God's mystery, which is the absolute exterior at one and the same time. And this greatest depth of God's mystery is precisely the Godhead as *Nichts* or *Ungrund*, not one God as *essentia* or *substantia*. The real solution of the paradox inevitable in the doctrine of two natures—that "God is dead on the cross and yet is not dead"—is also fully realized in understanding the Godhead as *Nichts*.

The death of Jesus on the cross is not a divine-human event, but most certainly a trinitarian event of the Father, the Son, and the Spirit. What is important in this regard is the total, personal aspect of the sonship of Jesus. This sonship of Jesus, however, is ultimately rooted in *Nichts* or *Ungrund* as the Godhead in "the unity of three persons in one God." Only here, but not in a trinitarian interpretation according to which

God is *una substantia* (one nature), can we say with full justification – as Moltmann does – that "in the cross, Father and Son are most deeply separated in forsakenness and at the same time are most inwardly one in their surrender."[54] Again, only here – when the sonship of Jesus is understood to be ultimately rooted in *Nichts* as Godhead – can the event of the cross of Jesus be understood truly as the event of an unconditioned and boundless love fully actualized for the Godless and the loveless in this law-oriented society.

In his book *Does God Exist?*, Hans Küng writes, "God in the Bible is subject and not predicate: it is not that love is God, but that God is love – God is one who faces me, whom I can address."[55] Can I not address God, however, not from the outside of God, but from within God? Again, is it not that God faces me within God even if I turn my back on God? the God who faces me and whom I address is God as subject. However, the God within whom I address as God and within whom God meets me is not God as subject but rather God as predicate. Or, more strictly speaking, that God is neither God as subject nor God as predicate but God as *Nichts*. In God as *Nichts*, God as subject meets me even if I turn my back on God and I can truly address the God as Thou. An I-Thou relationship between the self and God takes place precisely in God as *Nichts*. Because God as *Nichts* is the *Ungrund* ground of the I-Thou relationship between the self and God, God as *Nichts* is neither subject nor predicate but a "copula" that acts as a connecting or intermediating link between the subject and the predicate. This means that God as *Nichts* is *Nichts* as God: God is *Nichts* and *Nichts* is God. And on this basis we may say that God is love and love is God, because *Nichts* is the unconditional, self-negating love. This is the absolute interior of God's mystery, which is its absolute exterior at one and the same time. We may thus declare:

> God is love because God is *Nichts*;
> *Nichts* is God because *Nichts* is love.

Here, both human longing for salvation and the deepest mystery of God are thoroughly fulfilled. Here again, the event of the cross in God's being is understood in both trinitarian and personal terms most profoundly.

God as subject who meets one and whom one can address as Thou is incompatible with the autonomous reason peculiar to modern humanity, and is also challenged by Nietzschean nihilism and atheistic existentialism. The notion of God as *Nichts*, however, not only is compatible with but also can embrace autonomous reason because there is no conflict between the notion of God as *Nichts* (which is neither subject nor predicate) and autonomous reason, and because the autonomy of rational thinking, however much it may be emphasized, is not limited by the notion of God as *Nichts*. In the kenotic God who is *Nichts*, not only are modern human autonomous reason and rationalistic subjectivity overcome without being marred, but also the mystery of God is most profoundly perceived. God as love is fully and most radically grasped far beyond contemporary atheism and nihilism.

All this is implied when I stated earlier that God is not God; precisely because of this, God is truly God. And, as I also emphasized before, this statement of God cannot be properly understood without our own parallel existential realization that "Self is not self, and precisely because it is not, self is truly self."

DYNAMIC SUNYATA

Sunyata as the Buddhist Ultimate

Now I turn to Buddhism and discuss how Buddhism can overcome scientism and Nietzsche's nihilism, and can also open up a basis for dialogue with Christianity.

The ultimate reality for Buddhism is neither Being nor God, but Sunyata. Sunyata literally means "emptiness" or "voidness" and can imply "absolute nothingness." This is because Sunyata is entirely unobjectifiable, unconceptualizable, and unattainable by reason or will. As such it cannot be any "something" at all. Accordingly, if Sunyata is conceived as *somewhere outside of* or *beyond* one's self-existence, it is not true Sunyata, for Sunyata thus conceived outside of or beyond one's existence turns into *something* that one represents and calls "Sunyata." True Sunyata is not even that which is represented and conceived as "Sunyata." In Nagarjuna's *Mulamadhyamaka-karika*, Sunyata, which is dimly perceived, is likened to "a snake wrongly grasped or [magical] knowledge incorrectly applied."[56] Throughout its long history, Mahayana Buddhism has strongly rejected such a view of Sunyata—that is, Sunyata represented and thereby attached to as "Sunyata"—as "Sunyata perversely clung to," as a "literal understanding of negativity," or as a "view of annihilatory nothing-ness." Instead, Mahayana Buddhism emphasizes that "Sunyata is non-Sunyata (*asunyata*); therefore it is ultimate Sunyata (*atyanta-Sunyata*)."[57] Sunyata not only is not Being or God, but also *not* emptiness as distinguished from somethingness or fullness. Just as the attachment to being must be overcome, the attachment to emptiness must also be surmounted. Accordingly, however important the notion of Sunyata may be in Buddhism, following Martin Heidegger, who put a cross mark "X" on the term *Sein*, thus rendering it as Sein, in order to show the unobjectifiability of Sein, we should also put a cross mark "X" on Sunyata, and render it Sunyata. What has been said above indicates that Sunyata is not self-affirmative, but thoroughly self-negative. In other words, emptiness not only empties everything else but also empties itself. Sunyata should not be conceived of somewhere outside one's self-existence, nor somewhere inside one's self-existence. True Sunyata is neither outside nor inside, neither external nor internal, neither transcendent nor immanent. Sunyata completely empties everything, including itself. That is to say, the pure activity of absolute emptying is true Sunyata. Hence, the well-known passage in the Heart Sutra (Prajnaparamita-hrdaya-sutra):

> Form is emptiness and the very emptiness is form; emptiness does not differ from form; form does not differ from emptiness; whatever is form, that is emptiness; whatever is emptiness, that is form.[58]

As the Heart Sutra clearly indicates, the realization that "form is emptiness," however important and necessary it may be, is not sufficient; it must immediately be accompanied with the realization that "the very emptiness is form." And these two realizations are one, not two.

"Form" should not be grasped and attached to as something substantial but should be emptied as nonsubstantial or formless. We should not become attached to such discriminations as "mountains are mountains; water is water," but should awaken to the nonsubstantiality or emptiness of such discriminations by realizing that "mountains are not mountains; water is not water." At the same time, however, "emptiness" should not be grasped and attached to merely as something nonsubstantial or formless, for formless emptiness must itself be emptied and grasped in terms of form. Thus, we must realize discrimination through nondiscrimination—that is, "mountains are really mountains precisely because mountains are not mountains; water is really water precisely because water is not water."[59]

Accordingly, although the Heart Sutra states, "whatever is form, that is emptiness; whatever is emptiness, that is form," this does not indicate a static or immediate identity of form and emptiness. Nor does it signify an identity of form and emptiness that is set forth and represented before one's eyes. It is a dynamic identity that is to be grasped only in an unobjectifiable and pre-representational manner—through the pure activity of emptying. In the realization of true Sunyata, form is ceaselessly emptied, turning into formless emptiness, and formless emptiness is ceaselessly emptied and forever freely taking form. This total dynamic movement of emptying, not a static state of emptiness, is

51

the true meaning of Sunyata. If we conceive of this total dynamic movement of emptying as *somewhere outside* us or *some time beyond* our present self-existence, however, we fail to realize Sunyata. Sunyata is not outside us, nor are we outside Sunyata.

In one sense, we are right here, right now, *in* Sunyata. We are always involved in the ceaseless emptying movement of Sunyata, for there is nothing outside it. And yet, in another sense, we are always totally embracing this ceaseless movement of Sunyata within ourselves. We *are* Sunyata in each and every moment of our lives. For true Sunyata is not Sunyata thought by us, but Sunyata lived by us. In this living realization of true Sunyata, self and Sunyata are dynamically identical. That is to say, true Sunyata is nothing but the true self, and the true self is nothing but true Sunyata. Apart from the absolute present—right here, right now—this dynamical identity of self and Sunyata cannot be fully realized. Again, apart from the nonobjectifiable and pre-representational standpoint, the absolute present and the dynamical identity of self and Sunyata cannot be properly grasped. And this dynamic identity of self and Sunyata is equally true of everyone and everything throughout the universe. Consequently, although the term *Sunyata* or *emptiness* may sound negative, it has positive, soteriological meanings.

The Positive Meanings of Sunyata

The positive, soteriological meanings of Sunyata may be summarized in five points.

First, in Sunyata, regardless of the distinction between self and other, humans and nature, humans and the divine, everything without exception is realized *as it is* in its *suchness* (in Sanskrit, *tathata*, which may also be rendered as "is-ness"). The realization of the suchness of everything is an important characteristic of the dimension of Sunyata. This does not, however, indicate that in Sunyata the distinctiveness of everything is eliminated. On the contrary, in the locus of Sunyata the distinctiveness of everything is clearly and thoroughly realized without being reduced to any monistic principle such as Brahman, Substance, or God, and yet everything is *equally* realized in its as-it-is-ness or suchness.

In the realization of Sunyata in the light of suchness, both distinction and equality, distinctiveness and sameness, are fully realized. For example, in the locus of Sunyata you are thoroughly you as you are and I am thoroughly I as I am—with our distinctive individuality and without ending in a single ultimate principle—and yet you and I are equally sharing the sameness in that both you and I are equally realized in terms of being-as-we-are. This is true not only of you and me, but also of the self and any other, the self and nature, and the self and the divine. The self is the self, nature is nature, and God is God, all with their distinctiveness, and yet they all are equal in terms of "each is as each is" or "as it is." Accordingly, in the realization of suchness, there is no difference between human beings and nonhuman beings (nature and supernatural entities).

This emphasis on there being no difference between human and nonhuman beings in the realization of "suchness" should not, as is often the case, be misunderstood as signifying a disregard of the particularity of human (and divine) personality.

Like Christianity, Buddhism is primarily concerned with human salvation—that is, the deliverance of human beings from suffering. Unlike Christianity, however, Buddhism does not take the personalistic divine-human relationship (I-thou relationship) as the *basis* of salvation, thereby regarding impersonal nature as something peripheral, but instead takes as the basis of salvation the transpersonal, universal dimension common to human beings and nature. This is why in Buddhism the clear realization of impermanency or transiency common to everything, including humans and nature, is the turning point from samsara to nirvana. In this transpersonal, universal dimension, everything, human and nonhuman, is equally and individually realized in its as-it-is-ness.[60]

Furthermore, unlike Christianity, which talks about God as the ruler and the savior, Buddhism does not accept the notion of a transcendent ruler of the universe or of a savior outside one's self. A Buddha is not a supernaturally existing being, but is none other than a person who awakens to the Dharma, the truth, the suchness or as-it-is-ness of everything in the realization of Sunyata. This means that it is by a person—by an awakened one—that the suchness of everything is realized. But suchness thus realized by a person encompasses everything in the universe, including human beings, nature, and the divine, the secular and the sacred.

For the elucidation of the issue, we should make a distinction between salvation as such and the *basis* of salvation; that is, between the problem of what salvation is conceived to be in a particular religion and the problem of on what *basis* that salvation is understood to take place. The realization of the "such-ness" of everything as the basis of salvation entails the awakening of one's original nature together with the awakening of the original nature of everything else, and the emancipation from attachment to the self and others.

Second, Sunyata indicates *boundless openness* without any particular fixed center. Sunyata is free not only from egocentrism but also from anthropocentrism, cosmocentrism, and theocentrism. It is not oriented by any kind of centrism. Only in this way is "emptiness" possible.

Accordingly, in Sunyata there is no fixed dominant-subordinate relationship among things in the universe. Humankind is not simply subordinate to Buddha, nor is nature simply subordinate to humankind. In this boundless openness, everything without exception is dominant as subject over everything else, and *at the same time* is subordinate to everything else. Such a dynamic, mutual dominant-subordinate relationship is possible only in the locus of Sunyata, which is completely free from any centrism and is boundlessly open. This is a complete emancipation and freedom from any kind of bondage resulting from discrimination based on any kind of centrism.

We find an idea strikingly similar to this mutual dominant-subordinate relationship in Christianity where Martin Luther emphasizes the following two propositions in his treatise *The Freedom of a Christian.*

> A Christian is a perfectly free lord of all, subject to none.
> A Christian is a perfectly dutiful servant of all, subject to all.[61]

The essential difference between Luther and Buddhism in this connection, however, lies in two points: (1) In Luther the mutual dominant-subordinate (lord of all and servant of all) relationship is realized only between human beings but not between human beings and nature. By contrast, in Buddhism the mutual dominant-subordinate relationship is realized not only among *each and every human being* but also among *each and every thing* in the universe, including human beings and nature. There is no anthropocentrism as occurs in Christianity. (2) In Luther, the mutual dominant-subordinate relationship is based on union with Christ, sharing with each other the things of God. Faith in Christ, the word of God alone, justifies, frees, and saves people. Without this christocentric and theocentric basis, the mutual dominant-subordinate relationship is not possible for Luther. On the other hand, the Buddhist idea of the mutual dominant-subordinate relationship occurs because there is no centrism whatsoever in the boundless openness of Sunyata.

Whereas the freedom of the Christian is realized through faith in the gospel of Christ, the freedom of the Buddhist is found in the awakening to the nonsubstantiality and the interdependence of everything in the universe. If in Christianity, as I suggested earlier, not only the kenosis of Christ, but also the kenosis of God is fully realized, and God completely empties Godself, the dynamic relationship of mutual domination-subordination or mutual immanence and mutual transcendence between human beings and God, and human beings and nature, can be fully realized. This is possible only by overcoming the theocentrism innate in Christianity.

Third, Sunyata can be translated by *jinen* in Japanese, or *svayambhu* in Sanskrit, which means "self-so," "so of itself," "things as they are," or "spontaneity." It also means "naturalness," not as a counterconcept to human agency, but as the primordial or fundamental naturalness underlying both human beings and nature. It is the most basic original "nature" of things prior to the separation between human beings and nature, between the divine and the human. Accordingly, *jinen* is beyond any kind of will, including human will, God's will, and the will to power in Nietzsche's sense. *Jinen* is, however, not a motionless, static, fixed state, but rather a pure activity of the most dynamic spontaneity, because it signifies unconstrained spontaneity realized in Sunyata without any will, whether it be the will of self or other, human or divine. God's complete self-emptying (the kenosis of God) as the absolute self-negation of the will of God must be based on this spontaneity in terms of *jinen*. Indeed, *jinen* is the dynamic, open abode to which everything returns for its final rest, and from which everything comes forth spontaneously.

Fourth, in Sunyata, not only the interdependence and interpenetration but also the mutual reversibility of things is fully realized. This is a natural consequence of the previously mentioned mutual dominant-subordinate relationships among things. Even the unity of opposites is fully realized in Sunyata because Sunyata is the locus of the boundless openness without any center or circumferential limitation. Accordingly, not only can this and that, here and there, up and down, right and left, East and West (in terms of spatiality) be realized to be interpenetrating and reciprocal, but also beginning and end, before and after, past and future (in terms of temporality) can be grasped as interpenetrating and reciprocal. Accordingly, time and history are not simply understood to be linear and unidirectionally moving toward a particular end, but are understood to be reciprocal and even reversible. (See the section below, "Time and History in Buddhism.") In this way, each and every moment of time and history can be realized as the beginning and the end at once. Furthermore, in the locus of Sunyata, good and evil, right and wrong, beauty and ugliness, and all value judgments, without being fixed in their orders, but without losing their differences, can be realized to be interpenetrating and reciprocal. Hence, there is no supreme good or eternal punishment. Nirvana is realized amid samsara, and samsara, when its nonsubstantiality is realized, immediately transforms into nirvana.

Fifth, and of most importance, Sunyata contains the two characteristics of wisdom (*prajna*) and compassion (*karuna*). Positively speaking, Sunyata is wisdom in the light of which the suchness of everything is clearly realized in terms of distinctiveness and sameness. And, in the light of wisdom, the aforementioned *jinen* is also clearly realized.

Accordingly, in the locus of Sunyata, by virtue of wisdom, all things, including the natural, the human, and the divine, regardless of their differences, are each equally affirmed in their suchness and *jinen*. This is, however, not an uncritical affirmation of the given situation. On the contrary, it is a great and absolute affirmation beyond—and thus not excluding—any critical, objective, and analytical distinction. This is because the absolute affirmation realized in Sunyata is established through the negation of negation; this is the negation of nondistinction, which is in turn the negation of distinction in the ordinary sense.

This wisdom aspect of Sunyata is inseparably and dynamically connected with the compassion aspect of Sunyata. Sunyata is compassion in the light of which the dominant-subordinate relationship among things in the ordinary and relative sense is freely turned over, and moral and ethical judgments in terms of good and evil or right and wrong on the human, historical dimension are transcended in the ultimate dimension. Through compassion realized in Sunyata, even an atrocious villain is ultimately saved, even evil passions are transformed into enlightenment. In contrast to the ordinary statement "Even an evil person is born in the Pure Land, that is, can be saved, how much more so a good person," Shinran, the founder of Pure Land True Buddhism, declares, "Even a good person is born in the Pure Land, how much more so is an evil person."[62]

Zen, too, emphasizes the same reversal of moral order in the deeper religious dimension by saying, "The immaculate practitioner takes three kalpas (aeons) to enter nirvana, whereas the apostate bhikku (monk) does not fall into hell."[63] Such transmoral compassionate activities and universal salvation are possible because they come spontaneously out of the unfathomable depth of Sunyata and because they are based on the great affirmation of all things realized through wisdom.

In the above five points I described the positive meanings of the Buddhist notion of Sunyata. In our times, however, because of these characteristics of the Buddhist principle of Sunyata, a Buddhist cannot escape at least the following three criticisms often raised by Western and Christian friends.

First, if the realization of the suchness and *jinen* of everything, a realization that is beyond critical, objective, and analytical distinctions, is essential to Sunyata, how can human reason and intellect, so important in the modern world, work in the context of Sunyata? Are they merely to be disregarded? What is the relationship between Buddhism and science, Sunyata and rational thinking?

Second, if value judgments, including the distinction between good and evil, right and wrong, are completely reciprocal or reversible, how can human ethics be established? In particular, how is the problem of evil to be understood in the realization of suchness and *jinen*?

Third, if past and future are completely interpenetrating and reciprocal, how can history be understood to take place? How can we talk about the novelty of things in history and the direction and end or outcome of human history? In addition to this criticism, Christian friends often make the following point:

> Christianity also, to some extent, talks about the interpenetration of past and future, for example, in terms of the eternal creation and the realized eschatology, and talks about the reversibility of value judgment, for example, as we see in Jesus' words "I come not to call the righteous, but the sinner." In Christianity, however, Jesus Christ as the Messiah and God as the ruler of history provide a criterion of ethical judgment and the aim of history along with the sense of novelty. How does the Buddhist principle provide a criterion of ethical judgment and the aim and direction of human history?[64]

My response to these criticisms requires both some further basic considerations about Sunyata and some critical reflections. There are two basic considerations about Sunyata that need to be elaborated. First, Sunyata should not be understood as a goal or end to be attained in Buddhist life, but as the ground or the point of departure from which Buddhist life and activity can properly begin. Sunyata as the goal or end of the Buddhist life is Sunyata conceived outside one's self-existence, which, as I mentioned earlier, is not true Sunyata. True Sunyata is realized only in and through the self here and now and is always the ground or the point of departure for Buddhist life.

Second, Sunyata is fundamentally non-Sunyata—that is, Sunyata with an "X" through it (S̶u̶n̶y̶a̶t̶a̶). That is the true and ultimate Sunyata. This means that true Sunyata not only empties everything else, but also empties itself. Through its self-emptying it makes everything exist as it is and work as it does. In other words, through its self-emptying the realization of Sunyata reestablishes a dualistic view and value judgment clearly, without being limited by them. Sunyata should not be understood in its nominal form but in its verbal form, for it is a dynamic and creative function of emptying everything and making alive everything.

The Role of Human Reason in Buddhism

On the basis of these two basic considerations, I want to make three critical remarks concerning the Buddhist notion of Sunyata. Let us examine the role of human reason in Buddhism, the meaning of free will in Buddhism, and time and history in Buddhism.

First, the role of human reason in Buddhism. Throughout the long history of Buddhism, human reason or intellect has not been grasped positively. Human reason or intellect as a mental ability to think, to measure and discriminate objects, is called *vikalpa* or *parikalpa*, and it has been regarded as something to be overcome in order to attain awakening or wisdom (*jnana*).

This is significantly different from the Western tradition, in which, from ancient Greece to today, human reason has generally been regarded as something essential to attaining true knowledge. This is especially the case when *nous* or *intellectus*, which is distinguished from *logos* or *ratio* as the power of conceptual and discursive thinking, connotes higher activities of the human mind that can intuitively realize ultimate reality and strive for positive unity in thought and action.

In Kant, pure theoretical reason can provide synthetic a priori knowledge that makes pure mathematics and pure natural science possible. With his theory of pure theoretical reason, Kant gives a firm philosophical foundation to empirical knowledge of the phenomenal world. Although Kant clearly realizes the limitation of pure theoretical reason in that the "thing in itself" cannot be known even though it is "thinkable" by theoretical reason, he philosophically demonstrates the possibility of knowledge of metaphysical entities such as freedom, the immortality of the soul, and God, by pure practical reason. In Kant, ultimate reality is knowable not theoretically but only practically in ethics. And to him, ethics is to be based on pure practical *reason*.

Arguing that "what is rational, that is actual; and what is actual, that is rational,"[65] Hegel emphasizes the dynamic identity of the rational and the actual. To Hegel, philosophy is nothing but the reconciliation with actuality. He advances the notion of "absolute knowledge" in which the opposition between subjectivity and objectivity, between rationality and actuality, is completely overcome. But, because Hegel's philosophy was later criticized as a panlogism, it is not completely free from the superiority of rationality over actuality, subjectivity over objectivity, form over matter. This can be seen in the fact that Hegel himself calls his logic "Subjective Logic."[66] Through this brief excursion into the history of Western philosophy, one can see how strong and persistent the reliance on speculative reason is in that intellectual tradition.

In marked contrast, the Buddhist tradition espouses persistent distrust of human reason. Buddhism did not find in human reason an intuitive ability to grasp ultimate reality. Buddhism thus has not developed human reason in the direction of transcendental pure reason as Kant did, or in Hegel's direction of dialectical, speculative mind. As a result, pure science and pure theoretical philosophy did not emerge in the long tradition of Buddhism. This is because the primary concern of Buddhism is not to study the laws of nature or to comprehend reality through speculation, but pragmatically to emancipate people from the suffering caused by the fundamental ignorance innate in human existence, ignorance of ultimate reality, ignorance deriving from the conceptual, dualistic way of thinking peculiar to human reason. Buddhism insists that only by completely overcoming rational and conceptual thinking can one awaken to suchness, as-it-is-ness, or the original "nature" of everything in the universe, which is fundamentally unanalyzable, unconceptualizable, and unobjectifiable.

Inasmuch as this awakening to suchness is beyond discrimination, it is called in Buddhism *nirvikalpa-jnana*,[67] nondiscriminating wisdom. This, however, does not signify the absence of discrimination or the absence of thinking—that is, "not-thinking"—because "not-thinking" is a mere negation of thinking and is still discriminated from thinking. Wisdom that is truly nondiscriminating is free even from the discrimination between "thinking" and "not-thinking," between discrimination and nondiscrimination. Accordingly, nondiscriminating wisdom is called *hishiryo*,[68] that is, nonthinking thinking, beyond both *shiryo*, thinking, and *fushiryo*, not-thinking. Unlike not-thinking (*fushiryo*), nonthinking thinking (*hishiryo*) is not an absence of thinking, but rather primordial thinking prior to the distinction and opposition between thinking and not-thinking. It is also primordial thinking prior to the bifurcation between the thinking subject and object of thinking. This is why Dogen, a Zen master in thirteenth-century Japan, said, "Nonthinking Thinking itself is Right Thinking."[69] In nonthinking thinking there is neither subject nor object, neither self nor no-self. It indicates the realization of the True Self, which, being entirely unobjectifiable, is to be realized even more on the near side than self and no-self.

Nondiscriminating wisdom, another term for nonthinking thinking, signifies *satori*, the awakening to the true self. It is only in this nondiscriminating wisdom that the suchness or as-it-is-ness of everything in the universe is fully realized. In nondiscriminating wisdom, thinking and being are identical. And this identity is inseparably connected with the awakening to the true self. This dynamic identity of thinking, being, and the true self is possible because nondiscriminating wisdom is a characteristic of Sunyata. Accordingly, although nondiscriminating wisdom is subjectless and objectless, it is not a special psychological state, but can be realized only by completely turning over all possible rational thinking and by breaking through even what is called *nous* or *intellectus*.

Due to its dynamic character, nondiscriminating wisdom does not exclude thinking. Instead, being beyond both thinking and not-thinking, it includes both. It can include rational, discursive thinking and even pure theoretical reason. This is, however, only *potentially* so, for historically Buddhism has been hasty to go beyond human reason to arrive at the nondiscriminating wisdom because of the stance that human reason is merely discriminative. Thus Buddhism has not known the creative possibility of human reason developed in the modern West in terms of science.

Buddhism also failed to realize that transcendental pure reason as opened up by Kant and dialectical self-negating reason as advocated by Hegel can be developed and realized out of human reason. As a result, the traditional form of Buddhism contributes little to the problems of rationality and science. In my view, this historical fact derives from overlooking the dynamic character of the Buddhist notion of Sunyata. Unless the dynamic character of Sunyata is fully realized, nonthinking thinking is apt to turn into mere "not-thinking." But, as I suggested, the Buddhist notion of nondiscriminating wisdom can *potentially* include and operate human reason and thinking within itself. It is an urgent task for Buddhism to *actualize* this potentiality experientially and existentially in contemporary terms.[70]

In order to pursue this task, the dynamic structure of the Buddhist notion of Sunyata must be realized to the extent that it can legitimately recognize and embrace all possible rational thinking, including the transcendental pure reason in Kant and dialectical self-negating reason in Hegel, which are hitherto unknown to Buddhism. If transcendental pure reason and dialectical self-negating reason are fully embraced by the notion of Sunyata through its dynamism, however, then they are not maintained just as they stand, but *regrasped* radically as a part of nonthinking thinking in the light of wisdom. This means that the limitation of rational thinking—that is, the conceptual and speculative nature of rational thinking from which even transcendental pure reason and dialectical self-negating reason cannot be completely freed—must be clearly realized in the light of nondiscriminating wisdom, and rational thinking must be turned over from its ground and *revived* as thinking on the basis of "suchness" through the realization of nonthinking.

In Christianity, which is based on God's revelation, the conflict between divine revelation and human reason has been a persistent problem. In Buddhism, which is based on the realization of Sunyata, there is no issue equivalent to that conflict. But to embrace reason properly in its pure and transcendental or dialectical form, and to make it alive and useful, Sunyata must be grasped most dynamically through the clear realization of self-emptying.

Free Will in Buddhism

Like the issue of human reason, the notion of free will has never been grasped positively in Buddhism. In the modern intellectual history of the West, the importance of human free will has been strongly emphasized. It has been generally recognized that humans have a capacity to make free decisions over and against external necessity. Only through free decision, through the exercise of free will, can one's subjectivity and personality be legitimately established. In this regard, Kant is more radical, on the one hand, in rejecting all previous moral philosophies based on moral sense or moral reason as heteronomous ethical theories, and, on the other hand, in dispensing with the theonomous command and love of the Judaeo-Christian tradition. Kant thus opens up an entirely new and transcendental realm of noumena in which the autonomy of pure practical reason is grasped as authentic freedom. Kant's notion of "causality through freedom"—that is, the categorical imperative of morality as the autonomy of the pure will—gives a firm philosophical foundation to the modern view of human free will.

Unlike most of Western philosophy, Christianity regards human free will negatively as the root of original sin, while taking God's free will and God's word positively as the principle of creation, redemption, and last judgment. Although human beings are creatures, they alone were created in the image of God and are endowed with the Godlike faculty of free decision and speech. Consequently, God's omnipotence, including foreknowledge and divine free will versus human free will, has constantly been an important theological issue. This, however, indicates Christianity's strong affirmation of God's will as the fundamental principle of the divine-human and the divine-nature relationship. Even Nietzsche, who rejects Platonism, Christianity, and modern humanism, including Kantian transcendental ethics, emphasizes the will to power as the basic principle of his radical nihilism. Though viewed in different senses in humanistic, Christian, and Nietzschean standpoints, the notion of "will" has thus always been viewed positively in the West.

In sharp contrast, Buddhism has never taken the notion of will positively. Buddhism grasps will negatively, in that the problem of human free will is grappled with in terms of karma that must be overcome to attain enlightenment or awakening and thereby to achieve real freedom. Emancipation from karma does not lead us to a realization of the autonomous pure practical reason as in Kant, to the omnipotent will of God as in Christianity, or to the will to power as in Nietzsche, but rather to the awakening to Sunyata, which is entirely beyond any kind of will.

It is a realization of suchness or *jinen,* primordial naturalness or spontaneity without will.

In view of the problem of free will, the Buddhist notion of Sunyata as suchness or *jinen* has both positive and negative aspects. As for the positive aspect, in Sunyata (1) the distinction and opposition between humans and nature, which is caused by anthropocentrism based on the emphasis on the free will peculiar to human existence, is fundamentally overcome; (2) the struggle between flesh and reason in making decisions based upon free will, which is inevitable in human existence as the subject of free will, is also overcome; (3) original sin as the disobedience of human free will against God's will involved in theocentrism does not emerge in Sunyata.

The Buddhist notion of Sunyata as suchness or *jinen,* however, also has negative aspects in view of the problem of free will. The notion of Sunyata inescapably leads us to at least the following three questions: (1) How can the notion of free will, peculiar to human existence, be positively established in the locus of Sunyata, which is primordial naturalness without will? (2) How can the problem of evil be understood to take place in the locus of Sunyata, which is beyond any kind of will, and how can the problem be resolved there? (3) How can Sunyata, as agentless spontaneity in its boundless openness, incorporate a personal deity as the ultimate criterion of value judgment?

Unless these questions are adequately resolved, Buddhism cannot properly provide a ground for human ethics and modern rationality, nor can it overcome the problems raised by Nietzsche's principle of the will to power. To cope with these questions and to overcome the negative aspect of the Buddhist notion of Sunyata, Christianity may provide some helpful suggestions.

The Buddhist Notion of Karma

In order to deal with the above questions properly, it may be helpful to first discuss the Buddhist notion of karma. Karma means act or deed. An act here is not mere physical movement, but physical or mental activity oriented by volition, which is based on free will. As the Buddha himself said, "O bhikkhus, it is volition (*cetana*) that I call karma. Having willed, one acts through body, speech and mind."[71] Karma is primarily equated with volition, that is, mental or spiritual acts (*manasa*) and, being mental volition, karma leaves traces in the series of consciousness (*vijnana*).

As volition connected with free will and consciousness, such mental acts are a basic element in karma, but what one does after having willed is more important than the willing.[72] Hence the importance of bodily and vocal acts is emphasized:

> Once produced by a conscious and voluntary vocal or bodily act, it exists and develops of its own accord, without the agency of thought, unconsciously, whether a man is sleeping, waking, or absorbed in contemplation. It is part of the series that takes the place of the soul in Buddhism.[73]

As a "series" composed of thoughts, sensation, volition, and material elements, the soul, or ego, is nothing but a collection of various elements constantly renewed. In reality there is no agent but the act and its consequences. Thus, although karma is a causally efficient phenomenon, the effect (*vipaka, phala*) of an act is determined not solely by the act itself, but also by many other factors, such as the nature of the person who commits the act and the circumstances in which it is committed. Accordingly, even when two people commit similar, if not identical, evil acts, they may reap different consequences and in different ways. For the circumstances or factors surrounding the actions are very different.[74]

> Unlike the traditional Hindu view of karma the Buddhist doctrine of karma is not deterministic, but conditional and generative. Karma is not a mechanical but organic power. It grows, expands and even gives birth to a new karma. Our present life is the result of the karma accumulated in our previous existence, and yet in our practical life the doctrine of karma allows in us all kinds of possibilities and all chances of development.[75]

The Buddhist view of karma outlined above entails at least the following three points. First, being volitional action based on free will, karma is essentially action that can be morally characterized. Although the circumstances and external stimuli are recognized as factors of karmic causality, conscious motives rooted in volition play the most important role in the determination of karmic causality. Also, good and bad actions are characterized by whether or not they are performed by such conscious motives as greed, hatred, and delusion. In such cases the responsibility of the individual is evident. Accordingly, it is in one's moral life that the law of karma operates most clearly.[76]

Second, though the Buddhist notion of karma is morally qualified, this does not entail an individualistic view of karma. In other words, although karma is closely related to the problem of an individual's responsibility, this does not imply an exclusively individualistic view of karma, a view that good or evil acts committed by a person determine only his or her own fate without affecting the lives of others. Instead, the karmic effect of one's own actions clearly determines one's own future and that of others as well. In the Buddhist cosmology, the whole universe, with all its variety, is the outcome of acts, and these acts constitute the collective mass of the acts of all beings.

In his book *Outlines of Mahayana Buddhism,* D. T. Suzuki describes this sympathetic solidarity or contagious characteristic of karma.

> It [the universe] belongs to all sentient beings, each forming a psychic unit; and these units are so intimately knitted together in blood and soul that the effects of even apparently trifling deeds committed by an individual are felt by others just as much and just as surely as the doer himself. Throw an insignificant piece of stone into a vast expanse of water, and it will certainly create an almost endless series of ripples, however imperceptible, that never stop till they reach the furthest shore. The tremulation thus caused is felt by the sinking stone as much as the water disturbed. The universe that may seem to crude observers merely as a system of crass physical forces is in reality a great spiritual community and every single sentient being forms its component part.[77]

This sympathetic and generative character of karma is effective not only throughout the vast expanse of the present universe, but also throughout all human history. Again, as D. T. Suzuki says:

> [The] history of mankind in all its manifold aspects of existence is nothing but a grand drama visualizing the Buddhist doctrine of karmic immortality. It is like an immense ocean whose boundaries nobody knows, and the waves of events now swelling and surging, now ebbing, now whirling, now refluxing, in all times, day and night, illustrate how the laws of karma are at work in this actual life. One act provokes another and that a third and so on to eternity without ever losing the chain of karmic causation.[78]

Third, the moral and individually self-responsible character of karma and the sympathetic and collective character of karma are not contradictory but rather complementary to one another. From the Buddhist perspective, karma is ultimately rooted in *avidya*—that is, the fundamental ignorance that "begins" without beginning and is unfathomably deep. *Avidya* is the ignorance of the true nature of things, that is, of emptiness and suchness, which results in not recognizing the impermanency of worldly things and tenaciously clinging to them as final realities. Thus *avidya*, as the root of karma, is identical with *bhava-tanha*, the will or thirst to be, to exist, to continue, to become more and more, to grow more and more, to accumulate more and more.[79]

It is an unconscious, endless impulse, which Schopenhauer terms *blinder Wille zum Leben* (blind will to live). Since *avidya* as the blind will to live is the deepest root of one's karma, it is thoroughly individual and self-responsible and yet trans-individual by going beyond the realm of one's consciousness; and thus it is sympathetically leaving an ineffable, reverberating mark on the life of the universe.

Briefly put, in the unfathomable depth of *avidya* (ignorance) – that is, the blind will to live – the individual aspect and the collective aspect of karma are dynamically united. And one's own karma, particularly one's free will involved in karma thus grasped in the unfathomable depth of *avidya*, is understood by oneself to be a center of the network of karma extending throughout the universe.

In the individual aspect of karma, we are responsible for everything caused by *our own avidya* realized in the innermost depth of our existence, that is, for everything, including consequences affecting us by innumerable factors, known and unknown to us, in the universe. Our individual karma is not exclusively individualistic but also reflects effects made by the acts of other beings through the sympathetic character of karma. On the other hand, in the collective aspect of karma, that is, in terms of collective karma, we are responsible for everything caused by *human avidya* universally rooted in human nature – for everything, including what is apparently unrelated to us in the ordinary sense.

In our collective karma nothing happens in the universe entirely unrelated to us insofar as we realize that everything human is ultimately rooted in the fundamental ignorance, *avidya*, innate in human nature. In this fundamental ignorance innate in human nature, individual karma and collective karma inseparably merge with one another. When Buddhism talks about *jigo-jitoku*, that is, self-karma self-obtaining, it must be understood to include not only the depth of individual karma, but also the breadth of collective karma. Only when this fundamental ignorance is overcome and the self-centeredness involved in karma is broken through, can one awaken to the true nature of things, to emptiness and suchness.

The Problem of Evil in Buddhism

Now we must turn to the question of how the problem of evil takes place in the locus of Sunyata and suchness, and how the problem can be resolved there. According to the Buddhist doctrine of karma, one is free to act for better or for worse within the circumstances in which the action is committed. Acts motivated by greed, hatred, and delusion are evil acts producing unmeritorious karma, whereas acts motivated by opposite qualities are good acts producing meritorious karma. The consequences of karma may be experienced in this life or in future lives. However, both good acts and evil acts are regarded, in Buddhism, equally as *evil acts* in the deeper and fundamental sense because both of them are determined not only by external stimuli and internal conscious motives but also by a deeply inner unconscious blind will, and thus bind one to the world of endless life-and-death-transmigration. As we see in the words, quoted below, of the Chinese Zen masters Lin-chi I-hsuan (d. 866) and Tai-chu Hui-hai (d. 788), even to seek Buddha and Dharma, to try to attain nirvana, is regarded as evil karma. In his discourse Lin-chi said:

> Make no mistake! Even if there were something to be obtained by practice, it would be nothing but birth-and-death karma. You are saying, "The six paramitas and the ten thousand [virtuous] actions are equally to be practiced." As I see it, all this is just making karma. Seeking Buddha and seeking Dharma is only making hell-karma. Seeking bodhisattvahood is also making karma; reading the sutras and studying the teachings is also making karma.[80]

The following is an exchange between a monk-scholar and Tai-chu Hui-hai.

> Scholar: How can one attain Great Nirvana?
> Master: Have no karma that works for transmigration.
> Scholar: What is the karma for transmigration?
> Master: To seek after Great Nirvana is precisely the karma for transmigration. To abandon the defiled and take to the undefiled, to assert that there is something attainable and something realizable, not to be free from the practice of getting rid of evil passions—this is precisely the karma that works for transmigration.[81]

It is essential for Buddhists to seek Buddha and Dharma, to seek after nirvana by getting rid of evil passions. Even so, however, Lin-chi and Tai-chu mean that insofar as such religious practice is motivated by human volition, it is the karma of life-and-death-transmigration and is karma making hell. One should not take these words simply to indicate a radicalism peculiar to Zen. These words are nothing but an explicit expression of the basic Mahayana view of karma.

Suchness or *jinen* (primordial naturalness) in the realization of Sunyata is fully realized right here and right now when one is freed from all karmas (volitional acts), good and evil, religious and secular. The following words of Lin-chi and Tai-chu make this point in their own expressive ways.

> When your seeking mind comes to rest, you are at ease—a noble man. If you seek him [a Buddha], he retreats farther and farther away; if you don't seek him, then he's right there before your eyes, his wondrous voice resounding in your ears.[82]

Scholar: How can one be emancipated?

Master: No bondage from the very first, and what is the use of seeking emancipation? Act as you will, go on as you feel—without second thought. This is the incomparable way.[83]

This is not an animal-like instinctive spontaneity but a spontaneity deeply based on the primordial naturalness (*jinen*) that can be realized only by getting rid of karmic blind thirst.

How does evil take place in the realization of Sunyata? This question can be properly restated by another question: How does karma take place in the realization of Sunyata? For karma, with *avidya* as its root, is the source of all evil. As already repeatedly stated, true Sunyata is not a static state of emptiness but a dynamic movement of emptying everything, including itself. This emphasis on the dynamic character of Sunyata, however, always leaves open the possibility that the realization of Sunyata will remain in "emptiness," dwell in "emptiness," and lead to an attachment to "emptiness." Precisely because the realization of Sunyata is so essential to Buddhists, Sunyata is often reified through conception as *something* called "Sunyata." As stated before, however, the Mahayana tradition has always warned against such a conceptualized and reified view of Sunyata as "Sunyata perversely clung to." For as soon as Sunyata is conceptually grasped, substantialized, and attached to as "Sunyata," it turns into karma. Substantialization of Sunyata is no less than a denial of true Sunyata, and an obstacle on the path to the realization of authentic Sunyata. Whereas a realization of true Sunyata indicates enlightenment, attachment to Sunyata signifies unenlightened ignorance, *avidya*.

How does the ignorant conceptualization of Sunyata take place in the locus of Sunyata? According to *The Awakening of Faith in the Mahayana,* one of the most important classic treatises of Mahayana Buddhism, "Suddenly a conception arises. This is called *avidya.*"[84]

"Suddenly" (Chinese, *hu-jan*) in this context does not indicate "suddenness" in the temporal sense, but rather "without why" in terms of causality, because the reason for the arising of conception in the locus of Sunyata cannot be rationally analyzed and explained. And yet, it happens.

In this regard, it may be interesting to consider here the Genesis account of the Garden of Eden. According to the account, it is by means of the temptation of a serpent that Adam and Eve, originally innocent, committed sin by disregarding the words of God and partook of the fruit of the tree of knowledge. Without the serpent's temptation, Adam and Eve might not have committed sin. Where, then, did that serpent come from? One may say that the serpent appears "suddenly" in the

Garden of Eden created by God. The very serpent in the Garden of Eden may be regarded as a mythological analogy to the statement in *The Awakening of Faith in the Mahayana* that "suddenly a conception arises." In the Genesis account, however, the serpent is not the cause of sin but merely an opportunity or occasion for Adam and Eve to sin. It is true that without the serpent's temptation, Adam and Eve might not have committed sin.

But it is exclusively by means of Adam and Eve's free will that they accepted the seduction of the serpent and made its temptation possible as "temptation." Wherever the serpent came from, it is nothing more than an occasion for the committing of sin by Adam and Eve. It is within Adam and Eve that the cause or ground of their committing of sin is realized.

Here we see the profound meaning and profound problematic character of free will. Why does the cause or ground of committing sin lie in the innocent Adam and Eve created by God? It is a fact that is beyond sheer rational analysis, deeply rooted in the unfathomable depth of free will. This is the reality of human free will. Despite a serpent's temptation, it is Adam and Eve's responsibility that they were disobedient to God's will. And as Paul states, "through one man sin entered into the world, and death through sin, and so death passed to all men because all men sinned." That is, all of us sinned in and through Adam, and death passed unto all as the "wages of sin" (Rom. 5:12).

Likewise, for Buddhism, however suddenly a conception and *avidya* may arise "without why" within ourselves, we are not free from responsibility for its arising. Despite its suddenness we are thoroughly responsible for the arising of *avidya* because, though unconsciously deep and endless, *avidya* is a will or thirst to be and to live. And the arising of *avidya* is possible at each and every moment of our life. As soon as we attach to Sunyata in the process of its incessant movement of emptying, we are involved in *avidya* and thereby in karma. Because of our attachment and abiding at any moment, Sunyata turns into karma, and *vidya* (enlightenment) turns into *avidya* (unenlightenment, ignorance). If we continuously attach to and abide in karma thus arisen, that karma creates more karma, and we become further involved in the endless process of the development of karma, in samsara, the transmigration of life-and-death. If we, however, completely abandon our attachment and abiding, and empty our conception and its objects—that is, if we do not substantialize the self and its objects any longer and awaken to their nonsubstantiality—karma ceases and *avidya* is overcome.

Although this extermination of attachment must be deep enough to overcome the attachment to the unconscious blind will to be, the cessation of attachment can take place at each and every moment of our life. In other words, as soon as we become completely nonattached to the self and the world in the process of samsara, karma ceases and Sunyata and nirvana are fully realized. This is because just as "suddenly" conception arises and *avidya* emerges, "suddenly" conception ceases and enlightenment (*vidya*) takes place. As a result of our detachment and self-emptying, karma turns into Sunyata, and *avidya* (unenlightenment) turns into *vidya* (enlightenment). Thus, we must say, "Suddenly conception perishes; this is called enlightenment."

True enlightenment is always sudden enlightenment that takes place "without why," beyond rational analysis. Both *avidya* and *vidya* take place suddenly. It is always suddenly that *vidya* turns into *avidya*, *avidya* turns into *vidya*, Sunyata turns into karma, and karma turns into Sunyata. We are originally and fundamentally standing in the "suddenness." We stand neither in sheer *vidya* nor in sheer *avidya*. Nor is it that at the outset there is *vidya* and then it turns into *avidya*. Nor that at the outset there is *avidya* and then it turns into *vidya*, for this very understanding itself is again a conceptualization. In reality, we are standing in the "as-it-is-ness" of "*vidya-as-it-is-is-avidya, avidya-as-it-is-is-vidya*." And this "as-it-is-ness" is nothing but "suddenness." It is an instantaneous pivot from which incessant mutual conversion from *vidya* to *avidya* and from *avidya* to *vidya* is taking place.

It may be called "dazzling darkness." It is not half dark and half dazzling. It is thoroughly dark, and yet, as darkness, it is thoroughly dazzling at one and the same time; it is thoroughly dazzling, and yet, as it is dazzling, it is thoroughly dark at one and the same time. That we are fundamentally standing in this dazzling darkness indicates that we are thoroughly unenlightened and ignorant, and yet simultaneously we are thoroughly enlightened. This is why Mahayana Buddhism emphasizes "samsara as it is, is nirvana; nirvana as it is, is samsara" and "*bodhi* (enlightenment) and *klesa* (defilement) are one and nondual—nondifferentiated and equal."[85] Such a paradoxical situation is possible because it takes place in the locus of Sunyata, which is entirely nonsubstantial and unobjectifiable, being bottomlessly deep, and because it takes place right here, right now at each moment—that is, in the absolute present.

In short, evil and karma take place when one becomes attached to and dwells in Sunyata without emptying oneself and the objects of the self. The root of such an attachment is *avidya*, the endless, unconscious thirst to be. On the other hand, evil and karma can be overcome when one completely empties oneself and the objects of the self through the realization of Sunyata in its dynamism. With this awakening, *avidya* turns into *vidya* and emancipation is realized. Suchness and *jinen* are nothing but terms that indicate Sunyata in its dynamism.

Suchness, *Jinen*, and Evil

The problem of ethics in Buddhism, however, is not resolved by what I have said thus far. The above discussion only clarifies the *fundamental reason*—in terms of "without why"—for the arising and ceasing of evil in human existence, whereas the problem of ethics is involved in a more *relative* human situation, which is conditioned by society and history. Traditionally, when Mahayana Buddhism seeks to explicate "suchness" and *jinen* (primordial naturalness or spontaneity), it often refers to natural phenomena as examples:

> Mountains and rivers and great earth:
> everything reveals the Body of Dharma.

> From the start blue mountains never move;
> white clouds come and go.

> Bamboo shadows sweep the stairs,
> Yet not a mote of dust is stirred;
> Moonbeams pierce to the bottom of the pool,
> Yet in the water not a trace remains.[86]

This last phrase from the *Futoroku* (The Record of Universal Lamp) is highly appreciated and often quoted in Zen to indicate "suchness" and *jinen* as exemplified by the will-free, unconscious, spontaneous movements of bamboo shadow and moonbeam, which though sweeping the stairs or piercing to the bottom of the pool, do not disturb or injure others. However, natural evil such as earthquakes and tornadoes, which are also will-free, unconscious, and spontaneous activities, and the struggle for existence in the animal world in which the weak become the victim of the strong, have scarcely been mentioned as examples of suchness.

Although human moral evils such as lying, stealing, killing, adultery, and so forth have been a deep concern throughout Buddhist history, clear discussion concerning how these human moral evils are to be understood in terms of the realization of suchness and *jinen* has not been explicit enough. Further, a question arises about whether or not immense historical evil such as the Holocaust and Hiroshima is an exception to suchness and *jinen*, and, if not, how such historical evil is to be grasped in terms of suchness and *jinen*. Though inevitably to be grappled with by religious thinkers, such a question is scarcely discussed by Buddhists. If suchness and *jinen* are the essential dimensions of Sunyata as Buddhist reality, these notions must be equally applied to natural evil, physical and biological, and human moral evil, individual and collective, and to whatever degree of evil. In other words, earthquakes, one species devouring another in the animal kingdom, individual murder, and the Holocaust all must be grasped in light of suchness and *jinen*. How is this possible and how is this justifiable?

In order to answer these questions properly I must clarify that the issues include the following three different dimensions and that all issues are properly and legitimately understood *ultimately from the vantage point of the third dimension.*

1. A nonhuman, natural dimension represented by pure natural science.

2. A transnatural, human dimension represented by individual morality, and collective social and historical ethics.

3. A transhuman, fundamental dimension represented by religious faith or awakening.

Natural Evil, Human Evil, and Religion

From the vantage point of pure natural science — that is, in a nonhuman natural dimension — both earthquakes and sunshine are equally natural phenomena caused by natural law and are entirely indifferent to human interest. An earthquake happens as an earthquake due to its natural necessity; the sun shines brightly as it does due to its natural law. In nature, both earthquakes and sunshine simply occur in their "suchness," purely objectively, without human subjectivity. Accordingly, we most note that the "suchness" or "as-it-is-ness" of natural phenomena reflected in natural science is an abstraction from which the concrete, living context in which we human beings are involved is absent. The same is essentially true of the struggle for existence in the animal world. When a lion attacks a rabbit and a snake swallows a frog, they engage in these "cruel" acts from their instinctive impulse to survive. In the purely nonhuman, natural dimension, their acts are as natural as a flower's blooming and the wind's blowing. If we do not project human feelings and human interest upon natural phenomena, both physical and biological phenomena in the natural world take place entirely naturally and spontaneously in their "suchness."

In the human dimension, however, earthquakes are often unfavorable disasters causing suffering and damage to individuals and society at large, whereas sunshine is usually regarded as a favorable benevolent blessing offered to human beings. Relatively speaking, in the human context, an earthquake is evil, whereas sunshine is good, although both of them equally are products of natural law. Likewise, although we humans feel pleasure and appreciation about a flower's blooming and a bird's singing, we may feel "cruelty" in a lion's attacking a rabbit or a snake's swallowing a frog. Our usual judgment of the flower and bird is "good," whereas that of the lion and snake is "bad" or "evil."

Such good and evil judgments are clearer and more definite in the case of human acts, individual and collective. In the human ethical dimension, honesty, kindness, integrity, courage, responsibility, and so forth are regarded as good, whereas lying, stealing, betrayal, killing, and so forth are regarded as evil. In broader, societal terms, peace and harmony are esteemed as good, whereas war and discord are depreciated as evil. And what is important in the human ethical dimension is not necessarily an outcome of one's act but an inner motivation. It is imperative in human ethical behavior to be good and right in one's motivation regardless of whether one's given physical, psychological, and social conditions are favorable to that motivation.

Human beings, however, are not so simple as to be ruled completely by ethical and moral principles. On the contrary, a painful confession, "the good which I would I do not; but the evil which I would not, that I practice. . . . Wretched man that I am! Who shall deliver me out of the body of this death?" (Rom. 7:19, 24) is not peculiar to St. Paul, but is inevitable to all seriously reflective persons. However important ethics may be to human beings, ethics cannot stand by itself, because when carried out to its final conclusion it falls into a dilemma, as Paul's words show, and finally collapses. One must therefore go beyond the ethical dimension and enter into the religious dimension. Ultimately, the distinction between good and evil in the ethical dimension is relative, not absolute.

When we go beyond the human ethical dimension to a more fundamental religious dimension, however, the situation is quite different. In the religious dimension, even natural phenomena are grasped no longer objectively, but deeply subjectively and experientially, not merely in the human context, but from a much deeper, most fundamental point of view. For example, in the faith of theistic religion, an earthquake may be believed to be a divine punishment upon us and the sunshine a divine grace upon us. They are no longer relatively evil or relatively good to our interest, but may be equally accepted by a believer in the divine will as a manifestation of divine providence. In theistic religion, human ethical good and evil are also grasped essentially in a different way from mere ethics. In Christianity, for instance, unlike Greek philosophy, good and evil are not grasped in terms of human-human relationships, but fundamentally in terms of the divine-human relationship. And in this divine-human relationship, as Paul said in the Epistle to the Romans,

"I have already charged that all men, both Jews and Greeks, are under the power of sin; as it is written, there is none righteous, no, not one" (Rom. 3:9–10). And as Jesus said: "Why do you call me good? Only God is Good" (Mark 10:18).

In the New Testament, sin is not a separate evil act or the total of such individual evil acts, but human disobedience and rebellion against the law of God and particularly the lack of faith in Jesus (John 8:24). Sin is universal and common to all humankind. Jesus Christ, however, was sent into the world not to judge the world, but that the world should be saved through him (John 3:17).

> For as through the one man's disobedience the many were made sinners, even so through the obedience of the one shall the many be made righteous. And the law came in besides, that the trespass might abound; but where sin abounded, grace did abound more exceedingly.
>
> (Rom. 5:19–20)

Furthermore, in Paul, corruption and deliverance from its bondage are not limited to humankind but include the whole creation:

> For the creation was subjected to vanity, not of its own will, but by reason of him who subjected it, in hope that the creation itself also shall be delivered from the bondage of corruption into the liberty of the glory of the children of God. For we know that the whole creation groaneth and travaileth in pain together until now. And not only so, but ourselves also, who have the first-fruits of the Spirit, even we ourselves groan within ourselves, waiting for our adoption, to wit, the redemption of our body.
>
> (Rom. 8:20–23)

Here we clearly see in Christianity, at least as confessed by Paul, the whole creation, including mountains, rivers, trees and animals, viewed as groaning and travailing in pain together with us by being subjected to vanity and corruption, but now hopeful for deliverance through the salvific work of Jesus Christ.

Just like Christianity, Buddhism stands in the transhuman, fundamental dimension of religion. Unlike Christianity, however, Buddhism is *fundamentally* not theistic and does not accept one personal God as the ultimate reality but Sunyata. Therefore, the term "transhuman" mentioned above has a different connotation. As discussed before, in Christianity only God is good and there is not one that does good. All human beings have sinned in Adam, and the whole creation is subject to vanity. By contrast, in Buddhism, there is nothing permanent, self-existing, and absolutely good, for everything without exception is co-arising and co-ceasing, impermanent, without "own-being," empty. The doctrine of dependent co-origination, one of the most basic teachings

73

of Buddhism, clearly emphasizes that everything without exception is interdependent with every other thing; nothing whatsoever is independent and self-existing. Accordingly, the one God as the absolute good cannot be accepted in Buddhism because, speaking from the perspective of dependent co-origination, a notion such as the one God as the absolute good who must be independent is nothing but a reification and substantialization of something as the only entity that has its own being.

Of course, the Christian notion of the one God as the absolute good is not a theoretical or metaphysical one, but a deeply practical, devotional one, which is considered crucial to one's salvation from sin and death. Yet, from the standpoint of Mahayana Buddhism, which emphasizes "Do not abide in Nirvana" to attain true emancipation and cautions us about "Buddha-bondage"[87] by saying, "the Buddha way and the Devil way are both evil,"[88] the one God as the absolute good appears as a special form of attachment in the religious and transcendent dimension. For Buddhism, the ultimate reality is neither secular nor sacred, neither samsara nor nirvana, neither sentient beings nor Buddha, neither emptiness nor fullness. It is true emptiness dynamically identical with true fullness.

Accordingly, the "transhuman" religious dimension does not, in Buddhism, indicate the divine or the sacred that is believed to have sovereignty—however immanent—over the world, nor does it signify the absolute good that is beyond the relativity of good and evil. Instead, the transhuman religious dimension signifies that which is neither the divine nor the human, neither the sacred nor the secular, neither the supernatural nor the natural, and is neither absolutely good nor absolutely evil: Sunyata.

Accordingly, in Buddhism, though relatively in the human dimension an earthquake is evil and sunshine is good; absolutely speaking, in a transhuman religious dimension the two events have no own-being or substance as evil or as good, or as divine punishment or divine grace. Both earthquake and sunshine, with their clear value distinction in the relative dimension, are, in an absolute ultimate dimension, equally grasped as the appearance of Sunyata in their suchness. There is absolutely *no thing*, including divine providence, behind or beyond them. They happen just in their suchness. This "suchness," however, is not abstract suchness as seen in pure natural science, which is realized objectively excluding human subjectivity and indifferent to human interest. On the contrary, it is the most concrete "suchness" that is only subjectively and experientially grasped at the unfathomable depth of our existence through the realization of the interrelationship (dependent co-origination) between all natural phenomena and us, and the realization of emptiness (nonsubstantiality) of both nature and human beings.

In other words, even such natural phenomena as earthquakes and sunshine are not excluded from the sympathetic universality of karma, but are realized as a unitary dimension of karma pervading the entire universe, this cosmic unity of karma being now realized at the depth of one's realization of individual karma. The law of dependent co-origination throughout the universe and the emptiness of everything can be existentially realized through the clear realization of the sympathetic universality and the cosmic solidarity of karma. Only here at this juncture is suchness in its most concrete sense realized.

It is precisely in terms of this most concrete "suchness" that Mahayana Buddhism states, "Mountains and rivers and the great earth—everything reveals the Body of Dharma," and "From the start blue mountains never move; white clouds come and go." This should not be confused with nature mysticism, which lacks the realization of dependent co-origination between humans and nature and the realization of the emptiness of everything. And such biological phenomena as a lion's attacking a rabbit and a snake's swallowing a frog are not exceptions to this concrete "suchness," in that these biological phenomena are grasped as a part of collective karma in which we are also involved and as a manifestation of Sunyata without an unchangeable substance.

At this point, however, we should not forget that natural phenomena thus accepted at this present moment in terms of suchness as a part of collective and sympathetic karma and as an appearance of Sunyata *in the light of wisdom*, are also realized simultaneously *in the light of compassion*, which works for a better future from the unfathomable depth of Sunyata without attachment to individual interest. Here I find an echo in St. Paul when he says, "the whole creation groaneth and travaileth in pain together until now," and talks about "hope that the creation itself also shall be delivered from the bondage of corruption into the liberty of the glory of the children of God." In Buddhism, through the universal compassion inseparably connected with universal wisdom, one can work toward bettering both humans and nature most effectively and appropriately when unattached to human self-interest.

A Buddhist View of the Holocaust

I want to address now the specific evil situation of the Holocaust as centered in such concentration camps as Auschwitz during the Second World War. Speaking in terms of society and history, as a Japanese who was neither a German nor a Jew and who lived at that time on the opposite side of the world, I could be said to have had nothing to do with that terrible event. And it is easy for me to condemn the Holocaust as a diabolical, inhuman, atrocious event. But, however serious I may be in this attack and in attempting to change the given social and historical situation, insofar as I stand outside of the event, my total approach is entirely wrong. From the perspective of the Buddhist doctrine of karma, I am not free from responsibility for the Holocaust. I must accept that "Auschwitz is a problem of my own karma. In the deepest sense I myself participated as well in the Holocaust." It is indeed the problem of my own karma, not in terms of my individual karma in the narrow sense, but in terms of collective karma, in that the Holocaust is *ultimately* rooted in the fundamental ignorance (*avidya*) and the endless blind thirst to live inherent in human existence in which I am also deeply involved through my own individual karma. I am sharing the blame of the Holocaust because at the depth of my existence I am participating in the fundamental ignorance together with the overt assailants in the Holocaust.

I believe that only through the realization of the collective karma and fundamental ignorance inherent in human beings that is realized at the depth of each person's existence, and through fundamental enlightenment as the realization of fundamental ignorance, can one properly and legitimately cope with such a historical evil as the Holocaust.

This, however, does not signify a joint responsibility of the victims in terms of the humanistic sense of justice, which is realized in the second human ethical dimension but in terms of solidarity realized in the third, most fundamental religious dimension. Furthermore, even within the third, religious dimension, what I have said above does not signify our solidarity with the case of Auschwitz equally through the realization of guilt and forgiveness under the sovereignty of one God, whether God is coercive (as some traditional theologies insist) or persuasive (as process theology maintains). Here, in this regard, the religious dimension is based on a God who is loving and just. Instead, what I am saying in terms of the religious dimension signifies the boundless openness or emptiness that is neither God, nor human, nor nature, and in which all things, including the divine, the human, and the natural, are interrelated to and interpenetrated by each other. Accordingly, even such an atrocious event as the Holocaust, which is relatively unrelated to me, must be grasped as a matter of my own responsibility in terms of sympathetic and collective karma that reverberates endlessly and is unfathomably deep.

Not as an outsider humanist who attacks the Holocaust from the vantage point of social and international justice, nor as a religious subject who judges and acknowledges the Holocaust through dynamic interpretation of divine justice and the all-loving God, but as one who painfully realizes the collective karma deeply rooted in human ignorance as the ultimate cause of the event in Auschwitz am I aware of and accept joint responsibility for the Holocaust and find in this realization the *basis* from which I can properly cope with the case of the Holocaust.

The standpoint of justice, humanistic or divine, cannot be a proper basis for our coming to terms with the Holocaust, because the notion of justice is a double-edged sword. On the one hand, it sharply judges which is right and which is wrong. On the other hand, the judgment based on justice will naturally cause a counterjudgment as a reaction from the side thus judged. Accordingly, we may fall into endless conflict and struggle between the judge and the judged. All judgment, "just" or otherwise, may perpetrate further karma. Instead, the standpoint of wisdom and compassion, which is realized through the realization of collective karma and the realization of the nonsubstantiality of everything in the universe, can in my view provide a more proper basis to cope with the Holocaust without getting involved in an endless conflict. In this regard, a key point lies in recognizing that although the Holocaust was indeed a brutal, atrocious historical evil, we should not substantialize and cling to it as a fixed separate entity unrelated to the rest of the vast and endless network of human history. That is to say, we should realize the relationality and the nonsubstantiality (lack of self-being) in that event.

By saying this, my intention here is not to diminish the reality of the evil of the Holocaust and to disengage it from the specific agony of the victims. No, not at all! As I said before, in the depth of my own being, I painfully realize the universal or collective karma innate in human existence in which the Holocaust is also ultimately rooted. This is a realization that inevitably emerges from the Buddhist doctrine of karma.

Obviously, the Holocaust constituted unimaginable sufferings for the Jewish people under Hitler and the manifestation of unprecedented moral evil. It may even be said to be a historical event qualitatively different from all other historical events. In the ethical and relative dimension, responsibility for the Holocaust clearly resides in Nazi, not in Jewish, individuals. But the same Buddhist doctrine of karma teaches us that however extraordinary and unique an event the Holocaust may be, it is not an isolated, independent event unrelated to the vast and boundless network of human history. In an immeasurable way, even the uttermost evil of the Holocaust is related to the innumerable events in the past and present of human history in which all of us, assailants and victims alike, are involved.

When we are victims of a horrible suffering such as what occurred in Auschwitz or Hiroshima, we tend to absolutize the evil involved as if it happened to us passively, unrelated to our own karma. However, insofar as we return to the deepest depth of our existence, we unavoidably realize the root of human karma which is common to all human beings and in which all good and evil are interrelated in one way or another. Accordingly, in absolutizing a particular evil or a particular good, however conspicuous it may be, a *real* view of the event is lost by substantializing it.

This absolutization entails a serious problem, because in practice it always is accompanied by an emotional attachment to the event and the involved people in terms of hatred or love. Such emotional attachment based on substantialization of the event creates further karma, and thus we are more and more deeply enmeshed in the endless process of karma. To overcome this endless process of karma, it is necessary not to absolutize the event but rather to realize its relationality and nonsubstantiality.

This may be a Buddhist version of the kind of "reorientation" Irving Greenberg implies when, in "Judaism and Christianity After the Holocaust," he states, "the Holocaust cannot be overcome without some basic reorientation in light of it by the surviving Jewish community." I agree completely with Greenberg when he further observes:

> Just as refusal to encounter the Holocaust brings a nemesis of moral and religious ineffectiveness, openness and willingness to undergo the ordeal of reorienting by the event could well save or illuminate the treasure that is still in each tradition.[89]

While in a human, moral dimension the Holocaust should be condemned as an unpardonable, absolute evil, from the ultimate religious point of view even it should be taken not as an absolute evil but as a relative evil.

It is perhaps Emil L. Fackenheim who most accurately clarifies the uniqueness of the Nazi Holocaust in human history. By employing a series of negations Fackenheim discusses the uniqueness of the Holocaust from seven points of view. For instance, he emphasizes that "the Holocaust was not a war," because while war is "waged between parties endowed, however unequally, with power . . . the victims of the Holocaust had no power."[90]

What seems to me most important in this regard, however, is his following emphasis.

> The Holocaust was not a case of genocide. . . . The genocides of modern history spring from motives, human, if evil, such as greed, hatred, or simply blind xenophobic passion. This is true even when they masquerade under high-flown ideologies. The Nazi genocide of the Jewish people did

not masquerade under an ideology. . . . The ideal was to rid the world of Jews as one rids oneself of lice. It was also, however, to punish the Jews for their "crime" and the crime in question was existence itself.[91]

This emphasis becomes clearer: "In all other societies [than Nazi Germany], however brutal, people are *punished for doing*. In the Third Reich non-Aryans were *punished for being*."[92]

With these emphases Fackenheim clarifies that the uniqueness of the Holocaust lies in the fact that not for the "crime" of Jews, but for the "existence" of Jews, not for their "doing" but for their "being," did the Nazis intend the Holocaust of Jewish people. In this regard I recognize the essential difference between Auschwitz and Hiroshima. By the analysis of Fackenheim I fully realize how unique and terrible the Nazis' Holocaust was. However, I also realize that Fackenheim's discussion about the uniqueness of the Holocaust refers to only the second dimension I mentioned earlier, that is, a human dimension represented by individual morality and collective social and historical ethics, and does not refer to a more fundamental religious dimension.

Then, how does Fackenheim understand the problem of the Holocaust in the religious dimension? If I am not mistaken, *Tikkun* is a key term for Fackenheim in this regard. *Tikkun* means a mending of what is broken or ruptured.[93] Referring to such philosophers and theologians as Martin Heidegger, Karl Barth, Paul Tillich, and Rudolf Bultmann and their views of the Holocaust, Fackenheim states:

> For the first time in this world, we are faced with the possibility that the Holocaust may be a radical rupture in history—and that among things ruptured may be not just this or that way of philosophical or theological thinking, but thought itself.[94]

Furthermore Fackenheim emphasizes that the dilemma in the post-Holocaust *Tikkun* "in which we are placed is so extreme, so unprecedented, so full of anguish as to seem to tear us in two." This dilemma is clearly seen in the fact that "Holocaust theology" has been moving toward two extremes: a "God-is-dead" kind of despair, and a faith for which, having been "with God in hell," either nothing has happened or all has been mended. To this dilemma Fackenheim makes a significant comment: "However, post-Holocaust thought . . . must dwell, however painful and precariously, between the extremes, and seek a *Tikkun* as it endures the tension."[95]

He then discusses three elements that compose the *Tikkun* emerging from this tension: a recovery of Jewish tradition, a recovery in the quite different sense of recuperation from an illness, and a fragmentariness attached to those two recoveries that makes them both ever-incomplete and ever-laden with risk. Referring to these elements, Fackenheim emphasizes:

> Without a recovered Jewish tradition . . . there is no Jewish future. Without a recuperation from the illness, the tradition must either flee from the Holocaust or be destroyed by it. And without the stern acceptance of both the fragmentariness and the risk, in both aspects of the recovery, our Jewish *Tikkun* lapses into unauthenticity by letting theirs, having "done its job," lapse into the irrelevant past.[96]

Finally he states:

> We remember the Holocaust; we are inspired by the martyrdom and the resistance; and then the inspiration quickly degenerates into this, that every dogma, religious or secular, is restored as if nothing had happened. However, the unredeemed anguish of Auschwitz must be ever-present with us, even as it is past for us.[97]

In the preceding, I have tried to follow Fackenheim's discussion of the Holocaust and to understand it as much as possible. I strongly feel how radically and painfully the Nazi Holocaust terrified the Jewish mind and how seriously and distressfully Jewish thinkers have been struggling concerning the problem of the Holocaust.

To me as a Buddhist, however, three questions still remain. First, I fully understand the uniqueness of the Nazi Holocaust and its unprecedented evil in all human history. However, does this uniqueness mean to Jewish people that the Holocaust is an isolated event entirely unrelated to other events in the world and history, and thereby has a fixed, enduring absolute evil nature? If it has a fixed, enduring absolute evil nature, how can Jewish people come to terms with the Holocaust and with God, who ultimately allowed the Holocaust to occur?

Second, if the rupture caused by the Holocaust is not a rupture of this or that way of philosophical or theological thinking, but of thought itself, how is *Tikkun*—that is, a mending of the rupture—possible?

Third, if the Holocaust means a complete rupture in Jewish history, how is a recovery of Jewish tradition possible? When Fackenheim emphasizes the "return to revelation," what revelation and what God does he maintain in his mind?

Free Will and the Ultimate Criterion of Value Judgment in Sunyata

Earlier, I mentioned three issues that the Buddhist notion of Sunyata must confront: How can the notion of free will, peculiar to human existence, be positively established in the locus of Sunyata, which is primordial naturalness without will? How can the problem of evil be understood to take place in the locus of Sunyata, which is beyond any kind of will, and how can the problem be resolved there? How can Sunyata, as agentless spontaneity, incorporate a personal deity as the ultimate criterion of value judgment in its boundless openness?

In preceding sections, I have dealt with the second question in detail and treated the first question indirectly. In this section I will discuss the questions concerning free will and the ultimate criterion of value judgment in the locus of Sunyata. This issue may be restated, "How can Sunyata, which is free from any centrism, focus itself upon a particular center?" Unless this question is sufficiently resolved, Buddhism cannot properly ground human ethics or overcome Nietzsche's principle of the will to power.

As I have already tried to clarify, in Buddhism the problem of human free will is grappled with in terms of karma, which is ultimately rooted in *avidya*, fundamental ignorance, and *bhava tanha*, blind impulse or thirst to live, both deeply rooted in human existence. This means that in Buddhism, human free will is grasped as an endlessly self-determining, self-attaching, and self-binding blind power, which is the ultimate source of human suffering and which inevitably leads us to the final dilemma: to death in the absolute sense. However, when this endlessly self-binding blind power (karma) is realized as it is, through the practice of *dhyana* (meditation), one can be emancipated from it and awaken to boundless openness, Sunyata. It is good to note here that *dhyana* in this connection is not a psychological process but a religious practice or discipline through which one experiences death (Great Death) and resurrection (Great Life). In this awakening to Sunyata, human free will is realized entirely anew in its pure form by eradicating its self-attaching and self-binding character. Instead of producing a chain of causation and transmigration, free will, which is now based on the awakening to Sunyata, freely works in this phenomenal world without attachment, delusion, or bondage. It is just as Lin-chi describes the "non-dependent Person of Tao," that is, an awakened person:

> Entering the world of form, not suffering from form-delusion; entering the world of sound, not suffering from sound-delusion; entering the world of smell, not suffering from smell-delusion; entering the world of taste, not suffering from taste-delusion; entering the world of touch, not suffering from touch-delusion; entering the world of cognition, not suffering from cognition-delusion. Thus realizing the six worlds of form, sound, smell, taste, touch, and cognition to be all empty forms, nothing can constrict this non-dependent Person of Tao.[98]

Like Buddhism, in which human free will is usually understood to be bound by the chain of causality and karma, in Christianity, human free will is under divine law and is dominated by sin. But Christians who believe in the grace of God in Jesus Christ are freed from the law itself and so from sin and its wages, death. "There is therefore now no condemnation to them that are in Christ Jesus. For the law of the Spirit of life in Christ Jesus made me free from the law of sin and of death" (Rom. 8:1-2). "Where the Spirit of the Lord is, there is liberty" (2 Cor. 3:17). "Now being made free from sin and become servants to God, ye have your fruit unto sanctification, and the end eternal life" (Rom. 6:22).

Thus, both Christianity and Buddhism talk about freedom, or liberation from sin, death, or karma. In Christianity, however, this freedom is the gift of God and is based on the will of God. Liberation from sin and death is the divine work of God. On the other hand, liberation from karma in Buddhism is not based on any kind of will, divine or human. It is realized through the Great Death of the human ego and is based on nothing whatsoever. It is *jinen*, primordial naturalness, and agentless spontaneity that springs from the bottomless depth of Sunyata. As the *Vimalakirti-nirdesa Sutra* states, "From the non-abiding origin is produced all things."[99] It is a spontaneous action without a particular agent, human or divine. It is an action without an agent and, in this naturalness or spontaneity, action as it is is nonaction and nonaction as it is is action.

In this respect, Buddhism's notion of freedom is more akin to that of Nietzsche than that of Christianity. For Nietzsche's notion of freedom is based on *Unschuld des Werdens*, that is, the "innocence of becoming,"[100] which is without subject and object, and in which there is no "doer." Although Nietzsche clearly rejects the psychology of will that creates a right to take revenge, his philosophy is ultimately based on the will to power that is faithful to "life" in the deepest sense. His notion of "will to power" is clearly different from human free will in the ordinary sense, and the will of God in the Christian sense. It is the most fundamental will to live, which is functioning at the depth of the universe, and Nietzsche regards the notion of human free will and even that of the will of God as self-deception, as human fabrication created by a human's preservation instinct.

When we return to the most fundamental will to power through the realization of the self-deceptive nature of human will and God's will, Nietzsche insists, we enjoy the "innocence of becoming," and intuitively realize eternity—eternal recurrence. Despite its great similarity with the Buddhist notion of *jinen*—that is, primordial naturalness or spontaneity—Nietzsche's notion of the "innocence of becoming" lacks the realization of Great Death without which *jinen* cannot be properly realized. The realization of Great Death is needed to overcome even the will to power, the basic principle of Nietzsche. Only when the will to power is broken through to the boundless openness of Sunyata are Sunyata and its accompanying notion of *jinen* fully realized.

As I mentioned before, in the awakening to Sunyata, human free will is realized entirely anew in its pure form by getting rid of its self-attaching and self-binding character. This pure free will is "pure" and "free," but not in terms of transcendental pure practical reason as in Kant, or in terms of divine will of an all-loving God as in Christianity, or in terms of innocence of becoming as in Nietzsche. It is pure and free because this will is always self-emptying and self-negating, not self-assertive or self-affirmative; it is absolute "willing" without the subject of will and the object of will; it is cheerful, intentionless, even playful, and yet most serious and untiring. It is pure and free without clinging to either the secular or the sacred, the self or others, cause or effect. In short, it is free will revived and working in the locus of Sunyata.

Just as one's free will, deeply involved in both individual and collective karma, was the center of the network of karma extending throughout the universe, pure and free will now revived in the locus of Sunyata permeates a center or locus of boundlessly open Sunyata. It is a center realized by Sunyata in its self-emptying nature. In other words, in and through the self-emptying of Sunyata, Sunyata concentrates itself into a particular center as the pure and free will.

This pure and free will is thoroughly one's free will, and yet, at the same time, it is not one's free will, but the free will of Sunyata. This pure and free will is thoroughly Sunyata's free will, and yet, at the same time, it is not Sunyata's free will, but one's free will. This dynamic identity of one's free will and Sunyata's free will is true with anyone's free will in the locus of Sunyata. The implication is that unlike one's self-centered free will involved in karma, pure and free will revived in the locus of Sunyata is self-emptying and self-negating.

This pure and free will revived in, and realized as the center of, Sunyata functions in terms of a "vow" that is traditionally called *pranidhana*. It is a vow to save others, however innumerable they may be, as well as one's self, a vow in which the mind to seek enlightenment and the desire to save all sentient beings are dynamically one. This is because in Sunyata the wisdom aspect and the compassion aspect are always working together through Sunyata's self-emptying. Sunyata remaining with itself, without turning itself into a vow, is not true Sunyata. However, Sunyata that remains only at the level of a vow still cannot be true Sunyata either. Just as Sunyata must empty itself and turn itself into a vow, it must empty even the vow and turn itself into an "act" or "deed," which is traditionally called *carita* or *carya*. For a vow that does not turn itself into an act cannot be a true vow. In this way, in and through self-emptying, Sunyata always ceaselessly turns itself into a vow and into acts, and then dynamically centers itself in a focal point of this dynamism.

This development of Sunyata into vow and act, however, does not signify that Sunyata goes externally out of itself. This development takes place within the locus of Sunyata. For being boundless openness, Sunyata has nothing outside of itself. Rather, the development of Sunyata into vow and act signifies Sunyata's going internally into its own depth. More strictly and sufficiently speaking, in the development of Sunyata into vow and act, the outward movement and the inward movement, the centrifugal approach and the centripetal approach, are not two but dynamically one. This is true precisely because Sunyata is boundlessly open; in it, everything is interdependent and interpenetrating. This is the dynamism of Sunyata, and the focal point of this dynamism—which can be realized at each and every point of dynamism—is the "vow" to save one's self and all others and the "act" to pursue the vow. Traditionally, Amida Buddha in Pure Land Buddhism is one of the personifications of such a vow and action.

The vow and act realized through the self-emptying of Sunyata provide not only the center of boundlessly open Sunyata but also the ultimate criterion of value judgment. This judgment is to be made in terms of whether or not a thing or action in question does accord with the vow and act to make one's self and all others awakened. If the thing or action accords with the vow and act realized in the dynamism of Sunyata, it is regarded as valuable, whereas if it does not, it is deemed "antivaluable." Valuable things will be naturally encouraged and promoted, but even "antivaluable" things will not be simply rejected or punished. Clearly recognizing the "antivaluable" nature of a thing in question in the light of wisdom, one will transform it from within itself in the light of compassion. Both promoting "valuable" things and transforming "antivaluable" things are the work of vow and act as the self-emptying of Sunyata. Vow and act, as the center of Sunyata and as the ultimate criterion of value judgment, are clearly realized only when Sunyata is realized dynamically in its self-emptying nature.

Time and History in Buddhism

Buddhism has a unique view of time. Time is understood to be entirely without beginning and without end. Inasmuch as time is beginningless and endless, it is not considered to be linear as in Christianity or circular as in non-Buddhist Vedantic philosophy. Being neither linear nor circular, time is understood to be not irreversible but reversible, and yet time moves from moment to moment, each moment embracing the whole process of time.

This view of time is inseparably linked with the Buddhist view of life and death. Buddhism does not regard life and death as two different entities, but one indivisible reality—that is, living-dying. For if we grasp our life not objectively from the outside, but subjectively from within, we are fully living and fully dying at each and every moment. There is no living without dying, and no dying without living. According to Buddhism, we are not moving from life to death, but are in the process of living-dying. This must be clearly realized.

We must also realize that the process of our living-dying is without beginning and without end. The process extends itself beyond our present life both into the direction of the remote past and into the direction of the distant future. (This is the reason, for example, Zen raises the traditional question, "What is your original face before your parents were born?" as well as the question, "If you are free from life and death, you know where you will go. When the four elements [a physical human body] are decomposed, where do you go?") Due to the absence of God as the creator and the ruler of the universe, in Buddhism there is no beginning in terms of creation and no end in terms of last judgment. Accordingly, we must realize the beginninglessness and the endlessness of samsara—that is, the transmigration of living-dying. This realization is essential because it provides a way to overcome samsara and to turn it into nirvana. For if we clearly realize the beginninglessness and endlessness of the process of living-dying *at this moment*, the whole process of living-dying is concentrated *in this moment*. In other words, this moment embraces the whole process of living-dying by virtue of the clear realization of the beginninglessness and endlessness of the process of living-dying. Here, in this point, we can overcome samsara and realize nirvana right in the midst of samsara.

In this view of living-dying, time is understood to be beginningless and endless. And, as I mentioned above, in the clear realization of the beginninglessness and endlessness of the process of living-dying at this moment, the whole process of time is concentrated in this moment and, with this moment as a pivot, past and future can be reversed. (Otherwise an emancipation from karma is inconceivable.)

Because of this unique view of time, however, Buddhism is relatively weak in its view of history. Time is not directly history. Time becomes "history" when the factor of spatiality (worldhood, *Weltlichkeit*) is added to it. History comes to have meaning when time is understood to be irreversible and each moment has an unrepeatable uniqueness or once-and-for-all nature (*Einmaligkeit*). But because time is understood to be entirely beginningless and endless and thus reversible, the unidirectionality of time and the uniqueness of each moment essential to the notion of history are not clearly expressed in Buddhism.

Buddhism, however, can develop its own view of history if we take seriously the compassionate aspect of Sunyata, namely, the self-emptying of Sunyata. In the wisdom aspect of Sunyata, everything is realized in its suchness, in its interpenetration and reciprocity with everything else. Time is not an exception. Accordingly, in the light of wisdom realized in Sunyata, past and future are interpenetrating and reciprocal. Furthermore, the beginningless and endless process of time is totally concentrated in each moment. This is why in Buddhism each "now" moment is realized as the eternal Now in the sense of the absolute present. However, in the light of compassion, also realized in Sunyata, another aspect of time comes to be realized. Although all things and all persons are realized in their suchness and interpenetration in the light of wisdom *for an awakened one*, those *"unawakened" from their own side* have not yet awakened to this basic reality. Many beings still consider themselves unenlightened and deluded. Such persons are innumerable at present and will appear endlessly in the future. The task for an awakened one is to help these persons as well "awaken" to their suchness and interpenetration with all other things. This is the compassionate aspect of Sunyata that can be actualized only by emptying the wisdom aspect of Sunyata. As the generation of "unawakened" beings will never cease, this process of actualizing the compassionate aspect of Sunyata is endless. Here the progress of history toward the future is necessary and comes to have a positive significance.

In the light of wisdom realized in Sunyata, everything and everyone is realized in its suchness and time is overcome. In the light of compassion also realized in Sunyata, however, time is religiously significant and essential. And the endless process of the compassionate work of an awakened person trying to awaken others is no less than the aforementioned process of Sunyata turning itself into vow and into act through its self-emptying. At this point, history is no longer a "history of karma" in which persons are transmigrating beginninglessly and endlessly. It becomes a "history of vow and act" in which wisdom and compassion are operating to emancipate innumerable sentient beings from transmigration. Here we do have a Buddhist view of history.

It is not, however, an eschatological or teleological view of history in the Christian or Western sense. If we use the term "eschatology," the Buddhist view of history is a completely realized eschatology, because in the light of wisdom everything and everyone without exception is realized in its suchness, and time is thereby overcome. If we use the term "teleology," the Buddhist view of history is an open teleology because in the light of compassion the process of awakening others in history is endless. And the completely realized eschatology and the entirely open teleology are dynamically united in this present moment, now. This is a Buddhist view of history as I understand it.

All that I have said about Sunyata can be summarized by saying that true Sunyata is not static but dynamic—it is a pure and unceasing function of self-emptying, making self and others manifest their suchness. It is urgently necessary to grasp the notion of Sunyata dynamically to give new life to Buddhism in the contemporary world.

I have suggested that in Christianity, the notion of the kenotic God is essential as the root-source of the kenotic Christ, if God is truly the God of love. I have also suggested that in Buddhism, Sunyata must be grasped dynamically not statically, for Sunyata indicates not only wisdom but also compassion. And when we clearly realize the notion of the kenotic God in Christianity and the notion of the dynamic Sunyata in Buddhism—without eliminating the distinctiveness of each religion but rather by deepening their respective unique characters—we find a significant common basis at a deeper level. In this way, I believe, Christianity and Buddhism can enter into a much more profound and creative dialogue and overcome antireligious ideologies prevailing in our contemporary society.

NOTES

This essay was originally delivered at the second conference on East-West Religious Encounter, "Paradigm Shifts in Buddhism and Christianity," held in Honolulu, Hawaii, January 3–11, 1984. The author is grateful to Professors S. I. Shapiro, Joseph S. O'Leary, Steve Antinoff, and Christopher Ives for their revisions and valuable suggestions.

1. A good example of this development is John Cobb's book *Beyond Dialogue: Toward a Mutual Transformation of Christianity and Buddhism* (Philadelphia: Fortress Press, 1982). See also Masao Abe, "John Cobb's *Beyond Dialogue,*" *The Eastern Buddhist*, vol. 18, no. 1 (1985), pp. 131–37.

2. Masao Abe, "Buddhism and Christianity as a Problem of Today," *Japanese Religions*, vol. 3, no. 2 (1963), p. 15.

3. Thomas S. Kuhn, *The Structure of Scientific Revolutions* (Chicago: University of Chicago Press, 2d ed., 1970), pp. 66–76. Hans Küng, "Paradigm Change in Theology," unpublished paper, pp. 7–8.

4. For the author's view of Marxism and Freudian psychoanalysis, see Masao Abe, *Zen and Western Thought* (London and Honolulu: Macmillan and University of Hawaii Press, 1985), pp. 231–48.

5. Hans Küng, *Does God Exist? An Answer for Today* (New York: Random House, 1981), pp. 109–10.

6. Ibid., p. 124.

7. Ibid., pp. 123–24.

8. Ibid., pp. 124, 634, 635, 124.

9. This section on nihilism is largely taken from my essay "Christianity and Buddhism–Centering Around Science and Nihilism," *Japanese Religions*, vol. 5, no. 3 (1968), pp. 36–62.

10. Martin Heidegger, *Holzwege* (Frankfurt am Main: Klostermann, 1950), pp. 206, 199, 200.

11. Friedrich Nietzsche, *Wille zur Macht* (Stuttgart: Kröner Tachenausgabe, Band 78), p. 10.

12. *The Complete Works of Friedrich Nietzsche*, vol. 12, ed. Oscar Levy (Edinburgh and London: T.N. Foulis, 1911), p. 73.

13. Nietzsche, *Wille zur Macht*, p. 11.

14. My notions of "nihilism before religion" and "nihilism beyond religion" may roughly correspond to Nietzsche's notion of "passive nihilism" and "active nihilism."

15. Abe, "Buddhism and Christianity as a Problem of Today," p. 17.

16. *Interpreter's Bible*, vol. 11 (New York: Abingdon Press, 1955), p. 49.

17. Ibid., pp. 48–50.

18. Ibid., p. 50.

19. Karl Barth, *Church Dogmatics*, IV/1, ed. G. W. Bromiley and T. F. Torrance (Edinburgh: T. & T. Clark, 1980), p. 558.

20. Jürgen Moltmann, *The Crucified God* (New York: Harper & Row, 1974), p. 201.

21. Küng, *Does God Exist?*, pp. 684–85.

22. Ibid., pp. 690–91. In his notes, Küng calls the reader's attention to how Moltmann puts quotation marks in the title of the important chapter 6 of *The Crucified God*.

23. Keiji Nishitani, *Religion and Nothingness* (Los Angeles: University of California Press, 1982), p. 59.

24. Moltmann, *The Crucified God*.

25. Karl Rahner, *The Foundations of Christian Faith: An Introduction to the Idea of Christianity*, trans. William V. Dych (New York: Seabury Press, 1978), p. 222.

26. Karl Rahner, *Sacramentum Mundi*, vol. 2 (London: Burns and Oates, 1969), pp. 207f.

27. Rahner, *Foundations of Christian Faith*, pp. 220, 222.

28. Ibid., p. 222.

29. Ibid.

30. Küng, *Does God Exist?*, p. 133.

31. Rahner, *Foundations of Christian Faith*, p. 220.

32. Moltmann, *The Crucified God*, pp. 24, 207.

33. Ibid., pp. 204, 243.

34. Ibid., p. 203.

35. Barth, *Church Dogmatics*, II/2, pp. 167, 162.

36. Moltmann, *The Crucified God*, p. 20.

37. Ibid.

38. Ibid., p. 204.

39. Ibid., p. 245.
40. Ibid.
41. Ibid., p. 274.
42. Ibid., p. 205.
43. Ibid., pp. 244–45.
44. Ibid., p. 243.
45. Ibid., p. 244.
46. Ibid., p. 228.
47. Ibid., pp. 204, 244, 246.
48. Ibid., 246.
49. Ibid., p. 278.
50. Ibid., p. 246.
51. Ibid., pp. 204, 244.
52. Ibid., p. 244.
53. Ibid., pp. 205, 275.
54. Ibid., p. 244.
55. Küng, *Does God Exist?*, p. 64.
56. *Mulamadhyamaka-karika*, 24. See Frederick J. Streng, *Emptiness: A Study in Religious Meaning* (Nashville: Abingdon Press, 1967), p. 213.
57. *Prajnaparamita-sutra. Taisho shinshu daizokyo* (hereafter *Taisho*), ed. Junjiro Takakusu and Kaigyoku Watanabe (Tokyo: Taisho Issaikyo Kankokai, 1924–32), vol. 3, no. 223, p. 250b.
58. *Prajnaparamita-hrdaya-sutra. Taisho*, vol. 8, no. 256, p. 848.
59. Abe, *Zen and Western Thought*, pp. 4–24.
60. Ibid., pp. 31f.
61. *Martin Luther: Selections from his Writings*, ed. and with an introduction by John Dillenberger (Garden City, N.Y.: Anchor Books, 1961), p. 53.
62. *The Tannisho*, tr. Ryukoku Translation Center (New York: Weatherhill, 1966), p. 22.
63. *Zenmon Nenjushu*, vol. 2, ed. Seizan Yanagida (Kyoto: Hanazono University, 1960), p. 120.
64. Taken from conversations with several theologians.
65. G. W. F. Hegel, *Grundlinien der Philosophie des Rechts* (Hamburg: Felix Meiner Verlag, 1955), p. 14.
66. G. W. F. Hegel, *Science of Logic* (New York: Humanities Press, 1966), vol. 2, pp. 209ff.
67. *Mahayana-sutralamkara*, ed. Sylvain Levi (Paris: Librairie Honoré Champion, 1907), vol. 1. Index to the *Mahayana sutralamakara*, by Gadjin M. Nagao (Tokyo: Nippon Gakujutsu Shinkokai, 1958), p. 344.
68. *Shobogenzo*, "Zazenshin," in *Dogen*, vol. 1, *Nihon shiso taikei* (The Outline of Japanese Thought) (Tokyo: Iwanami, 1970), p. 127.
69. "Sanjushichibon-bodaibunpo," in *Dogen*, vol. 2, p. 190.
70. Abe, *Zen and Western Thought*, pp. 112, 119–20.
71. *Anguttara-nikaya*, ed. Devamitta Thera (Colombo: 1919), p. 590.
72. *Encyclopedia of Religion and Ethics*, vol. VII, ed. James Hastings (New York: Charles Scribner's Sons, 1915), p. 674.
73. Ibid.

74. David J. Kalupahana, *Buddhist Philosophy: A Historical Analysis* (Honolulu: University of Hawaii Press, 1976), pp. 48–49.

75. D. T. Suzuki, *Outlines of Mahayana Buddhism* (New York: Schocken Books, 1963), p. 198.

76. Kalupahana, *Buddhist Philosophy*, p. 47.

77. Suzuki, *Outlines of Mahayana Buddhism*, p. 193.

78. Ibid., pp. 207–208.

79. Walpala Rahula, *What the Buddha Taught* (New York: Grove Press, 1959), p. 31.

80. *The Record of Lin-chi* (Kyoto: Institute for Zen Studies, 1975), pp. 18–19.

81. D. T. Suzuki, *Essays in Zen Buddhism*, 3d Series (London: Luzac, 1934), p. 26.

82. *The Record of Lin-chi*, p. 19.

83. Suzuki, *Essays in Zen Buddhism*, p. 26.

84. *The Awakening of Faith*, tr. Yoshito S. Hakeda (New York: Columbia University Press, 1967), p. 50; adapted here.

85. *Shohomugyo-kyo*, *Taisho*, vol. 15, no. 650, p. 759c.

86. *A Zen Forest: Sayings of the Masters* (New York: Weatherhill, 1981), pp. 64, 81, 89.

87. *The Record of Lin-chi* (*Rinzairoku*), *Taisho*, vol. 47, no. 1985, p. 499c.

88. *Denshinhoyo*, *Taisho*, vol. 48, no. 2012A, p. 387a.

89. Irving Greenberg, "Judaism and Christianity After the Holocaust," in *Jews and Christians in Dialogue*, ed. Leonard Swidler, *Journal of Ecumenical Studies*, vol. 12, no. 4, p. 52.

90. Emil L. Fackenheim, "Foreword," in Yehuda Bauer, *The Jewish Emergence from Powerlessness* (Toronto: University of Toronto Press, 1979), p. vii.

91. Ibid., pp. vii–viii.

92. Ibid., p. viii.

93. Emil L. Fackenheim, *To Mend the World* (New York: Schocken Books, 1982), p. 252.

94. Ibid., pp. 192–93.

95. Ibid., pp. 309, 310.

96. Ibid., p. 310.

97. Ibid.

98. *The Record of Lin-chi*, *Taisho*, vol. 47, no. 1985, p. 500c.

99. *Vimalakirti-nirdesa Sutra*, *Taisho*, vol. 14, no. 475, p. 547c.

100. Friedrich Nietzsche, *The Will to Power*, ed. Walter Kaufmann (New York: Random House, 1968), p. 297.

PART II

RESPONSES TO MASAO ABE

I

Holocaust, Sunyata, and Holy Nothingness: An Essay in Interreligious Dialogue

RICHARD L. RUBENSTEIN

For thousands of years Jews have been sustained by the belief, diversely interpreted, that the omnipotent and omnibenevolent Creator of the universe had chosen them from among all peoples and sanctified them to his service. This conception of the divine-human relationship permeates every aspect of Jewish law, lore, liturgy, and ritual. Without it there would still be a Jewish people, given its shared historical experience, but the continuity of traditional Judaism would be shattered.

In the aftermath of the Holocaust, those who believe in the election of Israel must ask whether the Nazi assault was ultimately God's punishment of Israel for her sins, just as Jeremiah saw Nebuchadnezzar's conquest of Jerusalem in 586 B.C.E. and the rabbis saw the Roman conquest of Jerusalem in 70 C.E. Many traditional Jews and Evangelical Christians have come to that conclusion concerning the Holocaust, not out of malice, but because it accords with their reading of Scripture.[1] Such a belief was impossible for me because, of necessity, it interpreted the whole Nazi universe of death and extermination as the work of a just and righteous God. Nor did any of the liberal Jewish responses to the Holocaust possess greater credibility. On the contrary, they appear to be evasive mystifications that somehow manage to affirm the sovereignty of the biblical God and the election of Israel while in a hazy and obfuscating way denying his involvement in the Holocaust.

In this crisis of faith, there was no alternative but to rely on my own emotional and intellectual resources in attempting to formulate a coherent worldview. Of overwhelming importance in this process was the long and often distressing psychoanalysis undertaken in the 1950s and early 1960s. The combination of the therapeutic experience and a disci-

93

plined reading of both Freud and Hegel, especially the dialectic of the Master and the Slave, in connection with doctoral studies at Harvard led to reflections concerning the "primal crime" and the origins of Judaism and Christianity, the servile consciousness and its consequences in the history and culture of Judaism, sibling rivalry and its communal extensions, the religio-cultural role of the superego, ontogenetic and phylogenetic origins, matriarchy, patriarchy, and fraternity in religious belief and institutions, eros and thanatos, and being and nothingness. These ideas led in turn to theological concepts such as God as the Holy Nothingness, the world as the dialectical self-alienation and self-unfolding of Divinity, the interconnectedness of all things, and the nonsubstantiality of human existence. Although many of these ideas, so important for the mending of my shattered religious cosmos, can be found in Jewish mysticism, they are profoundly at odds with the mainstream of biblical and rabbinic Judaism.

From time to time I would encounter a Buddhist scholar in dialogue who would tell me that my ideas were close to Buddhism. This point was also made by Father Professor Klaus Rohmann in his systematic analysis of my thinking in his book *Vollendung im Nichts? Eine Dokumentation der Amerikanischen Gott-ist-Tod-Theologie.*[2] The turn to dialectical mysticism and to a position somewhat close to Buddhism came only after the collapse of my belief in the sovereign, transcendent Creator God of Scripture and the election of Israel. Even when the latter belief appears to use the language and symbolism of Scripture, it, like Buddhism, is the polar opposite of biblical religion, whether Jewish or Christian.

This opportunity to enter into dialogue with Masao Abe is therefore most welcome. My agreement is greatest with Abe's views concerning the ultimate nature of reality, but we differ when he attempts to apply his insights to concrete historical events such as the Holocaust. I am also compelled to take issue with his interpretation of kenosis, the self-emptying and self-abnegation of Divinity (Phil. 2:5–10). Here, I believe he narrows the gap between Buddhism and Christianity more than can be justified. In spite of their differences, Judaism and Christianity are biblical religions with a basic core of agreement concerning the Creator God. In biblical religion, the sovereign Creator God is the ultimate reality upon whom both the human and natural orders are dependent. In Buddhism, ultimate reality is neither God nor Being but Sunyata, literally, "emptiness," which can imply "absolute nothingness" (p. 50). Biblical religion knows nothing of dependent co-origination; instead it affirms *dependent origination*, beginning with creation itself. Moreover, Scripture depicts the Creator God as relating to humanity through a series of conditional pacts, or *covenants*, in which God as the superior party stipulates both the conditions under which he will extend his protection to his creatures and the dire penalties involved in a want of conformity with these conditions. The covenant at Sinai is, of course, the most important conditional pact in Scripture, although it is by no means the only one (Ex. 20:1–14). Every biblical commandment presupposes a covenantal relationship between God and humanity. Christianity does not differ from Judaism on the idea of a divine-human covenantal relationship. It differs in its proclamation that Christ alone enables humanity to fulfill its covenantal obligations.

This is evident in the way the biblical traditions concerning the Fall of Adam are treated in each tradition. Both normative rabbinic Judaism and Pauline Christianity insisted that humanity would not have been afflicted with sickness and mortality had Adam not violated the first commandment: "Of the tree of the knowledge of good and evil, thou shalt not eat of it" (Gen. 2:17, 18, KJV). Referring to Adam's sin, Paul of Tarsus declared, "By one man sin entered into the world, and death by sin" (Rom. 5:12, KJV). In one rabbinic tradition the Ministering Angels are depicted as asking God, "Why didst Thou impose the penalty of death upon Adam?" God replies, "I gave him an easy commandment yet he violated it."[3] Both Paul and the rabbis agreed that "the wages of sin is death" (Rom. 6:23, KJV).

In biblical religion, humanity's fundamental project is neither the death of the ego-self nor the realization of Sunyata but the restoration of humanity's radically impaired covenantal relationship with God. There is little, if any, disagreement between the two biblical religions on the need to restore the relationship; there is profound disagreement concerning the means. In Judaism faithful obedience to God's commandments, as interpreted by the rabbis, is regarded as the only valid method by which the divine-human relationship can be mended. Such fidelity is not easily achieved and can be achieved only by persons possessed of a strong ego and a disciplined sense of self. Neither dionysian letting-go nor the Buddhist death of the self can have a legitimate place in such a system.

The sheer perversity of the human will also serves as a barrier to fidelity, as Paul of Tarsus recognized. Even when Paul wanted to keep the commandments, he was unable to: "For the good that I would I do not: but the evil which I would not, that I do" (Rom. 7:19, KJV). Paul the Pharisee became convinced that he could never obey the commandments as God had intended and yearned for another way to restore the broken relationship between God and humanity. He came to believe that, in his infinite mercy and compassion, God had offered humanity the only effective promise of reconciliation, Christ's self-emptying abandonment of his own divinity in taking upon himself "the likeness of men," humbling himself, and becoming "*obedient* unto death, even the death of the cross" (Phil. 2:7, 8, KJV, italics added).

Among the many readings of the extraordinary passage in Philippians where Christ's self-emptying is affirmed, few are as interesting or as original as Professor Abe's (pp. 31–35). Nevertheless, I hold that this passage must be read in the light of biblical religion's theology of covenant and election. Paul disagreed with the majority of his rabbinic contemporaries who believed that *human* obedience would ultimately suffice to undo the consequences of the Fall.[4] Let us recall the classical definition of sin in biblical religion, *rebellion against the will of the Creator.* Paul's faith in Christ as Savior and Restorer rested on his faith in Christ's *superlative obedience* to God's will. In the kenosis passage in Philippians, Paul defines the nature of that obedience: it is "obedience unto death."

As noted, the corollary of the belief that "the wages of sin is death" in both rabbinic Judaism and Pauline Christianity was that a person perfectly obedient to the will of the Creator would never die. According to Paul, Christ was such a person. Because of his perfect sinlessness, Christ did not have to suffer death on the cross. Nevertheless, out of love for humanity, he emptied himself of his divinity and suffered that bitter, painful, and degrading death. Because Christ had no need to make reparation for his own sins, his death on the cross was reparation for the sins of Adam and his progeny. That is why Paul saw Christ as the Second Adam and the antitype of the first Adam, undoing by superlative obedience and sacrificial dying the consequences of the first Adam's disobedience. This is expressed by Paul:

> For if by one man's offence death reigned by one; much more they which receive abundance of grace and of the gift of righteousness shall reign in life by one, Jesus Christ. . . . For as by one man's disobedience many were made sinners, so by the obedience of one shall many be made righteous.
>
> (Rom. 5:17, 19)

Neither the covenant nor the theme of vicarious atonement is central to Abe's reading of Philippians 2:5–11. Instead, Abe interprets Christ's salvational function as essentially "self-emptying" and relates Christ's kenosis to the problem of the human ego: "All discussion of Christ as the Son of God will be religiously meaningless if engaged in apart from the problem of human ego, our own existential problem of the self" (pp. 33–34). Although I have much sympathy with Abe's insights concerning the path to *individual* awakening, I have great difficulty in discerning a fundamental symmetry between his reading and the fundamental theological intentions of Paul, the former Pharisee and pupil of Rabban Gamaliel.

To read Philippians as does Abe is to disconnect the Old and New Testaments, something neither Paul nor the Christian religious and theological mainstream were ever willing to do. Paul's religious problem was neither enlightenment nor the complete negation of the self but the restoration of the right relationship, defined by the covenant, between God and humanity.

Even Paul's declaration in Galatians 2:20, "I am crucified with Christ: nevertheless I live; yet not I, but Christ liveth in me," must be understood in terms of the Law, covenant, and election rather than as a Buddhist-like absolute negation of the self (p. 34). Galatians 2:20 is illuminated by Romans 6:3–4:

> Know ye not, that so many of us as were baptized into Jesus Christ were baptized into his death? Therefore we are buried with him by baptism into death: that like as Christ was raised up from the dead by the glory of the Father, even so we also should walk in newness of life.

Paul's position is that, as sinners incapable of fidelity to God's holy Law, we can expect no reconciliation. Only through *total identification* with the sinless and perfectly obedient Christ can we possess his merits and *through him* achieve perfect reconciliation with God. Identification is bestowed upon us by immersion in the baptismal waters where we pay sin's penalty by dying his death. Having paid the penalty, we arise from the baptismal waters resurrected as new creatures in Christ. The debt incurred under the Law has been paid not by our death but by Christ's and by our total identification with him. In Abe's interpretation, the transcendent, law-giving Author of the covenant has disappeared from Paul's horizon together with the disobedient sinner's need to pay his guilty debt. Instead, salvation consists in the "death of the human ego-self" (p. 34).

To repeat, there are many elements in Abe's thought with which I am in profound sympathy, such as the need to overcome fundamental ignorance (*avidya*) and dependent co-origination. Nevertheless, for me his interpretation of kenosis narrows the gap between Christianity and Buddhism more than is warranted by the fundamental perspectives of either tradition. It is, of course, possible to discern similarities between Buddhism and certain aspects of Jewish and Christian mysticism, but that is largely due to the subterranean elements of heresy and heterodoxy in mysticism, which, at the deepest level, represents a profound, albeit discretely disguised, rejection of the biblical conception of creation. This is obvious in the Kabbalah of R. Isaac Luria (1534–72), the mystic who has had the greatest influence on contemporary Jewish thinkers. In his religious behavior Luria was a devotedly compliant Orthodox Jew; his mystical teachings were among the most revolutionary ever taught within the Jewish community. In Lurianic Kabbalism the creation of the universe is the consequence of a cosmic catastrophe, a rupture in the Divine Ground identified by Luria as the "breaking of the vessels," in which a "part of God Himself was exiled from God."[5] Luria identifies *tikkun* as the process by which the exiled parts of God are ultimately to be restored to God so that the *En Sof* or *Urgrund* may once again be "all in all."

How distant is the notion of creation as cosmic catastrophe from the view of creation expressed in Genesis 1:31: "And God saw everything that he had made, and, behold it was very good." Writing of the tension between the conservative and revolutionary tendencies of the great Jewish mystics among whom Luria is preeminent, Gershom G. Scholem has observed:

> This tension . . . runs through the whole history of mysticism. When it becomes conscious it colors the personal behavior of the great mystics. But even when in full lucidity they choose a conservative attitude toward their tradition, they always walk the steep and narrow path bordering on heresy.[6]

Insofar as I agree with Abe, it is largely because my understanding of the terrible events of twentieth-century Jewish history has left me no credible option but to depart, as did the mystics, from the path of orthodoxy. By orthodoxy I do not mean institutional Jewish orthopraxy, which calls itself "Orthodox Judaism," but *orthodoxos*, "right opinion," in the case of Judaism, the theological mainstream.

Even more problematic than Abe's interpretation of kenosis is his interpretation of the Holocaust. Abe begins his discussion of the Holocaust by stating that he may share a measure of responsibility for the Holocaust. He observes that as a Japanese "who lived at the time on the opposite side of the world," he could easily claim that he had "nothing to do with that terrible event" (pp. 75–76). Nevertheless, in keeping with the Buddhist doctrine of karma, Abe accepts the fact that "in the deepest sense" he also participated in the Holocaust. Abe qualifies this statement by distinguishing his own individual karma from collective karma. The Holocaust, Abe tells us, is not his problem in the terms of his "individual karma in the narrow sense, but in terms of collective karma, in that the Holocaust is *ultimately* rooted in the fundamental ignorance (*avidya*) and the endless blind thirst to live inherent in human existence in which I am also deeply involved through my own individual karma. I am sharing the blame of the Holocaust because at the depth of my existence I am participating in the fundamental ignorance together with the overt assailants" (p. 76, Abe's italics).

I am struck, as have been other critics of Abe, by the ahistorical nature of Abe's avowal of responsibility. John Cobb is on target when he observes that "a specific event requires specific explanation" because "original sin and *avidya* have always been with us, but events like the Holocaust are fortunately not everyday occurrences."[7] In his avowal of responsibility Abe manifests an avoidance of the concrete facts of history and society that is by no means limited to religious thinkers of any particular tradition. On the contrary, on occasion such avoidance of the concrete appears to be an occupational hazard among religious thinkers. In the case of the Holocaust, it is my view that no attempt at theological interpretation will be adequate if it fails to offer an answer to the question "Given the power equation between the Jews and their European neighbors, why did the Holocaust take place in the twentieth century rather than at an earlier time?" Moreover, to be credible the answer must include some consideration of the concrete historical, demographic, religious, social, economic, and cultural factors involved in the relations between the Jews and their neighbors.

Abe is, however, correct when he observes that, from the perspective of the Buddhist doctrine of karma, he must accept the fact that "in the deepest sense [he] participated as well in the Holocaust" (p. 76). Abe's reason is that "all things in the universe are interdependent, co-arising, and co-ceasing—nothing exists by itself."[8] I also concur on the necessity to overcome *avidya*, which consists of "not recognizing the impermanency of worldly things and tenaciously clinging to them as final realities" (p. 64). The Buddhist understanding of how the laws of karma work, especially Abe's nondeterministic reading, reflects the same sense of the interconnectedness of all human and natural events that is an indispensable precondition of research in the natural and the social sciences.

Abe is also correct in asserting that the Holocaust cannot be seen as an "isolated event" but must be understood within the larger historical context in which it took place. In that sense, not only does Abe bear some measure of responsibility, however infinitesimal, for the Holocaust, so do I and all peoples and governments at the time. Leaving aside the issue of the Vatican policy of refusing to condemn the actions of the Nazis in Roman Catholic Poland, the World War II policies of the United States and Great Britain were, for example, at times close to passive cooperation with genocide.[9] Nevertheless, if all peoples and governments of the period shared a measure of responsibility for the Holocaust, Abe's responsibility is so infinitesimal that he unintentionally trivializes the very real responsibility of the leaders of the legitimately constituted German government, who actively planned and perpetrated the Shoah, and their many followers who willingly and obediently carried out the genocidal project. Even the sins of the Western governments were largely sins of omission; those of the German government were definitely sins of commission. Abe accepts responsibility even as he acknowledges that he had "no direct social or historical involvement in the Holocaust."[10] By contrast, to this day the perpetrators have almost universally denied responsibility, and their contemporary scholarly admirers even go so far as to attempt to deny that the Holocaust ever happened!

Although Abe appears to accept far more responsibility than he should, apparently John Cobb thinks that, as a Japanese, Abe accepts too little. Accepting a measure of responsibility as a Christian, Cobb chides Abe: "Japan was an ally of Nazi Germany. So far as I know, it did not protest the Nazi policies or use its influence to change them."[11] Cobb's comments about Japan and Nazi Germany are partly motivated by his desire to contrast his historical approach to the Holocaust with Abe's suprahistorical approach. I share Cobb's preference for the historical approach. I also recognize that Cobb is motivated by genuine good will and that he qualifies his statement with the phrase "so far as I know." Nevertheless, the historical record shows that during World War II the Imperial Japanese Government was responsible for saving thousands of Jews who might otherwise have perished.[12]

The fundamental policy of the Imperial Japanese Government toward the Jews was formulated at the conference on December 6, 1938, that came to be known as the Five Ministers Conference. Those present included the Prime Minister, Navy Minister, Minister of Foreign Affairs, Finance Minister, and Army Minister Seishiro Itagaki. The ministers issued a declaration which read in part:

> Our diplomatic ties with Germany and Italy require that we avoid embracing the Jewish people in the light of their rejection by our allies. But we should not reject them as they do because of our declared policy of racial equality, and their rejection would therefore be contrary to our spirit. This is particularly true in the light of our need for foreign capital and our desire not to alienate America.

The declaration further stipulated:

> 1. At present we will not reject the Jews living in Japan, Manchuria, and China, and *we will treat them equally with other foreigners.*
> 2. Jews to enter Japan, etc., in the future will be treated *under the same entry as other foreigners.*
> 3. We will not extend a special invitation to Jews to come to our territories, but capitalists and engineers will be mentioned.[13]
>
> [italics added]

The Five Ministers Conference "set the tone for the Japanese relations to the Jews for the next three years."[14] It facilitated the entry of almost 20,000 Jewish refugees into Japanese-controlled territory. The policy was angrily protested by the German Foreign Office, but the Japanese government reminded its ally that Japan was not a German client state. In July of 1942 SS Colonel Joseph Meisinger, the Gestapo chief for Japan, China, and Manchukuo (Manchuria) who had served in Warsaw in 1939, met with Japanese authorities in Shanghai and officially demanded that the Japanese exterminate their Jewish charges on Rosh Hashanah "like garbage."[15] Vice Consul Mitsugi Shibata found both Meisinger and his proposals revolting. He warned the leaders of the Shanghai Jewish community, urging them to use their Tokyo contacts to thwart Meisinger.[16] The Shanghai Jews succeeded in getting word to Foreign Minister Matsuoka. The Japanese government thereupon rejected Meisinger's proposals, although on February 18, 1943, the Japanese decreed that "stateless refugees" would be confined to a ghetto in the Hongkew section of Shanghai, one of the poorest sections of the metropolis. Nevertheless, within Hongkew, the Jews were never harmed. Admittedly, Japanese motives in rescuing the Jews were mixed. Some Japanese were motivated by humanitarian concerns; others likened the Jews to a *fugu* fish, a species that is a great delicacy when properly prepared but that can result in a painful death when improperly prepared. Nevertheless, Japan rejected National Socialist doctrines of racial supremacy and protected those Jews within the territory it controlled. It is hoped that this insertion of concrete historical facts into a theological discussion may help us realistically to assess Professor Abe's "responsibility" for the Holocaust both as an individual and as a Japanese.

As stated above, Abe qualifies his avowal of responsibility by stating that it stems from his realization of our collective karma in which "nothing happens in the universe entirely unrelated to us insofar as we realize that everything human is ultimately rooted in the fundamental ignorance (*avidya*) innate in human nature."[17] Abe believes that victim and perpetrator can achieve "solidarity" by awakening to the realization of our fundamental ignorance. He makes it clear that his views do not signify a "joint responsibility" of the victims in terms of the "humanistic sense of justice," which, he contends, is realized in the human ethical dimension. The "solidarity" to which he points is realized in terms of the most "fundamental religious dimension." Moreover, although recognizing the religious dimension in biblical faith in God, Abe explicitly excludes that faith from what he terms the *fundamental* religious dimension. Hence, he denies that "solidarity" can be achieved "through the realization of guilt and forgiveness under the sovereignty of one God

. . . who is loving and just." As understood by Abe, the most fundamental religious dimension "signifies the boundless openness or emptiness that is neither God, nor human, nor nature, in which all things,
including the divine, the human, and the natural, are all interrelated to
and interpenetrated by each other" (p. 76). Here and only here, where
we overcome *avidya* and realize dependent co-origination, is it possible
to achieve solidarity.

Abe's position on the Holocaust cannot be understood apart from his
belief in the fundamental qualitative difference between the "universal
religious dimension" and the "historical, ethical dimension" of human
existence. History and ethics concern "human-human" relationships;
religion concerns the "divine-human relationship."[18] Abe, of course,
takes issue with Judaism and Christianity, both of which reject the radical discontinuity between history and ethics on the one hand and "religion" on the other. If I understand Abe correctly, before we can come to
terms with the Holocaust we must transcend such ethical categories as
good and evil. Hence, Abe rejects the standpoint of justice, whether
humanistic or divine, as an inappropriate basis for coming to terms with
Auschwitz, for all judgment may provoke "a counterjudgment as a reaction from the side thus judged," leading to a never-ending conflict
between those who judge and those who are judged (p. 77).

I agree with Abe that the standpoint of justice cannot be the proper
basis for coming to terms with the Holocaust, but for somewhat different reasons that arise not out of Judaism or biblical religion but out of
the limited relevance of ethics to the behavior of the modern sovereign
state. In an earlier work I argued that "the Nazis probably committed no
crime at Auschwitz."[19] Crime is defined by Webster as "an act or omission forbidden by law." As horrible and obscenely indecent as were
their deeds, the perpetrators broke no laws of their country at the time.
On the contrary, the extermination project was largely assigned to the
so-called forces of law and order whose members were obedient to Nazi
law in carrying out their assignments.

Some Western theologians and moralists have argued that the Nazis
violated either natural law or law commanded by the sovereign Divinity. However, even if it could be shown that such a Divinity exists,
between 1939 and 1945 neither the Vatican nor the leaders of the German churches, both Protestant and Catholic, saw any reason to protest
the mass extermination they knew to be under way. And they were the
only European religious leaders remotely capable of influencing events
during the war. One must also ask, What penalties were inflicted upon
the perpetrators for breaking what some theologians now say was a

breach of divine law? Admittedly, Germany lost the war, but the vast majority of the perpetrators went on to live very comfortable lives in postwar Germany. With only miniscule exceptions, even those who were accused of mass murder received at most mere slaps on the wrist.[20]

Even if divinely ordained norms were violated, norms that can be violated with impunity are functionally equivalent to no norms at all. I agree with both Abe and such critics as Eugene B. Borowitz that the source of such norms would have to be a sovereign, transcendent Lawgiver. I agree with Abe that no such omnipotent Divinity exists. Hence, the standpoint of justice is irrelevant in coming to terms with the Holocaust.

The fact that legal and ethical concepts break down when confronted with an event such as Auschwitz in no sense minimizes my sense of horror and revulsion at what took place. Given the choice of freeing the leading perpetrators of the Holocaust and Germany's war of conquest against her neighbors or of preventing them from doing further harm by bringing them to trial, the right decision was made to hold the international war-crimes trials. Nevertheless, the Nuremberg trials resorted to the *ex post facto* fiction of "crimes against humanity," found neither in German nor Allied law books, in order to permit the victors to punish the perpetrators.

When, in responding to Abe, Eugene B. Borowitz criticizes my conception of God because it "did not provide a ground for qualitatively distinguishing between Nazis and Jews," he seeks that distinction in the realm of Divinity where it cannot be found.[21] Here I agree with Abe that the distinction between perpetrator and victim must be made in the dimension of history and society rather than Divinity. The way to stop genocide is not through fruitless religious appeals to would-be perpetrators or the prayers of those targeted as victims, but for the latter to learn from their terrible history and take realistic steps to defend themselves. That indeed has been the practical rationale for the establishment of the State of Israel. Israel will survive only as long as it is capable of defending itself. Should it ever lose that capacity, there is little reason to doubt that its enemies will make good their promise to drive the Jews into the Mediterranean. Borowitz discerns a qualitative difference between perpetrator and victim in the fact that "God is holy/good, the Holocaust is enduringly evil." I see no evidence for Borowitz's assertion that "God is holy—and that means, most closely, that God is good."[22] Like Divinity itself, the category of holiness is beyond good and evil. If we look to Divinity as the ground and source of being, we cannot avoid seeing, so to speak, Divinity as the ground and source of the endless war of species against species and even of man against man. Even if we accept belief in the sovereign Creator God of Scripture, the lion has yet to lie down with the lamb. Moreover, Scripture is not without the record of God commanding what were, in effect, holy wars of extermination. Borowitz is unable adequately to answer Abe's crucial question: "How can the Jewish people come to terms with God who ultimately allowed the Holocaust to happen?" Identifying himself with "almost-traditional Jewish believers," Borowitz replies on their behalf:

> Unable to sacrifice God's goodness, or power, or deny the reality of evil, they reluctantly sacrifice the certainty of logic in the face of what they know to be the ultimate commanding power of living in holy goodness. They believe, in their fashion, even though they do not understand in any ultimate way.[23]

Borowitz is to be commended for his honesty. Nevertheless, he and his many followers appear to make factual statements about the nature of Divinity and the divine-human relationship; yet, when faced with the contradiction between God's power and his alleged goodness, they defend their position by rejecting the relevance of logic and by confessing their inability to "understand in an ultimate way." In reality, Borowitz communicates a wishful, emotional determination to remain faithful to Jewish tradition no matter what the intellectual and theological obstacles. His position may indeed be a sociological necessity for the Jewish community, but, as Borowitz himself seems to admit, it is not a position that those seeking theological clarity concerning the religious significance of the Holocaust can find credible or illuminating.

Although Abe is correct in asserting that one cannot come to terms with the Holocaust from the standpoint of justice, one must ask what kind of "solidarity" between Jews and Nazis he has in mind. How could an understanding of our fundamental ignorance realistically bring about solidarity as he proposes? Since the end of World War II, there have been Jews, myself included, who have had no difficulty in becoming friends with and working with Germans without being judgmental in these relationships. Germans willing to enter into friendly or collaborative relations with Jews reject the idea that their nation or race has a fundamental obligation to exterminate Jews. Not so, Nazis and Neo-Nazis. To this day, they continue to seek the universal destruction of Jews even as they rejoice in their World War II "achievement" while publicly denying that the Holocaust ever happened. On the human, ethical level solidarity must be reciprocal to be meaningful. There can be no genuine reciprocity on that level between the unrelenting perpetrator and his victim.

What about solidarity on what Abe characterizes as the ultimate religious level? What does Abe mean by solidarity between Nazis and Jews on that level? As noted above, Buddhist teaching concerning overcoming *avidya* can be enormously helpful in personal life and in one's relations with others, but in what concrete way is overcoming *avidya* relevant in the political realm or in intergroup relations, where Nazi-Jewish relations would have to be worked out? I simply do not understand what Abe means when he writes concerning the Holocaust:

> Only through the realization of the collective karma and fundamental ignorance inherent in human beings . . . and through fundamental enlightenment as the realization of fundamental ignorance, can one properly and legitimately cope with such a historical evil (p. 76).

To attempt to achieve solidarity at the ultimate level seems to me to reduce solidarity to a meaningless abstraction. In considering the specific case of the Holocaust, I must await Abe's instruction concerning how solidarity could actually be achieved in the concrete, historical instance of Nazis and Jews.

One of the ways Borowitz deals with Abe's question concerning God and the Holocaust is to minimize the relevance of the question within Judaism. Thus, Borowitz erroneously argues that "the Christian death-of-God movement and, probably more importantly, its underlying cultural ferment were more responsible for bringing Holocaust theology into being than any indigenous demand by Jews for a fresh statement of their faith."[24] Borowitz is wrong on both theological and historical grounds. Can there be a more pressing theological question in the aftermath of the worst communal disaster in all of Jewish history than whether the Holocaust was a punishment inflicted upon Israel by the God who is alleged to have chosen Israel and to have promised the direst of misfortunes were Israel to disobey his commandments? The question was first raised as a public theological issue with the 1966 publication of the first edition of *After Auschwitz*.[25] Nevertheless, in raising the issue, *After Auschwitz* did no more than make manifest the unspoken question in the heart of almost every Jew.

Unlike Borowitz, Masao Abe understands that no extrinsic theological influence is required to ask of Jewish thinkers certain fundamental questions concerning the religious significance of the Holocaust. One of Abe's questions is whether the Jewish people see the Holocaust as "an isolated event entirely unrelated to other events in the world and history" and if it has such a fixed, absolutely evil nature, "how can Jewish people come to terms with the Holocaust and with God, who ultimately allowed the Holocaust to occur?" (p. 80).

Abe's question must be answered in two parts. First, almost all Jewish thinkers regard the Holocaust as a *unique* event in that it was the worst catastrophe in more than three thousand years of Israel's history. Nevertheless, to the best of my knowledge no responsible Jewish scholar views the Holocaust as an event *unrelated* to its larger historical context.

Second, some Jews have come to terms with God by becoming apocalyptic messianists, others by regarding the Holocaust as divine punishment. The messianists interpret the Holocaust as a decisive expression of God's action in history, the "birthpangs of the Messiah." As such, the Holocaust constitutes an indispensable part of the unfolding drama of the return of the Jewish people from exile to the "whole land of Israel" where they await the imminent arrival of the Age of the Messiah.[26] Nonmessianic Orthodox Jews have, as noted, tended to interpret the Holocaust as God's punishment of a sinful Jewish people. The sins include abandoning traditional Judaism, assimilation, Liberal Judaism, Zionism, and Marxism. Still others, such as Eugene Borowitz, have "come to terms with God" by returning to the "God of the covenant."

I find little credibility in any of the mainstream Jewish responses to the Holocaust. There are far more plausible historical explanations of both the Holocaust and the return from exile than the idea that it was the providential plan of an all-powerful yet omnibenevolent, sovereign Creator. For me, the only remotely plausible mainstream interpretation is the Orthodox view that Auschwitz was the just punishment inflicted by God upon a sinful Israel. Nevertheless, even this view is beset by insurmountable problems. It saves both the justice and the goodness of God by depicting the most religiously compliant prewar Jewish community, the Eastern European, as infinitely more sinful than they were in reality. What possible sins could the adults or their children have committed to justify inflicting Auschwitz upon them?

Still, both the radical messianists and the nonmessianic Orthodox traditionalists do offer a theologically consistent, if not an entirely plausible, account of the relationship between the biblical God and the Holocaust. The traditionalists understand the Holocaust in terms of God's covenant with Israel. Their view of the Holocaust is consistent with the terrible words spoken against Israel by the prophet Amos as God's mouthpiece: "You only have I known of all the families of the earth; therefore I will punish you for all your iniquities" (Amos 3:2, KJV).

As noted above, Borowitz claims that he and other "almost-traditional Jews" have come to terms with God after the Holocaust by returning to the God of the covenant. This return has been motivated by a search for a "more adequate ground of value" in a world in which "humanism" could no longer offer a substitute value structure for religion.[27] I have considerable sympathy for Borowitz's search. Although humanism cannot offer a substitute value structure, Borowitz's description of how "almost-traditional" believers come to terms with the Holocaust appears to raise more questions than it solves:

> Like classic Jewish pietists, they hope the goodness of God day by day will set the context for their confrontation with evil. Creating that day-to-day appreciation of God's continual goodness is more important to them than understanding the *limit case of gross suffering.*[28]

When Borowitz claims on behalf of "almost-traditional" Jews like himself that God's continual goodness is more important than the "limit case of suffering," he takes for granted the very issue in question, namely, whether it is possible realistically to speak of the continual goodness of God in what one historian has called "this Lear of a century." Moreover, when Borowitz refers to the "limit case of suffering," he seems to imply that the Holocaust is outweighed in significance by the far greater incidence of God's goodness in our times. He thus appears to solve the problem of God and the Holocaust by minimizing the importance of the single greatest disaster in all of Jewish history, a disaster that resulted in the extermination of the majority of Europe's Jews and the destruction of all the traditional Jewish communities of Eastern Europe. Yet we cannot be sure whether Borowitz actually means what he says, for he also tells us that almost-traditional Jews have "reluctantly" sacrificed "the certainty of logic" for their way of life if not for their beliefs.

From the Orthodox point of view, Borowitz and his followers lack seriousness when they speak of the God of the covenant as the ultimate source of their values. They believe that one can be serious about the God of the covenant only when one attempts diligently to observe the whole corpus of rabbinic law including the dietary laws, the laws concerning the Sabbath and Holy Days, and the laws of "family purity," especially as they apply to women. Unlike Borowitz, the traditionalists and the messianists are likely to agree with Abe that the Holocaust was not an absolute evil from the ultimate religious point of view. As divine punishment, the Holocaust could not be absolute evil but God's terrible but indispensable way to lead a remnant of Israel back to the true path of the Torah. For the radical messianists, the Holocaust as the birthpangs of the Messiah was a terrible but necessary step in the divine plan for Israel's redemption.

Like the messianists and the Orthodox, but for different reasons, Abe and I conclude that the Holocaust, hideous as it was, was nevertheless not an absolute evil. None of history's interrelated and interdependent events can be called absolute evil, because every event has unintended and unpredictable consequences. For example, absent the Holocaust, there would have been no state of Israel. Recognition of this fact does not minimize the horror of the Holocaust. Nevertheless, for an evil to be *absolute*, no good whatsoever could have come of it.

Abe's last question concerning the Holocaust is also divided into two parts.

First, Abe asks if, as Emil Fackenheim has argued, the Holocaust "means a complete rupture in Jewish history, how is a recovery of Jewish tradition possible?" (p. 80). I believe Fackenheim was in error on this point. One can speak of the Holocaust as a "complete rupture" with Jewish history only by ignoring the concrete facts of that history. The seeds of the Holocaust were planted in the first and third Christian centuries. In the first century, the Jews were defeated by Rome in two devastating wars and were thereafter condemned to adapt to life as a defenseless minority whose very existence depended upon the sufferance of others. With the triumph of Christianity, the Jews of Europe were condemned to dwell among people who regarded them as Satan's spawn and Christ-killers. Only by offering services in commerce and finance, not otherwise available in many parts of Europe before the onset of modernity, were the Jews permitted any kind of domicile. With the onset of modernity, the Jews, who had been a complementary economic class, found that they had become an economically competitive class. The newer economic competition was exacerbated by the older religious competition. With the disruptions of two world wars, their fate was sealed.[29] Nevertheless, there was a fundamental difference between the Holocaust and all previous Jewish disasters. The Holocaust constituted the first attempt by the government of any host people to undertake a program of unremitting extermination against the Jews. Jews had been persecuted, expelled, ghettoized, and the object of mob and even military violence, but before National Socialist Germany no government ever undertook a program of extermination.

Nor, as Fackenheim has argued, has Jewish tradition been lost. Jewish tradition has been maintained by the Orthodox, the messianists, and even by "almost-traditionalists" like Borowitz. If it has been lost, it has been by those Jews who, like myself, affirm the death of the God of covenant and election after Auschwitz. Yet, despite this theological perspective, Jewish tradition is my religio-cultural inheritance, and my involvement in religious life is primarily as a member of the Jewish community. I turn to Jewish rituals, traditions, and rites of passage to celebrate and commemorate the cycle of time and seasons and the crisis moments of life. Though the tradition as divinely mandated has lost its authority, it has by no means lost my reverent respect.

The second part of Abe's question concerns Fackenheim's proposed "return to revelation." Referring to Fackenheim, Abe asks, "What revelation and what God does he maintain in his mind?" Abe is, of course, on target. An Orthodox traditionalist would have no trouble answering Abe. He or she would reply that he or she believes in the God of Sinai and obeys the divine revelation as found in Scripture and as interpreted by the great rabbis of normative Judaism. Not so, Fackenheim, who, like Borowitz, can speak only rhetorically of a revelation lacking all specific content, which evaporates when one attempts to pin him down. Consider, for example, the following statement by Fackenheim:

> Revelation thus remains a mystery even while it is being revealed; and every single word spoken by any prophet is inexorably shot through with human interpretation.[30]

When Fackenheim speaks of revelation and Borowitz speaks of returning to the covenant, we are confronted with mystification, not theology. The reason for non-Orthodox Judaism's inability to extricate itself from mystification is its inability to face the fundamental theological problem arising out of the Holocaust: *There is no way to affirm the traditional God of covenant and election with affirming that God as the ultimate Author of Auschwitz.* That is the reason I have spoken of the death of the transcendent biblical God of the covenant and election whom both Scripture and rabbinical sources assert to be the ultimate Actor in the drama of Israel's history. In its place, I have spoken of God after the death of God, God, "the Holy Nothingness" as the Ground and Source of our being. This affirmation is close to the traditions of Jewish mysticism and to Abe's conception of Sunyata. There is a striking similarity between the following description of Sunyata by Abe and my view of God as *En Sof*, Omnipotent Nothingness, *Urgrund* and *Telos:*

> The ultimate reality for Buddhism is neither Being nor God, but Sunyata. Sunyata literally means "emptiness" or "voidness" and can imply "absolute nothingness." This is because Sunyata is entirely unobjectifiable, unconceptualizable, and unattainable by reason or will.
>
> (p. 50)

Like Abe, I hold this conception of the Ultimate because of my sense of the interdependence of all things, not as fixed substantial entities but as ephemeral, ever-changing processes. This conception of things is very close to the Buddhist sense of dependent co-origination from which even God is not excluded. Even when we disagree about the concrete world of history, I welcome Abe's reflections on the Holocaust and acknowledge my indebtedness to him.

NOTES

1. See Richard L. Rubenstein, *After Auschwitz: History, Theology, and Contemporary Judaism*, 2d ed. (Baltimore: Johns Hopkins University Press, 1992), pp. 3-13, 159-63. Chapter 1, "The Dean and the Chosen People," is especially relevant.

2. Klaus Rohmann, *Vollendung im Nichts? Eine Dokumentation der Amerikanischen Gott-ist-Tod-Theologie* (Cologne and Zurich: Benziger Verlag, 1977).

3. Talmud Babli, Shabbat 55b. According to Rabbi Ammi, "There is no death without sin, and there is no sin without iniquity" (Shabbat 55a).

4. I have discussed this issue in Richard L. Rubenstein, *My Brother Paul* (New York: Harper & Row, 1975).

5. Gershom G. Scholem, *On the Kabbalah and Its Symbolism*, tr. Ralph Mannheim (New York: Schocken Books, 1965), p. 107.

6. Ibid., p. 118.

7. John B. Cobb, Jr., "On the Deepening of Buddhism," in John B. Cobb, Jr., and Christopher Ives, eds., *The Emptying God: A Buddhist-Jewish-Christian Conversation* (Maryknoll, N.Y.: Orbis Books, 1990), p. 93.

8. Masao Abe, "A Rejoinder," in Cobb and Ives, eds., *The Emptying God*, p. 186.

9. In May 1939 England effectively closed the door to Jewish immigration to Palestine, a policy that was strictly enforced during most of the war, thereby condemning thousands of Jews to death at the hands of the Nazis. See Leni Yahil, *The Holocaust: The Fate of European Jewry* (Oxford: Oxford University Press, 1990), pp. 119-20, 624-30. In the case of the United States, with the exception of a small number of Jews from Germany and western Europe, the government of the United States steadfastly refused to permit even the temporary settlement of Jewish refugees in spite of the fact that it had extensive knowledge of the Holocaust. The State Department even went so far as to prevent messages from Gerhard Reigner, the Geneva representative of the World Jewish Congress, telling of the plight of Eastern European Jewry, from being delivered to Rabbi Steven S. Weiss, president of the American Jewish Committee. The hostility of the State Department toward any measure that would offer any help to Europe's Jews became so blatant that officials of the Treasury Department drew up a memorandum to Secretary of the Treasury Henry Morgenthau, Jr., "Report to the Secretary on the Acquiescence of This Government in the Murder of the Jews." Morgenthau then presented the contents of the memorandum to President Franklin Delano Roosevelt. Six days later on January 22, 1944, when most of Europe's Jews were already dead, Roosevelt set up the War Refugee Board (Yahil, *The Holocaust*, p. 609). Many other instances could be cited including the refusal to bomb the Auschwitz crematoria even though the I. G. Farben synthetic rubber and oil plant at Auschwitz was bombed. The policy of the U.S. War

Department was set forth in February 1944: "It is not contemplated that units of armed forces will be employed for the purpose of rescuing victims of enemy oppression unless such rescues are the direct result of military operations conducted with the objective of defeating the armed forces of the enemy." See David S. Wyman, *The Abandonment of the Jews: America and the Holocaust, 1941–1945* (New York: Pantheon Books, 1984), p. 291. Successful bombing of the Farben plant while avoiding the crematoria required precision bombing and a deliberate decision to permit the crematoria to continue in operation.

10. Abe, "A Rejoinder," p. 186.

11. Cobb, "On the Deepening of Buddhism," p. 93.

12. See Marvin Tokayer and Mary Swartz, *The Fugu Plan: The Untold Story of the Japanese and the Jews During World War II* (New York: Paddington Press, 1979).

13. David Kranzler, *Japanese, Nazis and Jews: The Jewish Refugee Community of Shanghai, 1935–1945* (Hoboken: KTAV, 1988), pp. 232–33.

14. Kranzler, *Japanese, Nazis and Jews*, pp. 232–33. In August 1940, Sempo Sugihara, Japanese Consul General in Kovno, Lithuania, issued transit visas that permitted thousands of Jews trapped in Soviet-occupied Lithuania to traverse Japanese-held territory on the transparent pretext that they were traveling to Curacao in the Dutch West Indies. Without Sugihara, these Jews would almost certainly have perished. Sugihara took action without consulting the Foreign Ministry, which nevertheless backed him up. Most of Sugihara's Jews reached Japan's port city of Kobe by way of Moscow, the Trans-Siberian Railway, and Vladivostok. When two thousand of their number found themselves unable to proceed because of the war, Foreign Minister Yosuke Matsuoka, who in 1936 had committed Japan to the Tripartite Pact with Nazi Germany and Fascist Italy, issued orders extending their visas. When the refugees' visa extensions ran out, they were sent to Shanghai where a total of about 17,000 Jews found themselves under Japanese protection. At the time no allied government was willing to take such a step.

15. Tokayer and Swartz, *The Fugu Plan*, pp. 222–26.

16. Kranzler, *Japanese, Nazis and Jews*, pp. 478–79.

17. Abe, "A Rejoinder," p. 186.

18. Ibid., p. 181.

19. Richard L. Rubenstein, *The Cunning of History* (New York: Harper & Row, 1975), p. 90.

20. Take, for example, the rather typical case of Dr. Otto Ambros, a leading German industrialist who was convicted at Nuremberg of the enslavement and mass murder of 200,000 inmates at Auschwitz. He served a sentence of three years, went on to a very prosperous career in both Germany and the United States at the highest levels of government and society. In the early 1980s Ambros served as a high-level technical advisor to W. R. Grace and Company and as a consultant to the U.S. Department of Energy. When his past conviction for mass murder became a matter of public knowledge in the United States in 1982, a White House spokesman declared that Ambros had "paid his debt to society." A spokesman for the W. R. Grace Company declared, "We do not feel there was anything wrong in employing this man in a technical position whatever he did." The spokesman added that J. Peter Grace, chairman of the board, "is extremely

proud" of his relationship to Ambros and did not find the appointment "embarrassing in any sense." See Lee Mays, "Reagan Expert Under Attack for Ties to Nazi War Criminal," *St. Petersburg Times*, April 25, 1982. The story is identified as having originated in the *Los Angeles Times*.

21. Eugene B. Borowitz, "Dynamic Sunyata and the God Whose Glory Fills the Universe," in Cobb and Ives, eds., *The Emptying God*, p. 84.

22. Ibid., pp. 84, 82.

23. Ibid., p. 86.

24. Ibid., p. 81.

25. Richard L. Rubenstein, *After Auschwitz: History, Theology, and Contemporary Judaism* (Indianapolis: Bobbs Merrill, 1966).

26. Rubenstein, *After Auschwitz*, 2d ed., pp. 211–13.

27. Borowitz, "Dynamic Sunyata," p. 86.

28. Ibid., italics added.

29. See Rubenstein, *After Auschwitz*, pp. 81–139.

30. Emil L. Fackenheim, "Can There Be Judaism Without Revelation?" in *Quest for Past and Future: Essays in Jewish Theology* (Indianapolis: Indiana University Press, 1968), p. 80.

2

The Fullness of History: A Response to Masao Abe

SANDRA B. LUBARSKY

A well-known passage of Talmud recalls the mourning of Rabbi Yohanan for his colleague, Resh Lakish. In an effort to comfort him, a fellow sage sitting with Yohanan sympathetically agrees with whatever he says. Unknowingly, he magnifies Yohanan's sense of loss. "Are you like Resh Lakish?" Yohanan cries. "Whenever I would state a law, he would put to me twenty-four objections; then from the questions and answers, the matter would be clarified. But you only say—'let me show you how right you are.' Do I need you to tell me I am right?" The Talmud continues, "He then stood up and tore his clothes, crying, 'Where are you Resh Lakish? Where are you Resh Lakish?'"[1]

Companionship in learning and the dialectic of questions and answers that comes from it are vital to the process of understanding. Happily, contemporary companionship need not be limited to one faith community, and as our partners increase, so do our questions and, with luck, our answers. It is with a sense of privilege that I participate in this reflection on Professor Abe's powerful essay. In the spirit of Resh Lakish and Rabbi Yohanan I offer my comments. I thank Professor Abe in advance for his companionship in this inquiry.

I would like to acknowledge an epistemological caveat that has been offered before by those who have attempted knowledge of other people's faiths: Language is not easily permeable. Especially in my thinking about Buddhism and the concept of dynamic Sunyata as presented by Professor Abe have I become aware of the dialogical demand for a "hermeneutic of humility."[2] At every juncture, my comments are conditioned on whether I have understood Professor Abe correctly. I cannot assume that I have; where I have not, I hope that there is something beneficial in having created the opportunity for correction.

"The only philosophy which can be responsibly practiced in the face of despair is the attempt to contemplate all things as they would present themselves from the standpoint of redemption."[3] This declaration by Theodor Adorno expresses, I believe, an idea that is deeply a part of Judaism. That there is a redeemer, that there are redemptive acts, that there is a promise of redemption—these are the facts that have fueled the lives of Jews. There is much within Jewish prayer and ritual that expresses the immense faith that a standpoint of redemption exists and, indeed, that assumes a glimmering of it. The Sabbath is redolent with redemption, and it is the Jewish intoxication with this fragrance that gives the Sabbath its strength. When it is said, "More than the Jews have kept the Sabbath, the Sabbath has kept the Jews," the theological reference is to the belief in a standpoint of redemption from which the shortcomings of this life are dignified and the despair of the hour counterpoised by eternity.

The idea of a "standpoint of redemption" seems to me to overlap in an important way with Abe's proposition that there is an "ultimate religious point of view" that surpasses our limited human understanding, in particular our understanding of suffering and evil. According to Abe, the religious point of view is the third of three dimensions of experience, the other two being a "nonhuman, natural dimension" and a "transnatural, human dimension." All phenomena, including natural and moral evil, are "properly and legitimately understood *ultimately from the vantage point of the third dimension*" (p. 71). For in the transhuman or religious dimension, things are grasped in their "suchness," or "as-it-is-ness"—no longer dislocated by time and personalities, no longer censored by the castellans of objectivity, no longer entangled by "centrisms" of any sort, and no longer consecrated or profaned by valuations of good or evil.

From both a Zen perspective and a Jewish perspective, then, there is a standpoint from which events are better understood than they are on the level of human understanding. For Jews, this is God's eye view; for Buddhists, it is the prism of Sunyata. The two traditions share in common the most significant opinion that life has a thickness to it.

I am struck, though—and attracted—by the great optimism on the Buddhist side that the more fundamental stratum of life can be fully ascertained. Abe talks about the "Self-Awakening of Zen" as a standpoint that can be achieved, in its dynamism, by human beings.[4] In contrast, Adorno's quotation continues like this:

> To gain the perspective of redemption is the utterly impossible thing, because it presupposes a standpoint removed, even though by a hair's

breadth, from the scope of existence, whereas we well know that any possible knowledge must not only first be wrested from what is, if it shall hold good, but is also marked, for this very reason, by the same distortion and indigence which it seeks to escape. The more passionately thought denies its conditionality for the sake of the unconditional, the more unconsciously, and so calamitously, it is delivered up to the world.[5]

Again, Adorno articulates the general sympathy of Jewish thought: that there is a transhuman perspective distinct from the human one and yet presentative to us only through history, and thus marred by history. The standpoint of redemption is a position that can be approached but not fully realized. Redemption touches us so that we are partially conditioned by it, but our conditionedness is not absorbed by it. Indeed, the attempt to overcome all our limitations is considered idolatrous. Its consequences are, as Adorno states, calamitous. The standpoint of redemption as a ground of being is reserved for God. The standpoint of redemption as a call for action and an assurance of transhistorical meaning is a resource for humanity.

Put this way, the two perspectives seem grossly at odds, with Zen promoting an unconditioned perspective on life and Judaism attacking such an aim as arrogant. But there is much more to be said than setting forth this opposition in such simplicity.

Within several modes of Jewish thought, there is the belief that self-transcendence is crucial to both intellectual knowledge and the experience of intense connectedness. For example, though there is the constant affirmation of the exhaustive nature of God's perspective on the world and, in contrast, the attenuated scope of human understanding, there is also the intense desire to ascend in some way to God. Jewish mystics speak of the effort toward "devekuth," or "mystical cleaving to God."[6] The rationalist Maimonides uses strikingly different language, but he too longs for a wider perspective on life that comes with knowledge of God: "One only loves God with the knowledge with which one knows Him. According to the knowledge will be the love."[7]

Moreover, knowledge of God and nonintellectual felt experience of God are not undertaken for the sake of the individual but rather out of love for God *and the world*, for they are paths of wisdom and hence of contribution to the well-being of God's creation. There is the desire to work *tikkun* (reintegration, healing) in the world—in Buddhist language, to end suffering and increase joy—for which self-transcendence is methodologically necessary. In these two ways, Judaism and Buddhism are not antipodal.

But how much self-transcendence is possible? Buddhism aims for "true emptiness dynamically identical with true fullness" (p. 74). Judaism encourages movement beyond one's particular self, yet the desire to transcend at least the ordinary limitations of human life is tempered by the recognition of important human limitations. Thus Maimonides urges that an individual "devote himself to the understanding and comprehension of those sciences and studies which will inform him concerning his Master, *as far as it lies in human faculties to understand and comprehend.*"[8]

In what follows I want to explore first, how the Buddhist emphasis on emptiness and no-self might temper the Jewish emphasis on particular historical events, and second, how the Jewish emphasis on history and relationships might modify the Buddhist emphasis on emptiness.

THE BUDDHIST EMPHASIS
ON EMPTINESS AND NO-SELF

Despite its position of limited self-transcendence, it seems to me that the Jewish perspective can benefit from some of the insights of the Buddhist notion of full self-transcendence, or emptiness and no-self. Abe's metaphysical assumptions include the notions of dependent co-origination and impermanence, and from these he concludes that there is no-thing, including no self, that is permanent and self-existing and absolutely good (p. 73). At least in regard to human nature, these insights can be upheld by a Jew as well as a Buddhist, and they offer an oft-needed corrective to the tendency in Judaism to hypostatize if not the individual self, then the community (e.g., "The State of Israel," "The People Israel," "Am Segula") or history (most recently, the Holocaust).

Despite prophetic warnings to the contrary, modern Jewish thinkers across the ideological spectrum often speak of the Jewish community as an eternal part of God's metaphysical order. In an essay on mourning, for example, the leading Orthodox thinker, Rabbi Joseph B. Soloveitchik, writes:

> The religious Jew, in particular, transcends his physical self by associating his life with the timeless covenantal destiny of the Torah community. . . .
> The individual is mortal, but *Knesset Yisrael*, the Jewish community, is enduring. The halakhic principle of *ein tzibbur metim*, "the community does not die" (Tem. 15b), is rooted in the concept that the existence of *Knesset Yisrael* as a metaphysical unity surpasses the physical existence of its individual members.[9]

Likewise, the eminent Reform Jewish theologian Eugene Borowitz, in an interesting explication of the need for balance between particularism and universality, recently wrote the following describing the particularistic side of the coin:

> In these years of danger and self-esteem, many of us partisans of human equality, who had eschewed making special claims for the Jewish people, found that we also believed that an absoluteness attached to Jewish survival and flourishing. . . . [M]any of us discovered that we believe that the Jewish people are indispensable, not merely to ourselves but to the universe and its scheme of things. We now knew that there was something transcendent about Jewish continuity.[10]

The danger of these statements becomes clear when they are juxtaposed to Abe's critique of a substance metaphysics. Having, at least on the theological level, evaded the snares of radical individualism, Jewish thinkers have often circumscribed self-transcendence within the boundaries of a sort of theological communalism. But the community can be idolized no less than the individual, indeed with even greater vigor—a fact that has scarred this century. To speak of the People of Israel or the Land of Israel as if it were a single, static entity whose historical existence masks its transhistorical essence is an extraordinary example of the fallacy of misplaced concreteness. Not simply a logical error, the ascription of actuality to an abstraction has, in this case, serious religious implications. When linked, for example, with the event of the Holocaust, such a mode of thought has produced what Emil Fackenheim calls the "614th commandment":

> Jews are forbidden to hand Hitler posthumous victories. They are commanded to survive as Jews, lest the Jewish people perish. They are forbidden to despair of man and his world, and to escape into either cynicism or otherworldliness, lest they cooperate in delivering the world over to the forces of Auschwitz. Finally they are forbidden to despair of the God of Israel, lest Judaism perish. . . . In ancient times, the unthinkable Jewish sin was idolatry. Today, it is to respond to Hitler by doing his work.[11]

Neither to give up hope nor to despair of God's existence is contemporary halakhah with commanding power. But the injunction that Jews survive "lest the Jewish people perish" is not, I believe, in the same category. Fackenheim expands on this idea with the statement that "Jewish survival, were it even for no more than survival's sake, is a holy duty as well," and he quotes with approbation the Israeli journalist Amos Kenan's statement "After the death camps, we are left only one supreme value: existence."[12]

Because of the loss of transcendent perspective and the reification of the Jewish people, survival is apt to become a value apart from other values and to eclipse the campaign against idolatry. It is, however, idolatrous to deem something absolute, complete, and eternal that is not. That was Hitler's sin, and that is the sin to fight against. What Sunyata

For Jews, the exemplification of God's historical activity is the covenantal relationship between God and the Jewish people. This covenant came to be understood as a binding relationship of *emmunah*, of loving trust. Despite the inequality of the partners, the covenant is a vessel of extraordinary mutuality in which the divinely transcendent God becomes personally immersed in the messy predicaments of history. So, for example, Abraham engages God in a negotiation over the fate of the Sodomites, and Moses successfully pleads the case of the Israelites. (In addition to being examples of divine-human intimacy, these are complex examples of the moral dimension that pervades the covenantal relationship.)

But at the same time as God is understood to be intertwined in personal events, it is also understood that the God who is known in covenantal relationship is not fully known. As God reminds Moses, God is not simply "the LORD, the God of your fathers, the God of Abraham, the God of Isaac, and the God of Jacob," but God is "I AM WHO I AM" (Ex. 3:14–15, RSV). God-in-relation is a partner with humanity, but God-in-Godself is independent. There is, then, the recognition that God's being transcends covenantal relationships, that God is somehow apart from history and time. But about this part of God's life, humans are ignorant and speculation on it has been sparse. When Jews, like Muslims, speak of the "mind of God," what has been meant is the "will of God," that is, what God intends for humanity. To the question "Is there a life of God apart from history?" Jews have given little thought; likewise to the question "Is there a life of humans apart from history and social relations?" The "Kingdom of God" is understood to be eventually *on earth*, offsetting the initial dualism between heaven and earth and transcendence and immanence.

Two of the reasons that seem to underlie Abe's desire to separate the historical realm from the religious are alien to Jewish thought. The first is the Pauline premise that human beings cannot do the good they intend to do, a premise that Abe states "is not peculiar to St. Paul, but is inevitable to all seriously reflective persons" (p. 72). The second is Abe's notion that "ethics concerns human-human relationships whereas religion concerns the divine-human relationship."[18] Both statements make clear that the sociohistorical dimension is flawed and limited.

Although there is no Jewish thinker that I know of who would assert that the world is perfect, such a position is held simultaneously with the belief in essential human goodness and in ethical monotheism. The foundation of Jewish belief is the ability of humans to "be holy" because they are made in the image of God who "is holy." Humans can "imitate" God (though they often mock God, instead), who is wholly good. Paul's confession, rephrased in a more characteristically Jewish way, would read, "For the good which I would I do not; *and* the evil which I would *also* do, that I practice—wretched man that I am!" I do not think that Jews reject the idea that too often the good that we intend has malignant consequences; rather, the emphasis is on the voluntary nature of much good and much evil. The source of this emphasis is the covenantal relationship in which Jews identify themselves as free partners with God, reflecting something of the divine image. Hence humans are not seen as *compelled* to do evil, but rather as able to carry out the ethical duties that follow from the divine-human alliance *within* history.

It is not clear to me why Abe has chosen to affirm the Christian notion of original sin except as a way of supporting his commitment to a discontinuous relationship between ethics and religion. For if there is "nothing permanent [and] self-existing," then there would not be such an enduring quality as original sin. Furthermore, if humans are indeed entrapped by sin, then it is not clear how they would be able to transcend it, break its yoke, and experience Sunyata. Indeed, it would seem that Christianity is correct here: if sin pervades the human psyche, then we are helpless to help ourselves.

The Jewish tradition also takes issue with Abe's exclusion of God from ethical relations. In the Talmudic era, rabbinic summaries of the essence of Torah illustrate the ontological connection between ethics and religion.

> Isaiah came and reduced them [the 365 commandments of Torah] to six [Isaiah 33:25–26]: (i) "He who walks righteously and (ii) speaks uprightly, (iii) he who despises the gain of oppressions, (iv) shakes his hand from holding bribes, (v) stops his ear from hearing of blood, (vi) and shuts his eyes from looking upon evil, he shall dwell on high."
>
> Micah came and reduced them to three [Micah 6:8]: "It has been told you, man, what is good, and what the Lord demands from you, (i) only to do justly, and (ii) to love mercy, and (iii) to walk humbly before God. . . ."
>
> Isaiah again came and reduced them to two [Isaiah 56:1]: "Thus says the Lord, (i) Keep justice and (ii) do righteousness."
>
> Amos came and reduced them to a single one, as it is said [Amos 5:43]: "For thus says the Lord to the house of Israel. See Me and live."
>
> Habakkuk further came and based them on one, as it is said [Habakkuk 2:4]: "But the righteous shall live by his faith."[19]

Although there is a moral order that is superior to the world, for Jews it makes no sense to talk of a moral order apart from the sociohistorical world. Moreover, morality is clearly both a divine-human relationship and a human-human relationship. Indeed, within Judaism to harm one's fellow human being is to harm God. The reverse is not necessarily the past. An outstanding example is the well-known and wonderful story of Moses, several hundreds of years after having received the Torah, trying to follow a discussion on the Torah led by Rabbi Akiba. Moses, the greatest of Jewish prophets, is hopelessly lost in the contemporary discussion (as no doubt Akiba would have been in a discussion with Maimonides and Maimonides in discussion with Mendelssohn). Like a child, Moses runs to God to complain that it doesn't seem right that he cannot follow the teachings of Akiba. What he likely wanted to hear was that the teacher was indeed mistaken in his exegesis, but what he was told instead was that this, too, was a part of the divine plan. The Torah itself should be vastly reinterpreted, to such an extent that it would become unfamiliar even to the great Moses. Nonetheless, Moses' role in history and the fact of the Torah are not lost. In the same way, events that were really evil remain evil past facts; they become relativized as they are enwrapped in the matrix of time.[22]

This dialogue having just begun, it seems that a conclusion is hardly in order. For now, let me reaffirm my thanks to Professor Abe for having initiated this discussion. It would have been much easier to speak in generalities or to set aside the Holocaust as a matter for Jews and Christians. I am very appreciative of Professor Abe's decision to bring the Holocaust directly into the orbit of Buddhist reflection. This seems to me to be truly an act of compassionate Sunyata.

NOTES

1. Babylonian Talmud Babya Mezia 84a.
2. Credit for the phrase "hermeneutics of humility" goes to Marcus P. Ford, who, as always, was of considerable help on this essay.
3. Theodor Adorno, *Minima Moralia: Reflections from a Damaged Life* (London: Verso, 1971), p. 247.
4. Masao Abe, *Zen and Western Thought* (London and Honolulu: Macmillan and University of Hawaii Press, 1985), p. 21.
5. Adorno, *Minima Moralia*, p. 247.
6. Gershom Scholem, *Kabbalah* (New York: Meridian Books, 1974), p. 174. Scholem points out that *devekuth* is, in the main, a matter of union with God but not absorption into the Godhead. "*Devekuth* results in a sense of beatitude and intimate union, yet it does not entirely eliminate the distance between the creature and its Creator, a distinction that most kabbalists, like most Hasidim, were careful not to obscure by claiming that there could be a complete unification of the soul and God. . . . Here and there ecstatic nuances can be found in the conceptions of *devekut* of other kabbalists" (p. 176). So, for example, Abraham Abulafia—according to Scholem, the "outstanding representative of ecstatic

Kabbalism"—goes so far as to say that one who has "felt the divine touch and perceived its nature . . . is no longer separated from his Master, and behold he is his Master and his Master is he; for he is so intimately adhering to Him [it is here that the term *Devekuth* is used], that he cannot by any means be separated from Him, for he is He ['he is He' being a famous formula of advanced Moslem pantheism]" (quoted in Gershom Scholem, *Major Trends in Jewish Mysticism* (New York: Schocken Books, 1954), pp. 123, 140–41. The bracketed comments are Scholem's.)

7. Moses Maimonides, *Mishneh Torah*, excerpted in *A Maimonides Reader*, ed. Isadore Twersky (New York: Behrman Hourse, 1972), p. 85.

8. Ibid., my emphasis.

9. Abraham R. Besdin, ed., *Man of Faith in the Modern World: Reflections of the Rav*, vol. 2, adapted from lectures of Rabbi Joseph B. Soloveitchik (Hoboken, N.J.: KTAV Publishing House, 1989), p. 121.

10. Eugene Borowitz, "Rethinking Our Holocaust Consciousness," *Judaism*, vol. 40, no. 4 (Fall 1991), pp. 400–401. It is important to note that Borowitz sees the task of postmodern theologians to "give a faithful, thoughtful explication" of the paradox of particularism and universalism and how Jews might live in affirmation of them both.

11. Emil Fackenheim, *God's Presence in History: Jewish Affirmation and Philosophical Reflections* (New York: Harper & Row, 1972), p. 84.

12. Ibid., pp. 86–87.

13. Masao Abe, "A Rejoinder," in John B. Cobb, Jr., and Christopher Ives, eds., *The Emptying God: A Buddhist-Jewish-Christian Conversation* (Maryknoll, N.Y.: Orbis Books, 1990), pp. 191, 174.

14. Ibid., pp. 175, 174. Abe notes that the two realms are "irreversible," though it is not clear what is meant by this in light of his statement that in Sunyata "the mutual reversibility of things is fully realized" (p. 55).

15. Actually, Abe has proposed not simply a dualism, but a "triism" consisting of the natural, human, and transnatural dimensions. I speak of a dualism, because I am concerned only with the relationship between the transnatural and the human dimensions. But one might also raise the question as to the relation of the human and the natural dimensions and of the transnatural and the natural dimensions.

16. Michael A. Meyer, *Ideas of Jewish History* (Detroit: Wayne State University Press, 1987), p. 7.

17. Arthur Green, "The Aleph-Bet of Creation: Jewish Mysticism for Beginners," *Tikkun* (July/August 1992), p. 46.

18. Abe, "A Rejoinder," p. 181.

19. Babylonian Talmud Makkot, 24a.

20. Meyer, *Ideas of Jewish History*, p. 21.

21. Abe's rejoinder to Eugene Borowitz that "in Judaism the realization of spiritual death ('the wages of sin is death') and great death (the complete death of the human ego) are absent" (Abe, "A Rejoinder," p. 185) is, I believe, not a valid statement if the doctrine of nonsubstantiality and interdependence can be affirmed apart from a dualism between the sociohistorical and the religious dimensions.

22. Indeed, Abe supports this very notion in his rejoinder in *The Emptying God* (p. 193). He writes: "We may be redeemed from our past sinful deed. Of course, this does not mean that our past deed becomes undone. But the meaning of that past deed to our life at this present moment may be changed through our repentance and God's forgiveness." Unfortunately, this interpretation of the "reversibility" of time is not clear in Abe's original essay.

3

The Convergence:
Sunyata as a
Dynamic Event

HEINRICH OTT

Masao Abe is a pioneer of interreligious dialogue in the specific context of modern globalism, scientism, and nihilism. Within the global framework in which contemporary humanity lives, scientism and nihilism, both of which reject the religious dimension altogether, must be resisted. This can happen only if religions learn to understand each other and discover their common denominators. (Abe is interested in Buddhism and Christianity because he believes there is a specific closeness, a spiritual affinity between them.) This does not imply that they would double their strength through an alliance. Such military or economic thought patterns cannot be applied at the religious level. Rather, a given religion is strengthened as a result of the encounter with its counterpart, which pushes it toward its deepest and most fundamental core and thus toward its greatest strength. Through the encounter with Buddhism, Christianity comes to a "kenotic" understanding of the reality of God himself (and not only to the dogma of the salvation-history events relating to the condescendence and kenosis of Christ, the Son of God and God-Man!); Buddhism, through its encounter with Christianity, comes to a "dynamic" understanding of its basic concept, Sunyata. Thus drawing on its inner strength, each religion is in a position to resist the threat both of scientism and nihilism. As a result, the latter do not surround and overtake religion; rather, religion, drawing strength from its inner core, surrounds and overtakes them. Christianity and Buddhism could become partners by respectively helping each other recognize their true strength. This does not imply a superficial approximation. On the contrary, as Abe stresses, the differences, the respective "Suchness" of both religions, emerge all the more distinctly.

The idea of mutual enlightenment and enrichment has become one of the great perspectives of interreligious dialogue today, shared by many thinkers interested in this question (one representative of this point of view is Raimundo Panikkar). However, the thought that the mutual strength gained in this way could help religion successfully combat the contemporary era's a-religious trends is new and original.

An open question remains, however, even for thinkers sympathetic to this approach: *What* actually happens *between* the religions in such an encounter? At this point Masao Abe offers in my opinion a helpful answer that opens up further lines of inquiry. He says that Sunyata is a *dynamic event*, a movement. "This total *dynamic movement* of emptying, not a *static state* of emptiness, is the true meaning of Sunyata. . . . Consequently, although the term *Sunyata* or *emptiness* may sound negative, it has positive, soteriological meanings" (pp. 51–52). Indeed, this may constitute the deepest essence of any genuine dialogue between religions: in such a dialogue we do not simply discuss objective differences between religious doctrines, but rather we experience—if we think the matter out thoroughly—a similar *movement*. If Sunyata is one dynamic event, then we should, indeed must, ask ourselves as Christians whether we experience a movement of Sunyata in our own Christian faith, too. Only the participation in this inner movement shows us ultimately what reality we are confronted with, even if we designate and interpret reality differently. This inner event points to the closeness between the religions, which is what makes a dialogical encounter possible and meaningful. If we wanted only to argue about objective doctrines and dogmatic decisions, the dialogue would be exhausted before it had really begun.

A dogmatic discussion about whether the statement of a specific passage of Scripture—the christological hymn in the second chapter of Paul's letter to the Philippians with its themes of the condescendence and kenosis of God's Son—is a dominating principle of the entire Christian faith or just a partial aspect of a larger whole would most likely lead only to fruitless controversies. On the other hand, one would come to a very different result by pondering the question of the most intrinsic religious experience of reality in Christianity and in Buddhism, and how it can be paraphrased and be made concrete and plausible to our contemporaries as a possible experience in their own lives. A religion always inspires a certain kind of perception of reality. In the process of such experience the truth of the ultimate and holy mystery emerges. This is how another important representative of the Kyoto School, Keiji Nishitani, defines religion in general in his work *Religion and Nothingness:* it is never a means to a given end, never "good for something," but rather is — independently of any purpose — in itself a certain kind of experience of reality. Nishitani pursues the question about the essence of religion further at this level and discovers proximities and affinities between the Christian and Buddhist traditions. Precisely the dialogue at this level (religion as the deepest possible experience of reality and the specific religions as specific ways of achieving this deepest experience of reality) is the place where Masao Abe attempts to make contact with Christianity. He sees an inner *closeness* here but does not pursue a harmonizing *approach* of the religions toward one another in an objective sense. This basic attitude of his seems appropriate. It aims at the core of religion. The core of religion does not consist in doctrine, but rather in contact with reality. Making contact in my heart with ultimate reality — God — or, better said, allowing myself to be touched by ultimate reality and communicating with it, is the central event of all religion, and not whether I make this or that statement about ultimate reality. (Speaking of God as ultimate reality constitutes a problem in itself. Such speech contains in itself, seen purely isolated, nothing at all. But it is, so to speak, drawn into that process of contact, and then it has, in this context, its own place and legitimacy.) It seems meaningful to me to follow the tracks of Masao Abe's project, for it offers perhaps the only real chance for an agreement, a way toward the experience of community between differing religions. Implicit in this is that each of the participating varieties of religion can and must be submitted to a "phenomenology of faith," that is, to a phenomenological analysis of the faith even as a phenomenon of consciousness. If we were to refuse to see faith, the specific manner of belief, (also) as a phenomenon of consciousness, we would lose touch with reality. In that case religion as reality would become "religious ideology" and "religious rhetoric," a mere means to an end that served a given set of interests. (I allow myself to speak in reference to Buddhism as "faith" — *sui generis* — just as on the other hand I do not hesitate to speak of the Christian faith as "enlightenment" — *sui generis*.)

Is it possible to discover something of the dynamic movement of Sunyata in the Christian faith as a dynamic event? I submit that it is indeed possible and agree with Masao Abe on this point. A similar movement can be recognized in the phenomenon of consciousness of the Christian faith, which is of course not surprising if one dares to think of all genuine religiosity as a result of contact with the one holy Mystery. The dogmatic question, to what extent one can think of the kenosis of the Son of God (a mythological notion) as a kenosis in the being of God himself, should be left to the search for agreement within Christianity on a specifically Christian self-understanding. For the present this question

129

should be left outside of the Buddhist-Christian encounter, because the latter deals with the much more fundamental question of the structure of religious experience itself.

If one desires to get involved in the Buddhist question of Sunyata, that is, of Emptiness, it is important first of all to comprehend a fundamental difference. Emptiness, or Nothingness, should not be understood the way it normally is in Western thought, that is, nihilistically. For Western—and also for traditional Christian—thought, Nothingness is pure negation, a dark night with no flickers of light, tohubohu, chaos as an absolute void. This conception has led to a deep misunderstanding in the West of the Buddhist faith. According to the Buddhist experience of reality, Nothingness, or Emptiness, is an open expansion, an open sky, a brightness that comprises and surpasses all known possibilities. A classical example of the consciousness of this great difference in recent Western philosophy is Martin Heidegger's dialogue "Aus einem Gespräch von der Sprache, zwischen einem Japaner und einem Fragenden" (from a conversation about language between a Japanese and a Questioner), in which Heidegger has his Japanese character say:

> This is why we in Japan immediately understood the lecture "What is metaphysics," upon the appearance in 1930 of its Japanese translation, fruit of the daring of a Japanese student who at that time was a hearer of your lectures. We still wonder today how the Europeans could make the mistake of interpreting the Nothingness of which you speak in the lecture nihilistically. For us, Nothingness is the highest name for that which you were describing with the word "Being."[1]

This difference in the concept of Emptiness should be kept in mind when thinking about Masao Abe's dynamic understanding of Sunyata. Becoming conscious of the difference eases our understanding as Christian theologians of the significance of Abe's thesis or vision. It helps us realize that in the analysis of our own Christian tradition we may indeed come across problems that we can solve more easily from the perspective of Sunyata, of kenosis, that is, of "emptying," than by using the thought patterns characteristic of Western metaphysics and Christian dogmatics.

In this context, the connection between Emptiness and suchness, as strongly emphasized by Abe in conjunction with his own tradition, is particularly interesting. It is precisely in the realm of Emptiness where suchness becomes possible.

To a thinker schooled in Western metaphysics, the thought that the *concretissimum*, the indissoluble, irreducible "that" and "thus," precisely the suchness of each discrete lived instant, "that what is as it is," should owe itself to Emptiness is admittedly odd at first. However, certain existential experiences can make this thought clearer and more understandable. Such experiences are found in the personal-ethical realm, in the "esthetic realm" (i.e., in the encounter with visible reality itself), and in the religious realm—notably in the Christian faith—in a person's surrender to faith in God and in "thinking oneself into" the truth of revelation. Nevertheless, our attempt to approach an understanding of the connection between suchness and Sunyata is served better by taking all of the realms we have just mentioned together: reality in its entirety (all phenomena) is included in the realm of Emptiness. Emptiness is what allows suchness to emerge in the first place. By suchness we mean the qualitative impenetrability in which, to use a figure of speech gleaned from mysticism, "nothing can be taken away and nothing added"—the rose has no "reason why." Emptiness means that everything that is, is "empty," that is, has no inherent substance of its own. If it is assumed to have a substance, as has been done in Western thought patterns from classical metaphysics all the way to modern technology, then it can be taken away and added to; real situations can be changed and the face of reality modified. This is indeed a fact of life in our daily experience and in our experience of our "technical" (in the widest sense of the word) abilities. This is why we tend to consider this thought pattern the only truly valid one. But, for example, a person's suchness, his or her ineffability, or the suchness, the impenetrable concreteness, of each instant that we live—these primary experiences that are prior to all others, in which we have always come up against true reality, fall through the cracks of this thought pattern. They slide out of sight.

Suchness, and with it ultimate reality, begins precisely beyond the realm of substantiality, in the realm of Emptiness. Thus the person, perhaps the most concrete reality there is, the *individuum ineffabile*, is empty. It is not possible to dig up a "substance," that is, an unchanging core of reality, around which the "accidents" would then crystallize. I cannot answer the question "Who am I?" Allow me simply to mention in this context Dietrich Bonhoeffer's poem entitled with the same words, "Who am I?" (in his *Letters and Papers from Prison*), as a specific Christian, religious testimony of faith. I do not know myself; I do not know who I really am. I appear to others and to myself sometimes one way and sometimes another. Only God truly knows me. This should not be taken to mean that only God in his omniscience possesses enough of the data necessary in order to understand me fully. (That would be a detour toward objectifying thought.) Rather, what this means is that I belong to God because only God is present within me, whereas I constantly slip through my own hands, so to speak. I am not "fixed" and therefore somehow perusable and graspable; even I cannot figure myself out. As Nothingness, I continually escape my own glance, even though I am to myself as an essentially empty "I," the most concrete, inevitable, "hardest" reality.

The same can be said about the person of the "other." The person in front of me is my "you," an *individuum ineffabile*, a reality just as originary, concrete, and "hard" as my own "I" is to me, existing in his suchness, that is, in that he is, he is a certain way, irrepeatably and irreplaceably thus. Similarities may exist: he may remind me of his father, of his brother, and so on, and yet he is in a unique way himself. And he is also essentially empty, lacking an inherent substantiality. He slips through his hands just as I slip through mine; he does not really know himself, just as I do not truly know myself.

Precisely this empty other (*l'autre*)—as spoken of by the great contemporary Jewish thinker Emmanuel Lévinas—is the source of ethics, my source of moral obligation. His claim to be himself has always been catching up with me. He already possesses me, and I am his "hostage." His "face" has always haunted me. 'The 'other' must be closer to God than I am myself. This is not a philosophical invention, but the first given in a moral consciousness which could be defined as the consciousness of the 'other's' priority in relation to myself. Correctly understood, justice begins with the 'other.'"[2]

To think of the person in categories of substance, that is, as a distinct, enduring ontic core around which "accidents" are grouped, and ultimately to think of God himself as a spiritual substance, was probably *the* intellectual mistake of Western metaphysics in trying to elucidate the scope of personal reality. Certainly, even if one tries to eliminate the concept of "person" altogether by reducing the "I" to complex brain functions, such thought remains no less trapped in categories of substance. The "substantial I" is denied and is replaced by "something" consisting of theoretically controllable and in this sense equally substantial processes. The concept of Emptiness goes beyond both of these positions, which are essentially akin to each other, and can perhaps help us get a glimpse of the reality of personal being. (In this way, a basic Buddhist experience may perhaps someday redound to the benefit of our Jewish-Christian personalism!)

In order to verify the Far-Eastern concept of Sunyata within the framework of our Western experience of thought and to make it clear and understandable, let us change our focus to (apparently) extrapersonal realms, such as the life of nature. Before we investigate nonhuman nature through science, before we make it into an object, we experience it. Nature belongs to our vital world, and, according to Husserl's later writings, the latter takes precedence over the objectified, mathematized world. Our access to nature by experience is primary and in a sense more objective than any other.

It seems to me – if it is possible for me as a scion of Western culture to understand the Japanese literary genre of haiku correctly – that the latter attempts to capture unrepeatable instants of the experience of nature in their uniqueness, in their suchness, and to catch hold of the depth of reality that, while remaining unutterable, reveals itself in a given unique situation:

> The old pond!
> The frog jumps in.
> The sound of water.
> (Bashō)

> Along this path
> no one walks
> on this autumn evening.
> (Bashō)

But the primary experience of reality manifests itself not only in poetry; we encounter the same content in painting. To Far-Eastern poetry we can thus add both Far-Eastern and European landscape painting (for example, Paul Cézanne) as manifestations that, as it were, make Sunyata visible. All art moves in the realm of Emptiness because the experience of nature, indeed nature itself, moves in the realm of Emptiness. Let us take haiku as an example: what it says is "nothing"; and what it reveals is not "something." There is nothing there of which it could "take hold." According to Nishitani, Emptiness is needed by poetry in order to live. "The saying known among us, 'a single leaf announces the autumn of the world,' is not a poetic utterance, but is rather spoken at a level at which a leaf's fall counts as an absolute fact; the falling leaf is touched and perceived in its *samadhi*. One could say that poetic truth and true poetry are only possible when a fact is spoken about at this level."[3]

In order to clarify this further, let us take some lines of European poetry from Joseph von Eichendorff:

> It was as though the sky
> had quietly kissed the earth. . . .

About what is this poem speaking? About "nothing," not about "something," not about fixed, substantial things. If it attempted to do so, it would cease to be a poem. Or let us think of the view or even the painting of a landscape. We see mountains, water, clouds, trees, houses, living beings, a certain light—all in a particular combination. No part of it can be changed. The suchness is as it is. Everything is dipped in Nothingness: nothing has a substance in and of itself. Only in the harmony of everything is the whole what it is. This suchness cannot be expressed by or dissolved into words. Neither do I myself, the observer, remain in myself; I go into the landscape and dissolve myself in it.

Suchness, as made possible by Sunyata, characterizes the primary experience of reality, whether it be the suchness of a situation at the personal level or the suchness of nature. There is no basic difference between them: the phenomena are there, as they are, created reality, imbued by their Creator and Savior. Suchness is the symbol and the form of the presence of eternity, of the Creator himself. The experience of suchness is the experience of God's presence. In Christian terms we could say that all of creation is contingence. It is as it factually is, held and inhabited by the Creator. (The Creator is not merely a "maker," not a demiurge, a supreme craftsman, or a motor! This is often misunderstood on the Buddhist side!) Nothing of that which is made is something in itself or for itself. It has no substance and is in this sense empty. And this means contingence.

Admittedly, this is not expressed in the language of Sunyata. But neither is it the language of metaphysics. Substantialism is gradually abandoned. Perhaps it is the beginning of a melting of horizons taking place between Buddhist and Christian language, between two ways of thinking that intend to learn to understand themselves and one another better and better. The Christian experience of God also knows the process of Emptying—of surrendering oneself to Emptiness, of transcending our daily reality, which at first we had thought to be graspable—and this experience is therefore moving in the direction of Emptiness.

This could doubtless be verified in each aspect of the Christian faith. I must limit myself here to a single example: *the forgiveness of sin* does not mean the mere elimination of sin, as though it had never existed. (Otherwise, what would the forgiveness of *sin* mean?) Neither does it mean an enduring memory of sin as something, so to speak, deleted. (Otherwise, what would the *forgiveness* of sin mean?) Both alternatives are equally flawed and make it impossible to gain an understanding of the forgiveness of sin. This disjunction only ceases to have validity in the realm of Emptiness, for there the false dilemma can be overcome and the gift of the forgiveness of sin can thus be more adequately understood.

I am thankful to Masao Abe for having taught me to understand Sunyata as a dynamic event.

NOTES

1. Martin Heidegger, *Unterwegs Zur Sprache* (Pfullingen: Günther Neske-Verlag, 1959), p. 108f.

2. Emmanuel Lévinas, *Die Spur des Anderen Untersuchen zur Phänomenologie & Sozialphilosophie* (Freiburg & München: Verlag Karl Alber, 1992), p. 200.

3. Keiji Nishitani, *Was ist Religion?* tr. Dora Fischer-Barnicol (Frankfurt: Insel, 1982).

4

Sunyata, Trinity, and Community

MARJORIE HEWITT SUCHOCKI

In "Kenotic God and Dynamic Sunyata," Professor Abe writes of Sunyata in a way that is also a manifestation of Sunyata. For Sunyata, he tells us, is a positionless position, a self-emptying whereby that which "is" is ever emptying itself into otherness — not in a Hegelian dialectical way, where self-emptying results in a new synthesis, but in an "absolute" way. Self-emptying becomes otherness, but otherness also enters the self-emptying process that is Sunyata, becoming yet again "itself" — except, of course, given Sunyata, there is no real "self" at all. If self-emptying is the stuff of selfness, then there is no self: all is emptying. And if all is emptying, then simultaneously, all is the ever-new fullness of absolute Sunyata.

The sense in which Professor Abe's essay is a manifestation as well as an explication of Sunyata is that Abe seemingly empties himself of his Buddhism in order to enter into Christianity. He enters, not at the edges, but at the very heart of Christian doctrine, the Trinity. Sunyata, emptied into Christianity, becomes a new way of expressing Christianity's central doctrine of the Trinity. Yet having done so, it cannot remain there, as if Sunyata finally comes to rest — far from it. For the conclusion of Abe's article shows Sunyata emptying once again, as indeed it must, so that it sheds its transformation into Christian Trinity to return to its Buddhist form (or nonform) in the realization of Sunyata.

Abe's entry point for interpreting trinity as Sunyata is not so much the Nicene or Cappadocian or medieval formulations of trinity, but the kenotic text of Philippians 2, that ancient hymn bespeaking God's own emptying in the incarnation that is a taking on of human form and likeness. But Abe is not content to remain with the explicit Philippians text. Like a good Christian theologian, he pushes the implications of the text into the fundamental question of how, on the basis of this text, we are to understand the nature of God. Here the self-emptying that appears as incarnation is pushed to become an everlasting self-emptying within the divine nature itself. The principle is Christian: the economic trinity must have its basis in the immanent trinity; or, as God acts, so God is. If God is the kenotic God in incarnation, then God is the kenotic God within God's own self: the economic trinity is but a manifestation of the immanent trinity, and the immanent trinity is wholly expressed in the economic trinity. The kenosis of God in this sense is not a once-upon-a-time historical event, but is an everlasting event whereby God is essentially sunyatic.

The language fails insofar as "God" connotes a sense of an ultimate self or force to Westerners, and "Sunyata" is the contradiction of this. A strict sunyatan reading requires either a dynamic reconceptualization of "self" or a simple dropping of the word, whereas within the Christian context the dynamic self remains a self even in its self-emptying. This is obvious in the long trinitarian tradition, where there is an ultimate irreducibility to each person, or foci, within the Godhead, so that self-emptying can never be exhaustive. In this respect, the sunyatan reading of trinity is an emptying that cancels the Christian meaning in order to preserve the necessary sunyatan dynamic. The paradox in such a case is that Sunyata has not fully emptied itself, for if it had, the essentially selfless nature of Sunyata would have fully embraced the "selfed" nature of trinity.

To a Christian, there is a sense of familiarity about this application of Sunyata to Christianity, and to the sunyatic movement whereby one religion empties into another, reinterpreting its host according to its own categories. Our own imperialism has left a trail of reinterpretations of various religions according to the criteria of whatever readings of Christ and salvation have been current among Christian proselytizers. Is Professor Abe's sunyatic reading of trinity an unintentioned variation on this theme? We have learned that it is unwise to interpret other religions in terms of Christian categories; is it any improvement to interpret Christianity in terms of Buddhist categories?

I will outline a brief history of Western travail concerning the issue of religious pluralism, and will then turn to Abe's respondents in *The Emptying God* to suggest that inserting one's own categories as interpretive principles for the tenets of another religion may be more productive of monologue than dialogue. Finally, I will suggest that what Abe has shown in his essay is that within Sunyata itself there is ample reason for the embrace of a true religious pluralism, apart from the weaving of one religious concept upon another. Likewise, the nonsunyatic Christian notion of the Trinity provides a dynamic within Christianity for embracing the integrity of each of the religious traditions. But if both Buddhism and Christianity respectively have deeply internal grounds and resources for the affirmation of one another, apart from any imposition of categories, then perhaps the truly dialogical way to embrace our goals of mutual understanding and world peace is through continued study of religions not our own with the respect such study engenders, and continued dialogue and cooperation in alleviating the suffering that is in the world.

A BRIEF SUMMARY OF WESTERN RESPONSES TO RELIGIOUS PLURALISM

Religious pluralism is hardly new to Christianity, as the tragic history of our relation to Judaism shows. Our fundamental response was not only to blame Judaism as a whole for the crucifixion of Jesus, but to deem the crucifixion as the culminating moral failure of the entire history of Judaism. We took the Jew to be the symbol of sin. This did not prevent us from borrowing from Judaism, but of course we considered ourselves to be the Jacob who receives the birthright originally promised to Esau. That which was good in Judaism, we said, receives its finest and truest form within Christianity. But despite our efforts, Judaism persisted in its own strength in a world where it was surrounded by a Christian power that on the whole wished it ill, and too often fulfilled its wish.

Islam fared somewhat better, but primarily because it was not geographically enclosed by Christianity. Again, Christianity borrowed from Islam, notably through Islam's preservation of valued texts from the Greek philosophers as well as from the philosophic writings produced within Islam itself. But as a religion, Islam like Judaism was given little merit. The fundamental response was the Crusades, bent upon showing the superiority of Christianity and upon wresting the Holy Land from Islam.

In the modern times of the late sixteenth and seventeenth centuries, voyagers returned to Britain and Europe with tales of religions in the Americas and in the Far East. It was the dawn of the age of Enlightenment, and the philosophers and philosophes were at great pains to find the "reasonableness" within all religions and so to account for a basic insight common to all—a rationalism expressed in piety toward God and decency toward one' neighbor. In order to prove Christianity's preeminent place in this growing pantheon of religions, reasonable zealots such as Toland in England and Fontenelle in France argued that Christianity itself was not at all mysterious, but stood its own preeminent ground as a model of rational religion, and therefore as the norm whereby the rational nature of all other religions was to be interpreted and, not incidentally, judged.

But at about the same time as the philosophically inclined were holding forth, the church was forming new missionary societies that would bring the revealed (yet reasonable) word of Christianity to the benighted heathen. Colonization and missionization went hand in hand, and Christianity indeed began to become a worldwide religion. In the process, the superiority of Christianity was naturally assumed. Why else would there be a mandate to convert the world?

While committed missionaries dedicated their lives to going where no Christian had gone before, those who dealt at all with the peculiarity of religions other than Christianity tended to take one of two routes. There were those who continued the tradition of Enlightenment rationalists in assuming a common core to all religions, although no longer necessarily the twin requirements of piety and morality. For example, in the nineteenth century Friedrich Schelling considered the core to be religion's object. Thus all religions described the same God in terms drawn from their own cultural sensitivities. Rudolph Otto placed religious universality in subjectivity, analyzing religion as the individual feeling of awe. Yet again, Arthur Schopenhauer identified the common core in metaphysics, so that each religion was to be understood as a manifestation of the pulsating world energy that blindly willed the actualization of various forms.

The second approach was a more explicit theological tendency to use Christianity as the norm of all religions. This tended to result in non-Christian religions being consigned to error and/or the flames of hell. Similarly, the worst of other religions was compared to the best of Christianity, or treatises were composed to show that those things in other religions that were indeed similar to Christianity were but poor imitations of insights grasped more clearly in the revealed truth of Christianity.

Each of these approaches has abated in recent years, giving way yet again to two quite different ways. The phenomenology of religion school originated first with sociologists such as Emile Durkeim, but grew to include structuralists such as Claude Levi-Straus and Mircea Eliade. This approach compared the various religions in terms of their sociological functions and intellectual structures. The assumption was not that there was a common essence underlying all religions, but rather that there were common functions and structures that applied to all religions. By studying the dynamics rather than the specific content of the religions, one would learn generally about the religious impulse of humankind.

The phenomenologists intended to leave aside questions of superiority or inferiority, seeking instead an illumination of religion through structures common to all. In actuality, they were unaware of the manner in which their own hidden cultural biases affected the dynamics and structures they identified, thus unwittingly skewing their results in favor of their own cultural perspectives. Meanwhile, the close intellectual kin of the phenomenologists were the history of religions scholars. For these, the concerns were not comparisons between one religion and another, but increased understanding of each religion in terms of its texts and in terms of its historical development within its cultural context. Insofar as possible, the historian of religion attempted to understand a religion on its own terms. However, with increasing sophistication, the problems of injecting one's own norms into the so-called objectivity of the study became apparent, promoting self-critical bracketing of one's own culture to whatever extent possible.

Concurrent with this latter approach, Christian theologians and/or philosophers of religion have struggled with the theological implications of religious pluralism. If one could name a patron saint for such a struggle, it would be Ernst Troeltsch, whose own journey was almost like a paradigm for his heirs to follow. His earliest work reflects the suppositions of Christian superiority common to most theologians of his period, but gradually he began to recognize the serious distortions such a supposition introduces into the attempt to understand other religions. In his final work, "The Place of Christianity Among the World Religions," Troeltsch recognized that Christianity is as culture-bound as are other religions, making comparisons invalid, and leading the faithful to the simple assertion, "it is true for me."[1] Inevitably, religions arise within, reflect, and perpetuate worldviews particular to the cultural history in which they are embedded.

It would take a half century or more before many theologians would begin to recognize the significance of Troeltsch for religious pluralism. Paul Knitter, in *No Other Name?*, fully embraces Troeltsch's point of view.[2] Knitter outlines the way in which most theologies continue to perpetuate the imperialism of judging other religions by Christian standards, or reinterpreting other religions into Christian categories. Neither form of imperialism adequately grasps the situation of religious pluralism, for it necessarily distorts other religions in the attempt to maintain Christian superiority.

Contemporary Christian wrestling with the issues might be epitomized in two contrasting books: *The Myth of Christian Uniqueness: Toward a Pluralistic Theology of Religions*, and a responding volume, *Christian*

Uniqueness Reconsidered: The Myth of a Pluralistic Theology of Religions.[3] The uniqueness of Christianity, as indicated in the titles, is the pressing issue, with proponents in the first volume following Troeltsch in developing the implications for Christian theology if Christianity is, like other religions, considered historically rather than cosmically unique. Contributors to the second volume argue in some sense for a retained cosmic significance to Christianity among the world religions.

DIALOGUE OR MONOLOGUE?

The essays in *The Emptying God* are contextualized by the above discussion. Each contributor is writing from the implicit or explicit normativity of his or her own religion. The possible exception is Thomas J. J. Altizer, whose essay seems to make Buddhism rather than Christianity the norm. But so long as any religion is taken as the norm for others, is there really a dialogue taking place? Or is it more the case that each tends to translate the other into her or his own categories, so that the discussion is more monological than dialogical? If the latter is so, then historical relativism seems to make it highly unlikely that we can truly hear otherness. I would like to suggest that when each religion can draw from its own categories a basis for open affirmation of other religions, then this might at least increase the hearing level by which we attend to one another. We might then jointly turn our attentions to the pressing needs of the world.

As suggested above, Abe reads Christianity in light of his prior Buddhist understanding of Sunyata, reading that notion in many ways into the somewhat idiosyncratic Philippians passage. His Christian and Jewish respondents then seem to read their own prior understandings into Abe's interpretation, either agreeing or disagreeing depending upon how easily Abe's interpretation can be blended into the prior understanding.

For example, Jürgen Moltmann has long understood God in terms of a primal openness, but he ordinarily develops the notion of trinity through faith categories rather than through metaphysical categories. In a sense, Abe gives Moltmann a metaphysics for what he wants to say, even though this metaphysics takes Moltmann further than he has yet gone. In all of his works, including *The Trinity and the Kingdom*, Moltmann deals primarily with the economic trinity.[4] The immanent trinity is but a shadowy background. The closest Moltmann comes to explicating its internal dynamic is through appealing to the traditional doctrine of perichoresis, or the sense in which each person within the trinitarian nature fully inheres in and thus communicates with the other two. But this perspective is adopted rather than developed in Moltmann.

For the most part, Moltmann's work is a rich and profound interpretation of the economic trinity and Christian faith toward the end of justice. For this purpose, God is from all eternity a sending God, and God is from all eternity open for God's own sending (and therefore, not incidentally, for God's own suffering). Moltmann reads Abe as giving a metaphysical accounting beyond that of perichoresis for grounding the sending God. However, he does not note in the process that the sense of justice and eschatology that figures so prominently in his development of the economic trinity is thereby severely undercut. From the point of view of Sunyata, justice is a Western dualistic concept that separates the judger and the judged. Eschatology is likewise dualistic in that it presumes a teleology separate from the world process, but governing the world process. Insofar as Moltmann requires both terms for the effectiveness of his economic trinity in history, his adoption of Sunyata as explicatory of the immanent/economic trinity introduces an insoluble tension into his previously developed theology. Until Moltmann responds to this issue, he is not fully in dialogue with Abe.

Schubert Ogden's response to Abe is perhaps at the opposite extreme from that of Moltmann. Ogden has no sympathy with the kenotic God because it simply does not fit with his Bultmannian position that Christian "faith is the unreserved trust and loyalty for which the ground of ultimate reality is the boundless love decisively represented through Jesus Christ."[5] Ogden's mode of thinking is one of the furthest removed from Abe, and his concise logical arguments against Abe make this clear. Abe's position does not meet with Ogden's own experience, and hence he finds it failing his own standards.

Eugene Borowitz, the Jewish respondent in the collection, also questions the use of Buddhist categories to interpret either Christianity or Judaism. He notes that "Abe's reinterpretation of Christ's kenosis seems to me quite utterly to transform it from what I have understood contemporary Christian theologians to be saying."[6] Borowitz's own response to Abe centers on Abe's comments concerning the Holocaust and its effects upon Judaism. Abe speaks to the intellectual effects, whereas Borowitz strongly emphasizes the ethical effects. Judaism's self-understanding is not primarily through theological systems, but through a way of living that manifests a covenant with a holy God. Within this covenant, Jews are called to be a holy people, thus bearing witness to the covenant with their holy living. Thus the Jewish response to the Holocaust is renewed commitment to this way of life for which so many died. Merely to "cope" with the Holocaust by reformulation of the nature of God is to sidestep the central Jewish identity of the covenantal call to holy living. Thus for Borowitz, Abe's suggestions for Judaism in effect parallel what Borowitz sees as Abe's suggestions to Christianity. That is, Abe's comments quite utterly transform Judaism from what contemporary Jews say and do.

Catherine Keller's response reflects her position concerning the self in *From a Broken Web.*[7] She insists that all talk of "selflessness" as a norm is unacceptable from a feminist perspective, given the substantive notion of a self that is presupposed even in the Buddhist term "selflessness." One must have a self to give a self. Sunyata, even in the Buddhist context, assumes the very male ego that it negates and therefore cannot apply to the experience of women. Because Keller refuses the basic supposition of Sunyata, she cannot accept its usefulness as a reinterpretation of the Christian notion of trinity.

John B. Cobb, Jr., perhaps more than any other Christian theologian, has incorporated Buddhist insights into his Christian understanding, so that he has at times called himself a "Buddhist Christian." But here he responds less by dealing with the sunyatic notion of God and more with the ethical considerations raised by Abe's article. This is certainly consistent with Cobb's strong turn toward the ethical over the past fifteen years. In this article, his long critique evolves into a moment of affirmation. Cobb claims that within Buddhism there is indeed a criterion – the Sambhogakaya – that enables a distinction between particulars, and thereby provides a basis for value. But in affirming the Sambhogakaya, is Cobb not reaffirming in a different language his own understanding of the initial aim of God as the principle of creative transformation?

Thomas Altizer's response is consistent with the position he first developed in the 1960s that God is totally emptied into the world. Because Altizer's views are so very close to Abe's views, sharing much common ground, there seems to me to be more actual dialogue both in his presentation and in Abe's response. They are talking the same language, but through different traditions, and therefore raise meaningful questions for each other.

David Tracy muses on the sunyatic interpretation of trinity, but finally decides on a more traditionally Western reading. He then offers to Abe a basis within the Christian mystic tradition for understanding compassion and wisdom. In effect, he responds to Abe's use of Buddhist categories to interpret the Trinity by offering Christian categories for the interpretation of compassion and wisdom. One might suspect that just as Tracy decides against the Buddhist formulation of trinity, even though he finds it interesting, Abe might decide against the Christian formulation of compassion and wisdom, even though he finds it interesting.

With the possible exception of Altizer, both Abe and each of the respondents in *The Emptying God* might be characterized as engaging in overheard monologues rather than dialogues.[8] Is it the case, then, that our attempts at interreligious dialogue are frustrated beyond compensation? Perhaps overheard monologues are the best we can do.

BEYOND MONOLOGUE

John B. Cobb, Jr., in his *Beyond Dialogue,* called for both Buddhism and Christianity to learn from those elements akin to themselves within the heart of each other, and so to deepen their own self-understanding through conversation with the other.[9] Each religion would thereby open itself to transformation, not simply through dialogue, but through interaction with the other insofar as it could see its own most revered categories reflected in the other. I have been suggesting that Abe's article, like many Christian attempts to read another religion through Christian symbols, reverses the process by reading Christianity through Buddhist symbols. Even if we succeed in transforming ourselves through our understanding of ourselves seen through the other, we are appropriating that other in terms of our own categories. Do we not risk remaining monological rather than dialogical?

All of this is to question the extent to which we really do want to impose our own categories upon each other. Is it not better to find ways within our own traditions to affirm the integrity of our differences? An affirmation of the integrity and uniqueness of each religion can clear the way for a dialogue in which we are not trying to read our own categories into each other's religious symbols and concepts, but are rather open to the full otherness of the other and to an openness that we will each remain other. Perhaps learning more fully about the other—even within the constraints of our perspectival knowing—will lead, in keeping with Cobb's intent, toward our own transformation. But this cannot be the only goal; it must remain the by-product. If appreciation of otherness is legitimate, the better goal is that we become conversational partners after the manner of friends. In such a fashion, we might transform the world into a community of communities, each with its own distinctiveness and richness deriving from its own ambiguities of times past and present.

I suggest that the categories with which Professor Abe works— Sunyata and trinity—offer resources from within the heart of Buddhism and Christianity respectively for affirming religious pluralism, and therefore open the way for just such a conversation. With regard to the affirmation of true otherness through Sunyata, I can only point to the way this is indicated in Professor Abe's essay. I take his application of Sunyata to trinity to illustrate the essential dynamic whereby Sunyata must affirm true otherness in order for its own emptying to occur. The more fully Sunyata is accomplished, the more fully the otherness of the other is brought into view—even though, in its own turn, the other empties once again into what is now its own otherness. Paradoxically, one might say that all things are other even while all things are the same, for the common denominator is Sunyata. If these insights derived from Professor Abe are correct, then Sunyata is indeed a fundamental affirmation of a full, though fluid, otherness. But again, it is more appropriate for one whose whole way of being in the world is informed by Sunyata to develop the sense in which there is an affirmation of otherness within Sunyata; it is only appropriate for me as an outsider—an other—to suggest.

From within my own Christian tradition, I can affirm otherness through that very trinitarian symbol that Abe interpreted through Sunyata, for the Christian understanding of the Trinity requires a unity through irreducible diversity. The Christian story is that the internal perichoretic relations of what is called the immanent trinity yield the external perichoretic work of the economic trinity. With regard to external relations, the perception is that God relates to us for our good. Our otherness to God is given: we are ourselves, and not God. Even though we can incorporate God's grace within our own becoming, we do so within the otherness marking the distinction between God and ourselves. Indeed, there are pantheistic strains within Christianity that understand the pervasive grace of God within the world to be the permeation of the world by God, thus undercutting its radical otherness. But this is a minor theme within Christianity: The major Christian self-understanding posits us as creatures who are other to God, and God as other to us.

With regard to the inner trinitarian relations, these are not interpreted according to the radical self-emptying of Sunyata, which appears to be an emptying without remainder. To the strong contrary, the coinherence signified by perichoretic union is one that requires the irreducible otherness within the trinitarian structure. Were there no *relata*, there would be no relation. Hence in the traditional language, the Father is always the Father and never the Son or Spirit; the Son is always the Son and never the Father or Spirit; the Spirit is always the Spirit and never the Father or Son. The Father generates the Son, who indeed mirrors the Father, and in the Western form of trinitarian expression, both Father and Son together spirate the Spirit.

Coinherence refers to the fullness of love, whereby there is interpenetration of knowing and willing. But this coinherence presupposes and requires the irreducibility of distinctions and has as its fullest reference the common nature. This common nature is not some fourth in whom all cohere, but is the very perichoresis of relation. Thus in this conceptuality, it is not the case that any member empties fully or otherwise into the others, nor is such an emptying possible. It violates the ground of trinity, which is the irreducible otherness within unity. The trinitarian notion is of God as an irreducible diversity within unity.

The notion of God as triune, therefore, can yield deep implications for any people naming this God as the one they serve. They will be called not to uniformity, but to many forms of diversity within community. Nor does the community of God dare to set limits to the types of diversity it can enfold. Men and women from all races and cultures, gathered as a community striving to ensure that each and all participate in love and freedom, are required in order for the Christian community to embody God's call to bear the divine image. But diversity need not stop with the varieties of peoples in the world; it may also address differences of theological expression. Thus the common naming of God as triune is a basis for the ecumenical nature of a church made up of diverse theological communions. If this church is called to be a people analogous to the mighty harmony of God's own being, then it is called to rejoice in its diversity and find its unity in its mutual care for the fullness of well-being among all its members.

Insofar as the community bears the image of God, it cannot be content with a fullness of love within its own borders. To the contrary, the very notion of God as triune carries the double notion of the immanent and economic trinity. That which marks God's own inner being finds its expression in God's acts beyond God's self. God's acts are in conformity with God's nature. If, then, there exists a community whose self-understanding involves being called to bear God's trinitarian image, then that community cannot rest content with the achievement of well-being simply within the boundaries of its own community of faith. Rather, like the God it serves, it must reach beyond its own borders in love. The goal would be that there be well-being throughout the created order. And if there is a value of diversity even within the community, there would be a value of diversity beyond the community's borders.

The image required for our planetary existence, therefore, is not simply of a community composed of various modes of diversity, but of a vision of the world as a community of communities, of a place where there are a variety of peoples, clustered around distinctive concepts, cultures, and religions. And these different communities are not antagonistic to each other, nor do they each demand that the other conform to its own mode of religion or culture. Rather, each reaches out in dialogue to the others, and all together look to a mutual task of seeing to the well-being of the whole created order.

This is, of course, a visionary development of the resources for affirmation of differences within the heart of the Christian notion of trinity. All who know the intolerant and imperialistic nature of Christian history will undoubtedly raise a quizzical brow at the reversal of this tradition that I am now suggesting in the very name of this tradition. Further, to envision the world as a community of communities encounters enormous practical problems. Differing concepts of what constitutes well-being can cause serious dissension—and so it must be, if we take seriously a valuation of diversity. By definition, diversity requires intellectual differences not only among individuals, but between cultures and countries. These differences cannot be romanticized, particularly when they are perceived to be differences that lead to ill-being for whole areas of this earth. The fundamental affirmation of diversity makes dialogue and diplomacy the only acceptable means of dealing with diversity. And yet dialogue and diplomacy, together with a commitment to well-being, are the makings of community—of a community of communities.

If Christians are fully informed by the triune notion of God as a complex diversity in unity, then the conceptual schemas by which we suspiciously evaluate other religions according to their compliance with our own standards must be supplanted with an openness toward new modes of community. The differing perceptions of God—or even of no God—are challenging, but not troubling. The very notion of trinity comes from our perception of how God has worked for us and with us. As such, it is marked as *our* story. Stories are for telling and sharing, not for enforcing. And because we cannot know God exhaustively, we cannot know exhaustively what stories God may be creating with other peoples in other traditions. One mode of knowing does not falsify another in a relational world; rather, contradictions can be turned to contrasts. As Troeltsch said so long ago, the God we know is the God for *us*.

AND THEREFORE . . .

Dialogue is not for the sake of converting us to each other's primary metaphors, but a way of more fully understanding the other and ourselves, so that we might appreciatively intuit the other's primal experience. Through dialogue we also have the privilege of entering into an assessment of our own primary experience from a sympathetic external point of view (much as goes on between Cobb and Abe). The goal is that through our conversations we might more fully know one another and care for one another, and together become influences to whatever degree possible toward a world where wisdom and compassion shape public as well as personal living.

It may be that the essays in *The Emptying God* must be taken in the mode of conversation, whereby one friend says to another, "Is it like this?" This interpretation of the other's experience in terms of one's own is not for the sake of giving a more authentic version of the other's categories, but for the sake of trying to understand the other, even though we must use our own categories for this purpose. The conversation proceeds through mutual clarification toward better understanding and deeper sharing.

The world is such that it supports a variety of interpretations, some of which are dualistic, some monistic. The inquiry for a metaphysical principle that is beyond dualism and nondualism, such as Sunyata, is one way of construing the stuff of existence, but it is not the only way. Indeed, the formation of consciousness in the Western tradition is such that a full nondualism seems to be an abstraction that is incongruent with our deepest experience, and therefore does not often address our religious sensibilities. The opposite is more often the case for those whose modes of perception have developed within Eastern traditions. To them, trinity most likely seems not only dualistic, but tritheistic, making Western perceptions incongruent with their experience and religious sensitivities. Through Sunyata, Buddhists develop the principle of nondualistic unity and practice the form of spirituality toward which it leads, in community and peace. Through trinity, Christians might also develop the principle of diversity in unity, and participate in community and peace.

If I read Abe correctly, Sunyata as well as trinity suggests an affirmation of difference, metaphysical as well as religious. Without the affirmation of differences, the ground for peace is tenuous. We must leave off trying to show each other how one way is superior to the other; we must cease trying to convert one another to our own way. We must begin with the wisdom of appreciative understanding through conversation and compassionate solidarity in furthering well-being. Having affirmed differences in religions among ourselves, perhaps we can broaden and share this affirmation toward the deeper realization of community in this troubled world.

NOTES

1. Ernst Troeltsch, "The Place of Christianity Among the World Religions," in *Christianity and Other Religions,* ed. John Hick and Brian Hebblethwaite (Philadelphia: Fortress Press, 1980), pp. 11–31.

2. Paul F. Knitter, *No Other Name? A Critical Survey of Christian Attitudes Toward the World Religions* (Maryknoll, N.Y.: Orbis Books, 1985).

3. John Hick and Paul F. Knitter, eds., *The Myth of Christian Uniqueness* (Maryknoll, N.Y.: Orbis Books; London: SCM Press, 1987); Gavin D'Costa, ed., *Christian Uniqueness Reconsidered* (Maryknoll, N.Y.: Orbis Books, 1990).

4. Jürgen Moltmann, *The Trinity and the Kingdom* (San Francisco: Harper & Row, 1981).

5. John B. Cobb, Jr., and Christopher Ives, eds., *The Emptying God: A Buddhist-Jewish-Christian Conversation* (Maryknoll, N.Y.: Orbis Books, 1990), p. 129.

6. Ibid., p. 80.

7. Catherine Keller, *From a Broken Web: Separation, Sexism, and Self* (Boston: Beacon Press, 1986).

8. Although I think this is arguable for Cobb's essay in *The Emptying God*, it is a questionable assertion with regard to Cobb's work as a whole. As indicated above, Cobb has been deeply informed by Buddhism and refers to himself as a "Buddhist Christian."

9. John B. Cobb, Jr., *Beyond Dialogue: Toward a Mutual Transformation of Christianity and Buddhism* (Philadelphia: Fortress Press, 1982).

5

God's Kenosis and Buddhist Sunyata in the World of Today

HANS WALDENFELS

Undoubtedly, it is Masao Abe who must be credited with having started a discussion between Eastern and Western scholars regarding the need to search in the international world of scholarship for a way of life between religion and secularism or scientism, between the hope of fulfillment and the threat of nihilism. The discussion has turned into a dialogue between Christian and Buddhist scholars. Moreover, Abe has not stopped inviting friends and scholars around the world to participate in the discourse.

This discussion started with Abe's first essay, "Buddhism and Christianity as a Problem of Today,"[1] which received many replies from all over the world.[2] Masao Abe in turn wrote a rejoinder and deepened his thought in a number of articles that were published in subsequent years.[3] Unfortunately, the results of the discussion could not be published so far. Nevertheless, the scholarly discourse has continued. Another step was the conference on "Heidegger, Mahayana Buddhism and Whitehead: Perspectives on Interfaith Dialogue," held in 1979 at the School of Theology at Claremont.[4]

In the context of a symposium on Buddhism and Christianity in the modern world, continued in various conferences held in the United States, and through Abe's own teaching at different universities in the United States, his understanding of the important comparison between Christian kenosis and Buddhist Sunyata grew. In the meantime, some of the more sensitive representatives of Christian theology joined in the discussion. Although I did not contribute to it directly since 1979 when I attended the Claremont conference, I realized with admiration how Abe himself attained an increasingly profound understanding of Christian thought in the process of the discussion, which, however, took place mainly in North American circles. I do not hesitate to repeat what Jürgen Moltmann commented about Abe's study of the kenosis of Christ:

> There are few Christian theological studies about the kenosis of Christ and the kenosis of God according to Philippians 2 that are so profound and precise as this work of a Buddhist scholar concerning the central topic of Christian faith. His presentation of the dynamic Sunyata is so lucid that every Christian theologian can understand it. Here reciprocal understanding is not only furthered, but Christianity and Buddhism in their immiscible difference are led into a common reality.[5]

However, reentering the discussion, I would like to return to questions that Masao Abe brought up in the correspondence we continued over the years and that he uttered in an international conference held in De Tiltenberg, Holland, in 1988. He insisted on the fact that in Catholic theology, too, the question of the kenotic God should have its own specific importance. Accordingly, he referred—as he did in "Kenotic God and Dynamic Sunyata" (pp. 37–40)—to the theology of Karl Rahner. Actually, he rightly complained that none of his respondents took up the point and reflected upon Rahner's point of view.

I will follow Abe's suggestions and return to Rahner's view later on. However, before doing so I call attention to another regrettable fact, which I have mentioned in an essay remembering the late Keiji Nishitani. There I wrote:

> I am somewhat saddened to report that the ongoing discussion on Buddhist *sunyata* and Christian *kenosis* taking place in the United States right now has failed to recognize Nishitani Sensei's fundamental contribution to the dialogue. After all, it was his understanding of *sunyata* and its comparison with God's emptiness—as it appears, according to St. Paul's Letter to the *Philippians* Ch. 2, in the life and death of Jesus Christ—which combined speculative thought with an ethical drive in a unique way. I learned from Nishitani Sensei that *anatman* (J. *muga*) in its full meaning is only partly comprehended by translating it into English as *not-self* or *non-ego*, and that it reaches its full realization only where it turns into the central mode of life, where *not-self* becomes *selflessness*. It is precisely God's self-emptying which leads to the understanding of divine love, just as it is the realization of Wisdom expressed in emptiness which marks the realization of Compassion at once.
>
> I would predict that the Buddhist-Christian encounter will reach its true point of convergence when the condition of self-forgetfulness is fulfilled, where people of both traditions meet in a practice of self-denial and self-surrender in service of all those who stumble blindly along the road whose end they do not know.[6]

Because I learned about the convergence of the two ideas central to Christianity (kenosis) and Buddhism (Sunyata) first from Nishitani and later on from Abe,[7] I want to return to Nishitani's inspiring presentation first. Moreover, I do this with good reasons because—at least according to my point of view—certain insights of Nishitani's view were overlooked during the later debate. If, at the end, some questions come up that I have dealt with earlier in the discussion, it results from the fact that I am more and more convinced that certain questions are difficult to be communicated; in fact, I still get the feeling that a number of questions I have uttered before are not yet considered and answered by Masao Abe. It is a problem of mutual respect that neither Christians try to reduce Buddhist teaching simply to the Christian point of view nor Buddhists try to reduce Christian teaching to the Buddhist point of view. In the meantime, we should make it a point of common effort to meet on the field of cross-religious encounter where mutual understanding will be the basic presupposition for an agreement or disagreement upon the question of whether we walk the same way or not.

NISHITANI'S VIEWPOINT

Keiji Nishitani developed his comparison of Buddhist Sunyata and Christian kenosis at some length in Chapter 2 of *Shukyo towa nanika* (*Religion and Nothingness*).[8] I would like to quote some paragraphs in detail to give an impression of Nishitani's approach.

What is it like, this non-differentiating love, this *agape*, that loves even enemies? In a word, it is "making oneself empty." In the case of Christ, it meant taking the form of man and becoming a servant, in accordance with the will of God, who is the origin of the *ekkenosis* or "making himself empty" of Christ. God's love is such that it shows itself willing to forgive even the sinner who has turned against him, and this forgiving love is an expression of the "perfection" of God who embraces without distinction the evil as well as the good. Accordingly, the meaning of self-emptying may be said to be contained within God himself. In Christ, *ekkenosis* is realized in the fact that one who was in the shape of God took on the shape of a servant; with God, it is implied already in his original perfection. That is to say, the very fact itself of God's being God essentially entails the characteristic of "having made himself empty." With Christ we speak of a deed that has been accomplished; with God, of an original nature. What is *ekkenosis* for the Son is *kenosis* for the Father. In the East, this would be called *anatman*, or non-ego.[9]

Regarding this text, I would like to add some observations. First, the problem of kenosis is to be seen in the broader context of Nishitani's reflection upon the personal and the impersonal. Unlike many other Asian thinkers, Nishitani is very well aware of the high esteem the concept of person enjoys in Western thinking and ethics. Accordingly he states:

> The idea of man as person is without doubt the highest conception of man yet to appear. The same may be said of the idea of God as person.[10]

Nevertheless, he calls attention to the fact that in modern Western thinking the Cartesian Ego is concealed behind the concept of human person. Actually, person-centeredness and ego-centeredness became identical and self-evident. Precisely this self-evidence is the point that he questions.[11] Consequently, the criticism of the concept of a personal God must also be judged from this perspective.

Second, for Nishitani kenosis is first a question of behavior and attitude, not of conceptualizing. This becomes evident in the first English translation, where *muga* or *anatman* is translated in the double way of "non-ego or selflessness."[12] Western people are tempted to speculate upon the deeper meaning of anatman in a rather theoretical manner—with the result that they overlook the fact that the notion, first of all, implies a way of acting, that is, bears an ethical connotation. In Nishitani's explanation, kenosis, the act of "making oneself empty," is nothing but the attitude of agape, or, in Buddhist terms, "nondifferentiating love." Whereas Abe's concept of love remains rather vague and abstract, Nishitani reads Philippians 2 in the horizon of some famous quotations taken from the Sermon on the Mount, Matthew 5:43–48. There are two sentences that deserve special attention:

> I say to you, Love your enemies and pray for those who persecute you, so that you may be sons of your Father who is in heaven; for he makes his sun rise on the evil and on the good, and sends rain on the just and on the unjust.
>
> (Matt. 5:44, RSV)

> You, therefore, must be perfect, as your heavenly Father is perfect.
>
> (Matt. 5:48, RSV)

The first sentence is at the same time a perfect expression of what in Buddhism is known as "nondifferentiating love beyond enmity and friendship," and the second is cited by Nishitani as an example of God's perfection.[13] It is the quality of nonego that brings the Buddhist feature of "nondifferentiating love" to the foreground:

> Non-ego (*anatman*) represents the fundamental standpoint of Buddhism, where it is called the Great Wisdom (*maha-prajna*) and the Great Compassion (*maha-karuna*) . . . the Great Compassionate Heart, the essential equivalent of the biblical analogy that tells us there is no such thing as

selfish or selective sunshine. The sun in the sky makes no choices about where to shine its rays and shows no preferences as to likes or dislikes. There is no selfishness in its shining. This lack of selfishness is what is meant by non-ego, or "emptiness" (*sunyata*). The perfection of God has this point in common with the Great Compassionate Heart of Buddhism. And the same divine perfection is then demanded of man.[14]

Third, it is important that agape is the "perfection," or the essence of God.[15] That is to say, nondifferentiating love is the very nature of God. In this sense Nishitani emphasizes that it makes sense to speak "of a perfect mode of *being* rather than of the *activity* of self-emptying or of *loving*":

> Although self-emptying, ego-negating love may be taken as characteristic of divine perfection, we point more expressly to that perfection when we speak of a perfect mode of *being* rather than of the *activity* of self-emptying or of *loving* that is typified in Christ and commanded of man. In other words, . . . the sort of quality we refer to as self-emptied can be seen as essentially entailed from the beginning in the notion of the perfection of God, and the activity of love as consisting in the embodiment or practice of that perfection. Considered in its relation to love as deed or activity, the perfection of God can also be called love.[16]

Fourth, because the modern concept of person includes the identity with the ego, there is, according to Nishitani, "no way around the conclusion that the perfection of God and love in the sense of that perfection point to something elemental, more basic than the 'personal,' and that it is as the embodiment or limitation of this perfection that the 'personal' first comes into being. A quality is implied here of *transpersonality,* or *impersonality.*" And in order to make clear that the term "impersonal" is not to be taken as the opposite of the "personal," Nishitani adds that he understands it paradoxically as the "personally impersonal."[17]

Fifth, this reminds us that Nishitani had discussed the topic of "personal-impersonal" before in Chapter 1 of *Religion and Nothingness,* where he reflects upon the personal relationship between God and man in a trinitarian context; here again it is less a question of speculative reflection than of an existential, "spiritual," or—as I would call it with Karl Rahner—"mystagogical" approach.[18] Nishitani writes:

> Compared to the usual meaning we find in the case of relationships like that between God and the soul, or some other "spiritual" relationship that is called "personal," what we are speaking of here would be considered as *impersonal.* But we are not using the term "impersonal" in its ordinary sense, as the antonym of "personal." The pantheistic notions of the life or creative power of the universe are instances of the impersonal in its usual sense. But when the omnipresence of God is encountered existentially as

the absolute negation of the being of all creatures, and presents itself as an iron wall that blocks all movement forward or backward, it is not impersonal in that usual sense.

. . . It is what we should call an "impersonally personal relationship" or a "personally impersonal relationship." The original meaning of *persona* comes close to what we are speaking of. In Christianity, the Holy Spirit has this characteristic. While being thought of as one *persona* of the Trinity, it is at the same time the very love of God itself, the breath of God; it is a sort of impersonal person or personal nonperson, as it were. But once such a point of view is introduced, not only the character of the Holy Spirit, but also that of God himself who contains this spirit, and of man in his "spiritual" relationship with God (as well as the character of that relationship itself), have to be seen on a new horizon.[19]

Jan Van Bragt has called Nishitani's work a *"theologia fundamentalis* of Zen Buddhism."[20] This implies on the one hand that it shows some similarities to Christian apologetics. On the other hand, by way of reflecting upon the formal preconditions of a true dialogue, it fulfills the conditions of dialogics (German, *"Dialogik"*). Christian fundamental theology also includes the consideration and handling of the various situations of human dialogue, but in the way of "spiritual theology" it cannot do without introducing what I like to call "God-experience." In analogy to that, I consider Nishitani's work on religion not only a philosophical reflection about the modern conditions of religion and religious life, but also a kind of invitation to seek a concrete way of reaching the unattainable and incomprehensible mystery that hides behind the term "emptiness."

Indeed, it was Karl Rahner's way of theologizing that enabled me to look at Nishitani's thought this way.

APPROACH TO KARL RAHNER

It is not possible to give a satisfying introduction to Rahner's theology. However, I would like to offer the following thesis as a starting point for a first approach. Karl Rahner's thought is grounded in the God-experience that was a constant undercurrent of his daily life until he died. It was his untiring effort to carry over the God-experience to the people of today, to translate it into their languages and understanding, and to open up their lives for their own existential experiences. Of course, this presupposes an acute awareness of modern human thought—of the needs, doubts, and desires of human beings. Among them the call for unity, peace, and simplicity is growing. However, the unity of the one world has to be realized within an immensely complicated variety of facets—in other words, in a world marked by pluralism.[21] In this situation the communication of a genuine "God-experience" becomes extremely difficult.

Moreover, Abe's difficulties with some phrases of Rahner dealing with the self-emptying God are rather small items against the existential calamities countless people all over the world are facing today.[22] I fully agree with Masao Abe when he insists that objectifying Sunyata destroys the very essence of Sunyata. Accordingly, he applies Martin Heidegger's suggestion to put a cross mark "X" on the term *Sein*, thus rendering it as S̶e̶i̶n̶, in order to show the unobjectifiability of *Sein*, and to S̶u̶n̶y̶a̶t̶a̶, thus proving that "emptiness not only empties everything else but also empties itself" (p. 51).[23] However, I cannot agree with Abe that for Karl Rahner "the kenosis of God, God's self-emptying, is still somewhat conceptualized or objectified" (p. 38). Rahner, too, is very much aware that human reasoning is unable to comprehend God and make him an object that we can fully grasp in a true concept.

In order to substantialize my statements, I have to repeat two texts of Rahner that I offered for consideration years ago. The first one refers to the understanding of mystical experience.

> I mean only (most modestly and hesitatingly) that the first and original experience of the Spirit of which I seek to speak is also the innermost core of what one may call mysticism. Hence, since what I mean by the experience of the Spirit is a faith-experience in its authentic and original sense, mysticism (in the usual sense of the word) is not a higher "stage" above normal faith but a definite kind of this faith-experience, one which belongs "as such," in itself, to natural psychology and to man's natural potentials for "meditation," concentration, the emptying of the mind, etc. If this "kind" of graced experience of the Spirit as such is explained as "natural" it is not thereby devalued. In fact someone can find God in His most immediate sharing of Himself in selflessly giving his soup to a poor man and going hungry himself. This very natural sort of helping one's neighbor can "in itself" be very natural and yet be the concrete process in which and through whose mediation the most radical acceptance of the sharing of the Spirit and experience of the Spirit which signifies salvation and eternity takes place. Thus the phenomena of meditation, of modelessness (*Weiselosigkeit*), of stillness, silence, emptiness, of the absolute loss of self, etc., can be ways in which and in whose midst the experience of God's silence and unspeakable sharing of Himself is more radically and "purely" accepted: in a radical freedom that gathers man completely together.[24]

I would like to add a second text where Rahner thematizes "the experience of God today." For him the difficulty of this topic consists in the fact that we are seeking to reflect upon an experience which is present in every man (whether consciously or unconsciously, whether suppressed or accepted, whether rightly or wrongly interpreted, or whatever the way in which it is present), and which involves the following factors: *on the one hand* it is more basic and more inescapable than any process of rational calculation in which we follow a line of causality leading from the egg to the hen, from the lightning to the thunder, in other words from the world to an originator, but which can also be broken off, leaving the conclusions which might have been arrived at unrecognized. *On the other hand,* however, this experience does not impose itself upon us irresistibly (as does the physical existence of a datum of sense experience or an organic sensation) in such a way that the transition from the experience itself to an explicit recognition of it in which we reflect upon, interpret, and express it, imposes itself upon us irresistibly.[25]

Reflecting upon the two texts, we reach various conclusions. First, Rahner's theological conception cannot be grasped by way of merely reflecting upon the conceptual system he uses; rather, we have to begin with the experiential basis of his theological thought. Moreover, the fundamental human experience is not limited to space and time but continues working throughout one's life. In a way, Rahner's starting point indicates the challenge every thought system is facing today, namely, that it has to reflect the fact that any human thought is grounded in the existential experiences of human life.

Second, being related to the concrete existence of human life includes two basic tensions: (a) the tension between the concrete experience and its communication in language, and (b) the tension between theory and action, word and deed, "ontology" or metaphysics and ethics.

Regarding the first tension, in ordinary life we encounter the other in the realm of language. This is true, even if we, beginning in the realm of language, realize that it is part of our existential hermeneutics to reach out beyond language into the realm of nonverbal communication. In the Western world it is precisely the destruction of a common way of thinking in a rather monolithic culture that leads to a deep awareness of the dissolution of common thinking into a variety of independent thought systems. It also calls attention to the limitations of human speaking. Thus we are forced to talk about something that never can be an object of our knowledge, in the way that an object belongs to the peculiarities of human speech.[26] The classical definition of truth, which consists in the adequacy of a subject matter and its expression, stands the test less and less. The result is that an increasing number of people distrust the ability of languages with regard to ultimate reality.

The situation becomes even more threatening when we turn our attention to the variety of foreign languages, cultures, thought patterns, and religions. Here again it is the thread of pluralism that calls for profound consideration. Concentrating on religion, actually we face a twofold thread: On the one hand, the single religion is menaced in its very identity, which not seldom leads to a hasty retreat into what is called today "fundamentalism." On the other hand, the multifold encounter of people belonging to different religions calls for mutual understanding in theory and practice. Where, however, the practical questions come to the foreground, the single identity can easily be sacrificed on the altar of "syncretism."

Third, in view of the situation marked by a deep sense of finitude and anxiety, doubt and uncertainty, which could be explained in more detail with regard to the use of languages, today religion must be seen again as a way of *reductio in mysterium*, a reduction or a return of human beings into the mystery. This is exactly what I have called the "mystagogical task of theology." In fact, we are facing a radical change of theology. Certainly, "theo-logy" will continue to work and reflect upon the equivalent "translations" of the basic experience. And yet, it is even more important to prove that behind all the religious teachings there is a true and vivid experience that renders all teaching meaningful. Neither can we avoid the reproaches contained in the various arguments of religious criticism; nor can we simply repeat religious argumentation without restoring its connection to the original experiences that open up the way of salvation and fulfillment.

Whoever is really acquainted with the biography of Karl Rahner knows that, besides his Christian identity, his personal experiential background was stamped by his membership in the Society of Jesus, a religious order founded by Ignatius of Loyola. This implies that his spirituality was formed by practicing the *Exercitia Spiritualia*, the "Spiritual Exercises" of the founder of the Jesuit Order.[27] If we look for any spiritual locus dealing with the difference between the experience itself and the "time after" the experience, we have to pay attention to the Rules of Discernments of Spirits.[28] I regret that I can offer only this hint.

Fourth, the experiential core of Rahner's God-relation is trained by the contemplation of the mysteries of the life of Christ.[29] What Masao Abe quotes from Rahner's writings is nothing but certain abbreviations and summaries of what Rahner has learned by contemplating the life of Christ. Indifference, abnegation, self-denial, theology of the cross, attaining of love—all of these are central notions of the Ignatian Retreat.

Beyond all doubt, Jesus crucified is the gateway to the Christian understanding of God. That remains true even though we leave aside the question of the uniqueness of Christ with regard to all other beings.

Rightly, Nishitani continues thinking from the ekkenosis of Christ to the kenosis of God. Although he did not know Karl Rahner at that time, he comes astonishingly close to his thought and approach.

Fifth, there is, however, one point that needs special attention because the connection between the most radical human experience as described in the two texts of Rahner quoted above reveals another tension that evidently plays only a minor role in Abe's Buddhist approach. Whereas in Christian understanding it is the life story of Christ that demands for the most fundamental human experience a place *inside* of human history, the concrete history of man and mankind, in ups and downs, in good and evil occurrences, although not missing completely in Abe's essay, is not very much elaborated there. Accordingly, the historical figure of the Buddha and its significance for future history is left out of consideration.

Combined with this part, I would like to warn against a confusion of philosophical and theological treatment of the God-question. Those who reflect about the kenotic God according to Philippians 2 enter the realm of theological thought. From a Christian point of view, theology (the doctrine of God, Christology, the doctrine of Christ) and anthropology (the doctrine of the human being) are indissolubly one unit. This can be gathered easily from the modern understanding of God's revelation, which in various respects is exposed as God's self-communication, self-surrender, self-denial, self-abnegation, self-emptying, and the like. The shift of emphasis from a more positive to a more negative expression is partly because the powerlessness of theodicy in view of the Jewish *Shoa* leads to a reconsideration of God's omnipotence, a reflection that is supported by the modern Jewish-Christian dialogue.

Sixth, the brief allusions to the development of Christian teaching should not lead the second tension into oblivion, namely, the tension between theory and action, word and deed. It was an exciting discovery that the basic concept anatman (J. *muga*) is to be understood in the twofold meaning of *nonego* and *selflessness*. I regret that what is a truism for a Japanese is not insisted upon more urgently in the procedure of the discourse.

I personally would like to insist on this point all the more because Abe himself did not hesitate to mention the Buddhist weakness in ethical thought.[30] Because they were not expressed later on in such a convincing way, I will quote Abe's reflections here again.

> Buddhism must face the following difficult problem: how can it account for man as "person" distinguished from "nature," with his freedom and hence his possibility to do evil? Where can Buddhism find the basis of

ethical responsibility and man's social and historic action? Buddhism is certainly concerned with human values, with the problems of right and wrong, truth and falsehood, good and evil, etc. However, when Buddhism grapples with the problem of good and evil, it is not treated as an ethical problem pure and simple, but rather as the problem of discriminative mind which is considered the basis of the good-and-evil distinction. Accordingly, it teaches that the true way to realize the non-discriminating Wisdom, which is Wisdom, which is at the same time *mahakaruna* (The Great Mercy), is to do away with the *avidya* (fundamental ignorance). Therefore, although Buddhism is concerned with ethical problems, it does not always struggle with them seriously enough as *ethical problems*. . . .

Where man's personality and responsibility with regard to individual and social life, and history is concerned, the following question must be asked; how can an individual person (however firmly he may be grounded in his own existence) deal with the social and historical conditions which cannot be derived from the *ground* of his own existence? For man's social life and history are not simply made up of an aggregate of individual persons. Through the centuries Christianity has seriously struggled with the problem. Its personalism and its clear distinction between God and man give Christianity an advantage in this respect. It has offered its own solution of the problem in the ethic of good-Samaritanism derived from divine love and a view of history based on eschatology. Up to the present, it seems that Buddhism has not wrestled with this problem successfully. Only rarely has Buddhism even raised a basic question about it. The time has come for it to ask whether and how the problems of ethics and history can be solved from the standpoint of *jinen*, which is entirely nondichotomic. In order to be able to answer this basic question, Buddhism must break through its traditional patterns of thought and rethink the whole matter from the depth of its genuine spirit.[31]

RETURNING TO MASAO ABE

Finally, I will return more directly to Masao Abe and his "Kenotic God and Dynamic Sunyata." The issues of kenotic God and dynamic Sunyata, together with the "problem of today," form a triangle. On purpose we first considered the points in question, as they are reflected in Keiji Nishitani's and Karl Rahner's approaches. The most significant outcome of our consideration is that for them both issues—kenotic God as well as dynamic Sunyata—are less a problem of different concept systems than a problem of modern life, namely, how to cope with the existential questions of human self-realization in a world that struggles between the search for unity and the drive to disunity and dissolution.

I finished my discussion of Nishitani and Rahner with a lengthy quotation of Abe's essay, which stands as the starting point of a symposium that still goes on. I find it exciting how Abe succeeds in putting the central Christian teaching about "emptying oneself" in the logic formula of *sokuhi*, how he rightly insists upon the "emptying of the emptying" (pp. 35, 39–40, 50). Although I admit that the questions regarding history and ethics are treated in some length, to my mind it is a fact that Abe often uses basic Buddhist statements in a rather dogmatic way, such that he is prevented from the elaboration of a more sober and convincing analysis of the modern world situation. Because of the situation of pluralistic views, however, we are obliged to distinguish between the factual data and the various ways of interpreting them, and to separate them. Only if there is some basic unity in the estimation of facts does it make sense to proceed to the question of evaluation and ways of reform.

Some progress is made when Abe divides the attitudes to the worldly reality into three dimensions: (1) the nonhuman, natural dimension, (2) the transnatural, human dimension, and (3) the transhuman, fundamental dimension (p. 71). The application of "pure natural science" only to dimension one, of "individual morality, and collective social and historical ethics" only to dimension two, and of "religious faith and awakening" only to dimension three does not meet the standards of scientific thinking today. The main objection is to be raised against a restriction of ethics to the second dimension. Neither is it allowed—to give only one contemporary instance—after Hiroshima and other bloody experiences with murderous weapons—to exempt the realm of natural sciences from ethical norms and standards; nor do we do justice to most of the world religions if we separate faith from ethics. In a way, the division offered by Abe proves the insufficiency of the foundation of formal and concrete ethics as proposed from a Buddhist point of view.

That does not mean that self-emptying is not the highest form of self-realization in the various dimensions of life. However, because human beings are bound to live in the concrete ambients of this-worldliness and therefore have to realize self-emptying or radical openness of mind inside the innumerable mass of people and the vast plurality of situations, Buddhism has to explain how to live the requested attitude *inside* the world, and not by way of escapism. The borderline between nonego as overcoming any way of wrong egotism and a new form of subtle egoism as withdrawal from any other person is extremely delicate. Considering the calamities in the world, I would rather sin against the demand of total nondualism than become insensitive to the uncountable amounts of need, distress, anguish, and despair among the peoples of the world. My main difficulty with the further process of the debate is the lack of progress in light of the problems of today.

I offer a final observation. Masao Abe closes his essay with this observation:

> I believe Christianity and Buddhism can enter into a much more profound and creative dialogue and overcome antireligious ideologies prevailing in our contemporary society (p. 87).

I would like to return to the question: Is "dialogue" the final word we have to offer, or is not the "self-emptying of the self-emptying" demanding not that we look so much at each other but that we turn our eyes away from us and fix them *together* on the suffering people in the world of today? The "self-emptying of the self-emptying" calls for a radical shift of view. That seems to be the central conclusion of kenotic Christology and of the dynamic Sunyata, as I learn it from Masao Abe, as well.

NOTES

1. "Buddhism and Christianity as a Problem of Today," in *Japanese Religions* (hereafter *JR*), vol. 3, no. 2 (Summer 1963), pp. 10–22; no. 3 (Autumn 1963), pp. 8–31.

2. Cf. "A Symposium on Christianity and Buddhism—A Reply to Professor Abe," *JR*, vol. 4, no. 1 (December 1964), pp. 5–52; no. 2 (March 1966), pp. 3–57 (among them my own first reply, pp. 13–25).

3. "Answer to Comment and Criticism," *JR*, vol. 4, no. 2, pp. 26–57; "Christianity and Buddhism Centering Around Science and Nihilism," *JR*, vol. 5, no. 3 (July 1968), pp. 36–62; "Man and Nature in Christianity and Buddhism," *JR*, vol. 7, no. 1 (July 1971), pp. 1–10; "Religion Challenged by Modern Thought," *JR*, vol. 8, no. 2 (November 1974), pp. 2–14. The symposium went on in *JR*, vol. 8, no. 4 (October 1975); and vol. 9, no. 1 (March 1976). (The last includes my second contribution: "Searching for Common Ways," pp. 36–56.)

4. The lectures were published in *JR*, vol. 11, nos. 2 and 3 (October 1980). At that occasion Abe discussed "Substance, Process, and Emptiness" (pp. 1–34); I set forth "The Search for Common Ground: Being, God, and Emptiness" (pp. 113–43).

5. Jürgen Moltmann, "God Is Unselfish Love," in *The Emptying God: A Buddhist-Jewish-Christian Conversation*, ed. John B. Cobb, Jr., and Christopher Ives (Maryknoll, N.Y.: Orbis Books, 1990), p. 116.

6. Hans Waldenfels, "Remembering Sensei," *The Eastern Buddhist* (new series), vol. xxv, no. 1 (Spring 1992), p. 145.

7. Cf. Hans Waldenfels, *Absolute Nothingness: Foundations for a Buddhist-Christian Dialogue* (first published in Germany in 1976) (New York: Paulist Press, 1980).

8. The English version of Keiji Nishitani's internationally important work *Shukyo towa nanika* (Tokyo 1961) appeared first chapterwise in *Philosophical Studies of*

Japan and *The Eastern Buddhist* (new series) before it was published as a book, *Religion and Nothingness* (Berkeley: University of California Press, 1982). The various translations demonstrate the common effort of author and translators to reach for a more comprehensive understanding of such basic concepts as *sunyata* (J. *ku*), *anatman* (J. *muga*), *kenosis, ekkenosis,* and *agape.*

9. Ibid., pp. 58f.

10. Ibid., p. 69.

11. Ibid., pp. 69ff and 13–22.

12. Waldenfels, *Absolute Nothingness,* pp. 86f, where I refer to the first translation. Also the German translation, *Was ist Religion?* tr. Dora Fischer-Barnicol (Frankfurt: Insel, 1982), which follows the first English translation, uses two terms: *"muga, d.h. non-ego* oder Selbst-Losigkeit" (p. 117). The new English translation definitely makes for a smoother reading, however, at the cost of avoiding some of the crucial points rather alien to the Western mind. The coincidence of an ontological and an ethical notion in one and the same concept of *muga* is a good example.

13. Nishitani, *Religion and Nothingness,* p. 58.

14. Ibid., p. 60.

15. In the same way, Abe states: "Kenosis or emptying is not an *attribute* (however important it may be) of God, but the fundamental *nature* of God" (p. 39).

16. Nishitani, *Religion and Nothingness,* p. 59.

17. Ibid., pp. 59–60.

18. Cf. Hans Waldenfels, *Kontextuaelle Fundamentaltheologie* (Paderborn: F. Schöningh, 1988), pp. 16, 30ff, 139–52, 320f, 449f, and 462ff.

19. Nishitani, *Religion and Nothingness,* pp. 40–41.

20. Waldenfels, *Absolute Nothingness,* p. 62.

21. Cf. in more detail Hans Waldenfels, *Begegnung der Religionen* (Bonn: Borengässer, 1990), pp. 336–59.

22. See pp. 36ff, where Abe himself to a great extent remains in the field of conceptualization. I ask myself constantly how he will seriously cope with the urgent question of plurality in our pluralistic society. I understand well that Jews as well as women can feel very much offended by what—from their standpoint—they must call insensitivity with regard to their existential questions.

23. Cf. Waldenfels, *Absolute Nothingness,* pp. 77ff.

24. Ibid., pp. 126–27.

25. Ibid., p. 144. See in more detail Part III, pp. 121–62; also K. P. Fischer, *Der Mensch als Geheimnis: Die Anthropologie Karl Rahners* (Freiburg: Herder, 1974), which is still considered one of the most profound introductory studies of Rahner's theology.

26. I refer to ordinary or scholarly modes of speech that are expressed in sentences. That does not mean that we have no modes of speaking that both serve as expressions of the limitations mentioned and still carry beyond, for example, poetry, lyric, and so forth.

27. Note that a mere reading or studying of the small book will never lead to an existential understanding. Accordingly, a discussion on the basis of common reading remains unsatisfying. It is a similar situation when the Zen experience is debated on the basis of insights gained by reading books concerning Zen.

28. Cf. *Exercitia Spiritualia*, nos. 313–36.

29. Ibid., 2–4.

30. Cf. Waldenfels, *Absolute Nothingness*, pp. 96–99.

31. *JR*, vol. 3, no. 3 (1963), pp. 29ff.

6

The Return to the Relative: Sunyata and the Realm of Ethics

CHRISTOPHER IVES

Masao Abe's essay on the kenosis of God and the dynamism of Sunyata features provocative treatment of a range of issues, especially concerning Christian and Buddhist notions of ultimate reality. His discussion of the forces challenging religion in modern times and of kenotic theology as a point of reference for dialogue with Christianity is both insightful in itself and valuable as a resource for those working to revitalize Christian contemplative life threatened since the Reformation. On the Buddhist side, his discussion of ethical aspects of Sunyata highlights key facets of the Buddhist tradition and begins to expound on several topics in Buddhism about which his Christian and Jewish dialogue partners have long wondered, including the will, evil, and history. His discussion of the natural, human, and transhuman dimensions, and his distinction between relative, ethical responsibility and absolute, religious responsibility for such historical events as the Holocaust are especially intriguing. Although his discussion provides answers to questions often asked about Buddhism, it triggers several other questions, Abe's future answers to which may further advance the important line of comparative thought in his essay.

Abe's exposition of Sunyata and its ethical implications seems strongest in the sections dealing with Sunyata as the Buddhist ultimate, the positive meanings of Sunyata, and karma. He offers a clear articulation of the Buddhist call for people to "empty" themselves in such a way that karma is broken through and ignorance turns over into wisdom and of how this shift entails a move beyond the realm of ordinary discriminating thought and the accompanying realm of ethics with its distinctions between good and evil, right and wrong. In the latter regard, Abe writes,

"One must . . . go beyond the ethical dimension and enter into the religious dimension. Ultimately, the distinction between good and evil in the ethical dimension is relative, not absolute" (p. 72). On this basis he sets forth a distinction between the relative and the absolute and formulates his three-dimensional scheme. Given the Buddhist critique of human entanglement in ordinary discriminating thought, Abe's emphasis on the need to go beyond discrimination and its dualistic distinctions situates him in the mainstream of Buddhist—especially Zen—thought.

My questions for Abe concern the next step of his exposition—the return to the relative, ethical dimension from the absolute, religious dimension of Sunyata. Highlighting a central distinction between these two dimensions, Abe writes, "While in a human, moral dimension the Holocaust should be condemned as an unpardonable, absolute evil, from the ultimate religious point of view even it should be taken not as an absolute evil but as a relative evil" (p. 78). Though this perspective with its criticism of the substantializing or reifying of historical events as absolute entities with fixed, essential natures appears to undermine ethical evaluation, Abe points out that the realization of Sunyata—with its facets of "suchness" and nonthinking (*hishiryo*)—is simultaneously a realization of the collective nature of karma, ignorance (*avidya*), and, by extension, personal responsibility for events ordinarily seen in the relative dimension as unrelated to oneself. In Abe's words, "in the collective aspect of karma, that is, in terms of collective karma, we are responsible for everything caused by *human avidya* universally rooted in human nature—for everything, including what is apparently unrelated to us in the ordinary sense' (p. 65), and "as one who painfully realizes the collective karma deeply rooted in human ignorance as the ultimate cause of the event in Auschwitz am I aware of and accept joint responsibility for the Holocaust and find in this realization the *basis* from which I can properly cope with the case of the Holocaust" (pp. 76–77).

The first questions that arise here concern the realization of collective karma and the consequent "coping." Does a realization of collective karmic responsibility constitute a sufficient ethical response to such a radically evil historical event as the Holocaust? Does the Buddhist recognition of such responsibility also lead to responsiveness or to an active "response ability"? And if so, does the realization of Sunyata equip one sufficiently to discern and formulate adequate, effective responses, or is something else needed as well, such as a serious encounter with and sustained study of concrete, historical "facts" and processes, however nonsubstantial they may be?

Moreover, prior to raising these issues, one might ask whether Abe's formulation of "joint responsibility" holds up to scrutiny. Useful here is a distinction between relationship (or connection) and responsibility (in the sense of being both a causal factor and, by implication, an agent with ethical responsibility). Given the notions of Sunyata and the virtually synonymous (at least in the Mahayana tradition) notion of dependent co-arising, an argument that people are related or connected to myriad events – however distant – in a web of ongoing, processive interrelationships has solid footing. But the leap to the claim that because of collective karma and shared ignorance all people must "accept responsibility" for events like the Holocaust appears dubious. If "responsibility" does imply causal agency and some sort of ethical burden, how can Abe argue that we *all* are responsible? Although this argument might serve the valuable purpose of drawing self-complacent or self-righteous observers into greater ethical awareness and engagement, it undermines the distinction between those who are related to an event and those who caused it and hence must take ethical responsibility for it. Does not Abe's use of the term "responsibility" trivialize the important ethical distinction between, for example, a Jewish infant and a Nazi guard at Auschwitz? In what meaningful sense must that infant "accept responsibility" for the Holocaust? Though it might be safe to say that at some level Jewish infants or adults experienced the kind of basic ignorance (*avidya*) underlying the actions of Nazis, it does not logically follow that they therefore share responsibility for the particular way in which Nazis actively expressed that ignorance through the catalyst of a set of concrete historical conditions impacting them and others who fell in behind Hitler.

In balance with his emphasis on the move to the absolute, religious dimension, Abe works to maintain the significance of the relative ethical dimension by arguing that rational thinking is "*revived* as thinking on the basis of 'suchness' through the realization of nonthinking" (p. 60) and that "[i]n the light of wisdom realized in Sunyata, everything and everyone is realized in its suchness" (p. 86). The key question here is that of the nature of this revival and the realization of things – including conventional ethical distinctions between good and evil – in their "suchness." What sort of stance does this revival of rational thinking and realization of things lead to as one reenters the ethical realm? In Japanese history, how have awakened Zen Buddhists given practical, ethical application to that rational thinking and their insight into the suchness of existing things? Judging from the historical record in Japan, ostensibly awakened Zen figures have tended to accept if not promote conventional, largely Confucian ethical norms and social arrangements, some of which have stood in tension with Mahayana Buddhist principles. This empirical historical evidence indicates that the realization of

Sunyata does not necessarily transform the personal ethical stance that one has transcended in moving to the absolute, religious dimension, but may simply reaffirm it in one's return to the relative, ethical dimension. In short, where is the empirical, historical evidence that the realization of Sunyata leads to the kind of transformation of ethical being implied in Mahayana Buddhist talk of the awakened individual (a Bodhisattva, as it were) returning from the absolute dimension to serve others with wisdom and compassion? And, if such a transformation can be demonstrated to occur necessarily, as opposed to occasionally, is there any specific pattern to it, or is it simply haphazard with a range of newly taken ethical stances (as appears to be the case historically)?

Abe addresses this issue in part by arguing that the "ultimate criterion of value judgment" is "whether or not a thing or action in question does accord with the vow and act to make one's self and all others awakened" (p. 84). Though this might seem to constitute a Zen formulation of a way to discriminate good from evil, it focuses on the religious dimension rather than the ethical dimension; and as Abe himself acknowledges, they sometimes stand in tension, as Kierkegaard realized in his treatment of the story of Abraham and Isaac in terms of the "teleological suspension of the ethical." As indicated by *upaya* (skillful means of leading others to awakening) stories in such Mahayana texts as the Lotus Sutra and by such Zen stories as Nan-ch'üan's killing of the cat, actions that lead oneself or others to awakening are not necessarily ethically acceptable at the relative level. For this reason, Abe's "ultimate criterion for value judgment" does not pertain to value judgments in general but to *religious* value judgments and hence might actually be an unacceptable criterion for *ethical* value judgments.

Even if we assume or actually demonstrate that the revived rational thinking and the insight into the suchness of things—including "good" and "evil"—do lead to a viable criterion for ethical value judgments or to a new, uniquely Zen ethical formulation of what is good and evil as opposed to conventional formulations, we are still left with the question of whether this will also lead to active ethical engagement. Abe speaks to this issue when he writes that "Sunyata remaining with itself, without turning itself into a vow, is not true Sunyata. However, Sunyata that remains only at the level of a vow still cannot be true Sunyata either. Just as Sunyata must empty itself and turn itself into a vow, it must empty even the vow and turn itself into an 'act' or 'deed,' which is traditionally called *carita* or *carya*. . . . In this way, in and through self-emptying, Sunyata always ceaselessly turns itself into a vow and into acts" (pp. 83–84). Abe's assertions here are ambiguous. He claims that Sunyata "must" empty itself and thereby give rise to vows and acts, but does "must" mean that it *necessarily* will do so, or that *if* Sunyata is to generate active religious and/or ethical engagement in the world it *will have to* empty itself? Judging from his statement at the end of the above quotation that "Sunyata always ceaselessly turns itself into a vow and into acts," the former appears to be his stance. Assuming this to be the case, however, how might Abe square this claim with the fact that many supposedly awakened Zen Buddhists historically have been socially passive, which might indicate the lack of a necessary connection between Sunyata and action (unless one restricts "vow" and "act" to the soteriological arena)? Further, how might Abe square his claim with supposedly awakened Zen Buddhists who supported Japanese militarism in World War II, that is, Zen Buddhists who have engaged in acts—and perhaps even vows— that seem to run contrary to the type of acts Abe's discussion implies one can expect from awakened Buddhists (de facto Bodhisattvas)?

This discussion of Zen formulations of good and evil and action based on Sunyata connects to the larger issue of the ends to which such formulations and actions are to be directed. Abe indicates that the ultimate goal is to lead all others to awakening while paradoxically realizing that people will continually and endlessly be born with the karma and ignorance Buddhism works to overcome. Though not explicitly outlined by Abe, this also implies an ethical telos as well; but as indicated above Abe seems to put forth a religious criterion for ethical action and thereby commit a category mistake and conflate two dimensions he works hard to distinguish in other parts of his essay. Regardless of the extent to which his essay implies an ethical teleology, his discussion of time throws a major obstacle in the way of his efforts to delineate and develop ethical dimensions of Sunyata. In his essay he writes that "Buddhism has a unique view of time. . . . Being neither linear nor circular, time is understood to be not irreversible but reversible," and that "past and future can be reversed" (pp. 84–85). For Abe, this reversibility has crucial salvific significance, for without it "an emancipation from karma is inconceivable" (p. 85). Unfortunately, "Kenotic God and Dynamic Sunyata" does not sufficiently outline what this reversibility entails.

Given his statements to the effect that, in the context of Sunyata, reversible time does not destroy linear, irreversible time, his reversibility does not seem to imply a literal flow of time backwards into the past or a possible obliteration of past events such as the Holocaust or the nuclear attacks on Hiroshima and Nagasaki. But what does it connote, then? Given the reference to emancipation from karma, one might suppose that it points to a religious recontextualization or reevaluation of past events in a liberating manner not unlike the effects of repentance as construed by certain Christian theologians. If Abe indeed is ultimately referring to such a discovery of a new interpretation of or meaning in past events, the appropriateness of "reversibility" needs to be questioned. Whatever his intent, the sense in which "past and future can be reversed" is in need of clarification.

Although the issues discussed above are those that emerge most prominently in my reading of Abe's essay, several other points call for consideration. First, Abe asserts:

> The standpoint of justice, humanistic or divine, cannot be a proper basis for our coming to terms with the Holocaust, because the notion of justice is a double-edged sword. On the one hand, it sharply judges which is right and which is wrong. On the other hand, the judgment based on justice will naturally cause a counterjudgment as a reaction from the side thus judged.
>
> (p. 77)

Does this characterization do justice to the various meanings of "justice," theological or otherwise? Further investigation of various formulations of justice and the way in which biblical notions of justice relate to God's love or mercy and to theological virtues would prove useful here.

Second, early in his essay Abe states that "Buddhism does not accept the notion of a transcendent ruler of the universe or of a savior outside one's self" (p. 53). How can this statement be reconciled with the piety toward Amida Buddha that characterizes the faith of Pure Land Buddhists, the largest group of Buddhists in Japan? Although Abe and Pure Land thinkers might argue that Amida is not a savior but rather a compassionate helper who simply makes a Pure Land believer's rebirth in the Pure Land possible (at which point the believer practices with fewer hindrances than in the ordinary defiled land here and eventually awakens), is it not the case that many Pure Land Buddhists do in fact accept a notion of a savior? Here a distinction between "Buddhism" *in its ideal form* as portrayed by thinkers or representatives of the tradition and "Buddhism" *in its actual historical forms* needs to be clarified and kept in sharp focus. (This point connects with my earlier discussion of the Bodhisattva ideal and the actual behavior of ostensibly awakened Zen Buddhists in Japanese history, and it is often overlooked in highly philosophical interfaith dialogue carried on largely in terms of ideal—as opposed to actual or common—concepts, practices, and values in traditions.)

Third, the above quotation about how Buddhism does not accept a savior also stands in tension with Abe's later concern about how Sunyata can "as agentless spontaneity in its boundless openness, incorporate a personal deity as the ultimate criterion of value judgment" (p. 62).

If as a Buddhist Abe does not accept the notion of a transcendent ruler of the universe or of a savior, how does one account for his concern about incorporating a personal deity? Does Buddhism need God in some sense or not? Is Abe simply allowing for the possible existence of a personal deity, albeit as something subsumed by and by implication of lower metaphysical status than Sunyata? Further, in a dialogue with other Zen Buddhists, would Abe make this point about incorporating a personal deity?

It is my hope that the general issues raised in this response will serve to draw out further groundbreaking exposition from Professor Abe. I look forward to his rejoinder, particularly its development of his valuable discussion of the key issue of Sunyata and ethics.

PART III

A REJOINDER

A Rejoinder

MASAO ABE

Spanning a wide range of issues, all of the above responses to my essay present substantial and penetrating critiques. Although I cannot respond fully to each issue they raise, I would like to consider the following eight that I deem most important for our dialogue.

1. The Problem of Kenosis
2. The Holocaust and Responsibility
3. God as the Holy Nothingness
4. God and History
5. Sunyata, Trinity, and Community
6. Karl Rahner in Dialogue
7. Sunyata and Ethics
8. The Reversibility of Time

THE PROBLEM OF KENOSIS

In the beginning of his response, "God's Kenosis and Buddhist Sunyata in the World of Today," Professor Hans Waldenfels points out that despite its importance, Keiji Nishitani's interpretation of the Christian notion of kenosis has been somewhat neglected in Buddhist-Christian dialogue. Waldenfels clarifies the uniqueness of Nishitani's viewpoint, arguing that to Nishitani (1) agape is the act of "making oneself empty"; (2) in the case of Christ, "making himself empty," or ekkenosis, is realized in the fact that one who was in the shape of God took on the shape of a servant; and (3) in the case of God, the meaning of self-emptying is contained within God in that self-emptying is part of the original nature of God. Further, what is ekkenosis for the Son is kenosis for the Father, a distinction crucial to an understanding of the Christian notion of kenosis. In "Kenotic God and Dynamic Sunyata," following Nishitani's interpretation I tried to clarify the distinction between the ekkenosis of Christ and the kenosis of God. I rejected the usual Christian understanding that the Son of God became a human without God ceasing to be God.

> Is it not that the kenosis of Christ—that is, the self-emptying of the Son of God—has its origin in God "the Father," that is, the kenosis of God? Without the self-emptying of God "the Father," the self-emptying of the Son of God is inconceivable. In the case of Christ, kenosis is realized in the fact that one who was in the form of God emptied "himself" and assumed the form of a servant. It originated in the will of God and the love of God, which is willing to forgive even the sinner who has rebelled against God. It was a deed that was accomplished on the basis of God's *will*. On the other hand, in the case of God, kenosis is implied in the original *nature* of God, that is, love.
>
> (p. 37)

Waldenfels discusses several other respects in which he considers Nishitani's understanding of kenosis unique, two of which I, too, would like to discuss. First, to Nishitani, kenosis is a question of behavior and attitude, not of conceptualization. As the act of "making oneself empty," kenosis expresses an attitude of agape or nondifferentiating love. Second, agape is the "perfection" or the essence of God. Because nondifferentiating love is the very nature of God, we should speak of it as a perfect mode of *being* rather than as *the activity* of self-emptying or as a perfect mode of *loving*. Further, the perfection of God is more fundamental than the "personal"; it is a sort of transpersonality or impersonality. In this connection, Nishitani offers the unique notion of an "impersonally personal relationship," or a "personally impersonal relationship," to indicate the absolute immanence and absolute transcendence of God in the "ontological" relationship between human being and the being of God.

To my interpretation of Christ's kenosis, Richard Rubenstein's reaction is ambivalent. He writes:

> Among the many readings of the extraordinary passage in Philippians where Christ's self-emptying is affirmed, few are as interesting or as original as Professor Abe's. Nevertheless, I hold that this passage must be read in the light of biblical religion's theology of covenant and election.
>
> (pp. 96)

He also states:

> There are many elements in Abe's thought with which I am in profound sympathy, such as the need to overcome fundamental ignorance (*avidya*)

and dependent co-origination. Nevertheless, for me his interpretation of kenosis narrows the gap between Christianity and Buddhism more than is warranted by the fundamental perspectives of either tradition.

(p. 97)

The central point of Rubenstein's criticism of my interpretation of kenosis is my emphasis on the abnegation of self at the expense of the notions of covenant and vicarious atonement. He writes: "Paul's religious problem was neither enlightenment nor the complete negation of the self but the restoration of the right relationship, defined by the covenant, between God and humanity" (p. 97). I fully accept Rubenstein's criticism because Christ's kenosis must be understood in the biblical theological context of covenant and election. However, is not the most crucial point of Christ's kenosis the "self-emptying" of divine prerogative in order to take the form of a servant, to engage in self-negation to the extent of becoming "obedient unto death, even death on a cross" (Phil. 2:8, RSV)? Christ's kenosis is the deepest condescension, which is simultaneously his exaltation. It is through this condescension and exaltation of Jesus Christ that the covenantal relationship between God and humanity can be restored.

My emphasis on the negation of the human ego-self in connection with Christ's kenosis does not indicate, as Rubenstein contends, that salvation consists of the death of the human self and enlightenment without the vicarious atonement of Jesus Christ. My statement, "All discussion of Christ as the Son of God will be religiously meaningless if engaged in apart from the problem of human ego, our own existential problem of the self," connotes that Christ's kenosis and vicarious atonement should not be taken objectively as nonexistential events, but subjectively and existentially in relation to our own self-negation. For this reason I write after the above statement:

> The notion of Christ's kenosis or his self-emptying can be properly understood only through the realization of our own sinfulness and our own existential self-denying. Jesus himself emphasizes, "He that finds his life shall lose it; and he that loses his life for my sake shall find it."

(pp. 33–34)

These words of Jesus clearly indicate that the denial of our life or the death of our self is necessary for our own new life in Christ Jesus. Even though we should construe Christ's kenosis in the light of the biblical theology of covenant and election, this existential approach is necessary, for one is hard-pressed to argue successfully that the restoration of the covenantal relationships between God and humanity and the vicarious atonement of Jesus Christ are achieved without the complete negation of the self on the human side of the relationship.

THE HOLOCAUST AND RESPONSIBILITY

After discussing my understanding of kenosis, Rubenstein argues, "Even more problematic than Abe's interpretation of kenosis is his interpretation of the Holocaust." He contends that my avowal of responsibility for the Holocaust is "ahistorical" because it avoids concrete sociohistorical facts in offering a suprahistorical, religious interpretation (pp. 98–100). And in response to my claim that people must overcome *avidya* to come to terms with the Holocaust and attain human solidarity, Rubenstein asks, "In what concrete way is overcoming *avidya* relevant in the political realm or in intergroup relations?" (p. 105).

Faced with his first criticism, I have the impression that Rubenstein's understanding of individual and collective karma is insufficient. Apparently he understands individual karma and collective karma to be two different categories, such that individual karma refers to specific, concrete, historical events and collective karma refers to a universal, suprahistorical, religious reality. However, the individual aspect of karma and the collective aspect of karma are inseparably and dynamically united in the unfathomable depth of *avidya*, the fundamental ignorance innate in the human existence. Accordingly, it is not the case that individual karma is involved in history whereas collective karma is simply ahistorical or transhistorical. Both individual karma and collective karma are equally historical/transhistorical or specific/universal. They indicate a return to the deepest root of the Holocaust and point to the *basis* on which the problem of the Holocaust can be properly addressed.

I do agree with Rubenstein when he writes, "No attempt at theological interpretation [of the Holocaust] will be adequate if it fails to offer an answer to the question 'Given the power equation between the Jews and their European neighbors, why did the Holocaust take place in the twentieth century rather than at an earlier time?'" (pp. 99). However, we should clearly realize that an answer to such a historical question is essential not as a *basis* or *ground* for the solution of the problem of the Holocaust but as a *condition* or an *occasion* for that solution. We should clearly realize the distinction between the *conditions* of the Holocaust and its *ground*.

Rubenstein agrees with me in asserting that one cannot come to terms with the Holocaust from the standpoint of justice and that it is important to overcome human *avidya*. But he raises the second criticism mentioned above: "In what concrete way is overcoming *avidya* relevant in the political realm or in intergroup relations, where Nazi-Jewish relations would have to be worked out?" (p. 105). In order to answer this question properly, I must explain my understanding of the structure of human existence. From my perspective, human existence consists of two dimensions: the horizontal dimension, which refers to the sociohistorical aspect of human existence conditioned by time and space, and the vertical dimension, which indicates the transspatial and transtemporal metaphysical or religious aspect of human existence. The former is the realm of immanence, whereas the latter is the realm of transcendence. These two dimensions are essentially and qualitatively different yet inseparably connected in the living reality of human existence. We are a dialectical existence oriented physically and metaphysically, temporally and eternally, culturally and religiously. We are always living at the intersection of the horizontal and the vertical dimensions, and each and every event, regardless of its scale or importance, takes place at that intersection.

In this regard, we must not forget that although the sociohistorical dimension and the religious, transhistorical dimension are indispensable for human existence, the latter dimension is *more fundamental*. The religious dimension is indispensable as the *ground* or *source* of human existence, whereas the sociohistorical dimension is indispensable as the *occasion* or *condition* necessary for human existence. Without the religious dimension as the ground, the sociohistorical dimension is groundless and rootless, and without the sociohistorical dimension as a condition or occasion, the religious dimension does not manifest itself.

Returning to Rubenstein's question about the concrete way of overcoming *avidya* in order to attain solidarity between Jews and Nazis, I must answer that my primary and basic concern in this context is the ground or foundation for solidarity between Jews and Nazis and not necessarily the concrete method or program leading to this solidarity. The ground of solidarity is more fundamental than programs that produce solidarity, and without a clear realization of the ground of solidarity, one cannot properly establish such programs. For this reason, I emphasized fundamental enlightenment—rather than the standpoint of justice—as the proper basis for dealing with the problem of Holocaust.

However, I frankly admit that I have written almost nothing about concrete programs needed for solidarity between Jews and Nazis on the horizontal sociohistorical dimension. To do so requires objective knowledge about relations between Jews and Nazis in the context of European history, economics, and politics. Such objective knowledge cannot be derived directly from the vertical, religious dimension. However fundamental religion may be, it must be supplemented by inquiries in the social sciences.

But this does *not* mean that, as Rubenstein suggests, "to attempt to achieve solidarity at the ultimate level seems to me to reduce solidarity to a meaningless abstraction" (p. 105). Solidarity is not reduced to meaningless abstraction by the attempt to achieve solidarity at the ultimate level, but it is when the attempt to achieve solidarity at the ultimate level is mistaken for an avoidance of concrete, historical facts and an escape to an ahistorical realm. As I emphasized earlier, a return to the ultimate religious level is a return to the basis from which one can properly work on the sociohistorical level.

The return to the religious level as the ground for solidarity is a realization that the Holocaust is ultimately rooted in the collective karma innate in human existence, which means that responsibility is shared by all people, not just the perpetrator. But, does this realization of collective karma and shared responsibility at the *ultimate* level of human existence reduce the uniqueness of the Holocaust and obscure the particular evil of the Nazis? Should we reject such a realization at the ultimate level, move to the sociohistorical level, and persistently label the Holocaust the absolute evil? If we do, how can we solve the problem of the Holocaust without falling into the endless dilemma of hatred and counterhatred? Is not the religious realization the only legitimate *basis*—as opposed to a *condition*—on which we can solve the problem of the Holocaust and work cooperatively to build a better world in the future?

GOD AS THE HOLY NOTHINGNESS

With regard to Fackenheim's discussion of the Holocaust, I posed the question, If the Holocaust "means a complete rupture in Jewish history, how is a recovery of Jewish tradition possible?" (p. 80). To this Rubenstein directly responds, "I believe Fackenheim was in error on this point" (p. 108). Rubenstein views the Holocaust as fundamentally different from all previous Jewish disasters because it "constituted the first attempt by the government of any host people to undertake a program of unremitting extermination against the Jews," and he contends the Jewish tradition has not been lost. He writes: "Jewish tradition has been maintained by the Orthodox, the messianists, and even by 'almost-traditionalists' like Borowitz. If it has been lost, it has been by those Jews who, like myself. affirm the death of the God of covenant and election after Auschwitz" (p. 108). However, I encounter complexity in Rubenstein's position when he writes immediately after the above statement:

Yet, despite this theological perspective, Jewish tradition is my religio-cultural inheritance, and my involvement in religious life is primarily as a member of the Jewish community. I turn to Jewish rituals, traditions, and rites of passage to celebrate and commemorate the cycle of time and seasons and the crisis moments of life. Though the tradition as divinely mandated has lost its authority, it has by no means lost my reverent respect.

(pp. 108–109)

How should I understand and reconcile the apparent inconsistency here? It seems to me that Rubenstein stands inside and outside of Judaism at one and the same time. His is a challenging and provocative standpoint that can be creative as well as destructive.

Rubenstein has been regarded as a Jewish "Death of God" theologian. In *After Auschwitz* he argues:

When I say we live in the time of the death of God, I mean that the thread uniting God and man, heaven and earth has been broken. We stand a cold, silent, unfeeling cosmos, unaided by any purposeful power beyond our own resources. After Auschwitz what else can a Jew say about God? . . . I see no other way than the "death of God" position of expressing the void that confronts man where once God stood after Auschwitz.[1]

I realize with empathy how Rubenstein and other thoughtful Jews, facing the slaughter of six million Jews by the Nazis, feel painfully compelled to reject the traditional notion of God as the author of history and of Israel as his chosen people. Unlike the traditional Jewish response to the problem of evil—namely, that evil can be understood as a "punishment" for sin, or that suffering is regarded as an "affliction of love" in the service of a higher purpose—Rubenstein is the first major Jewish theologian to declare the death of God in response to the atrocity of the Holocaust. For Rubenstein, the Holocaust dealt the final blow to belief in a moribund God of history reigning over a progressing humanity. He argues:

If I believed in God as the omnipotent author of the historical drama and Israel as His chosen people, I had to accept [the] . . . conclusion that it was God's will that Hitler committed six million Jews to slaughter. I could not possibly believe in such a God nor could I believe in Israel as the chosen people of God after Auschwitz.[2]

Contrasting his view of the problem with that of Dietrich Bonhoeffer, Rubenstein once stated that his problem is *not* "how to speak to God in an age of no religion . . . [but rather] how to speak of religion in an age of the absence of God."[3] This statement is extremely important. Semitic religious traditions are theistic, being based on faith in the existence of a personal God, and as a result "faith" and "religion" are almost inter-changeable. With the above statement, however, Rubenstein breaks through the traditional theistic framework and opens up a path to an "atheistic" religion. Thus he approaches "atheistic paganism," certain types of mysticism, and Buddhism.

Emil Fackenheim and Richard Rubenstein are two of the most out-standing Jewish theologians engaged in Holocaust theology. Whereas Fackenheim's response to the Holocaust is to seek refuge in the Jewish people, Rubenstein's is to seek refuge in religion. Rubenstein's shift to atheistic paganism derives from his encounter with the death camps. Unlike Fackenheim, he does not focus exclusively on the victimization of the Jews, leaving room for the possibility that the suffering of others needs to be part of Israel's self-understanding. To him, Judaism interpreted as "mystical paganism" in the absence of God is the only adequate response to the primitive atavism of our humanity fully exposed by Auschwitz. "In the time of the death of God a mystical paganism which utilizes the historic forms of Jewish religion offers the most promising approach to religion in our times."[4]

What is most important in this connection is Rubenstein's notion of God as the "Holy Nothingness." In *Morality and Eros* he argues:

> I believe there is a conception of God . . . which remains meaningful after the death of God-who-acts-in-history. It is a very old conception of God with deep roots in both Western and Oriental mysticism. According to this conception, God is spoken of as the *Holy Nothingness* [and in Kabbalah, as the *En-Sof*, that which is without limit and end]. When God is thus designated, he is conceived of as the ground and source of all existence. To speak of God as the Holy Nothingness is not to suggest that he is a void. On the contrary, he is an indivisible *plenum* so rich that all existence derives from his very essence. God as the Nothing is not absence of being but superfluity of being.[5]

This notion of God as the Holy Nothingness is strikingly similar to the notion of Sunyata (Emptiness) as the ultimate reality in Buddhism. Sunyata is no void or emptiness standing as the counterpart to fullness, and it is unobjectifiable, unconceptualizable, and unattainable by reason and will. It is beyond emptiness and fullness in the relative sense and yet embraces them. Accordingly, Buddhists claim that "True Emptiness is Wondrous Being," for Sunyata is the source of everything. In any case, with his notion of God as the Holy Nothingness, Rubenstein breaks through the traditional framework of Judaism and emerges into the open horizon that is common even to Buddhism.

From a Buddhist perspective, however, I pose the following four questions: (1) Although I personally affirm the uniqueness of the Holocaust, I wonder why Rubenstein considers it to be "uniquely evil"? Why do the death camps challenge God's existence any more directly than, say, the destruction of the First Temple, which was the first and perhaps most surprising trauma in Jewish history? (2) If God is not the author of the historical drama and Israel is not his chosen people, how is history to be understood? How should one view the peoplehood of Israel? (3) If God to post-Auschwitz Jews is the Holy Nothingness, are the God who acts in history, the Jewish covenant with God, and ultimately Judaism itself completely dissolved in that Nothingness? If not, how do the covenant and history come to have meaning in the current world? (4) In Buddhism, through its self-emptying, Sunyata is working in terms of wisdom and compassion and thus is working soteriologically. What are the soteriological activities of "Holy Nothingness" as the post-Auschwitz notion of God?

In his response, "The Convergence: Sunyata as a Dynamic Event," Professor Heinrich Ott accurately grasps my approach to dialogue and expresses his agreement with it clearly:

> Precisely the dialogue at this level (religion as the deepest possible experience of reality and the specific religions as specific ways of achieving this deepest experience of reality) is the place where Masao Abe attempts to make contact with Christianity. He sees an inner *closeness* here but does not pursue a harmonizing *approach* of the religions toward one another in an objective sense. This basic attitude of his seems appropriate. It aims at the core of religion.
>
> (p. 129)

Emphasizing the importance of making contact in our hearts with ultimate reality—rather than doctrinal discussion—as the central event of all religions, Ott evaluates my approach and states:

> It seems meaningful to me to follow the tracks of Masao Abe's project, for it offers perhaps the only real chance for an agreement, a way toward the experience of community between differing religions.
>
> (p. 129)

Moving a step further as a Christian theologian, Ott impressively raises a question:

> Is it possible to discover something of the "dynamic movement" of Sunyata in the Christian faith as a dynamic event? I submit that it is indeed possible and agree with Masao Abe on this point. A similar movement

can be recognized in the phenomenon of consciousness of the Christian faith, which is of course not surprising if one dares to think of all genuine religiosity as a result of contact with the one holy Mystery.

(p. 129)

Based on the above understanding, Ott discusses the fundamental differences in the understandings of the notion of "nothingness" or "emptiness" in the East and the West.

Emptiness, or Nothingness, should not be understood the way it normally is in Western thought, that is, nihilistically. For Western—and also for traditional Christian—thought, Nothingness is pure negation, a dark night with no flickers of light, tohubohu, chaos as an absolute void. This conception has led to a deep misunderstanding in the West of the Buddhist faith. According to the Buddhist experience of reality, Nothingness, or Emptiness, is an open expansion, an open sky, a brightness that comprises and surpasses all known possibilities.

(p. 130)

In this regard it is very impressive and suggestive to see that Ott emphasizes the importance of becoming conscious of the above difference in the concept of Emptiness not only to reach a better understanding of Buddhist thought but also to help realize that

in the analysis of our own Christian tradition we may indeed come across problems that we can solve more easily from the perspective of Sunyata, of kenosis, that is, of "emptying," than by using the thought patterns characteristic of Western metaphysics and Christian dogmatics.

(p. 130)

Along this line Ott proceeds to focus on the connection between "Emptiness" and "suchness," which I emphasized in the Buddhist tradition because suchness becomes possible precisely in the realm of Emptiness. Ott also argues that "suchness, and with it ultimate reality, begins precisely beyond the realm of substantiality, in the realm of Emptiness" (p. 131). And rejecting the substantialization innate in the Western spiritual tradition, Ott surprisingly states:

To think of the person in categories of substance, that is, as a distinct, enduring ontic core around which "accidents" are grouped, and ultimately to think of God himself as a spiritual substance, was probably *the* intellectual mistake of Western metaphysics in trying to elucidate the scope of personal reality.

(p. 132)

In order to "verify" the Far-Eastern concept of Sunyata within the framework of Western experience of thought and to make it clear and understandable, Ott refers to nature. A highlight in his response is his quoting of Bashō's haiku,

> The old pond!
> The frog jumps in.
> The sound of water.

as an example of an attempt "to capture unrepeatable instants of the experience of nature in their uniqueness, in their suchness, and to catch hold of the depth of reality that, while remaining unutterable, reveals itself in a given unique situation" (p. 133).

Toward the end of his response Ott offers a unique interpretation of suchness that will open up a deeper common ground for Buddhism and Christianity.

> Suchness is the symbol and the form of the presence of eternity, of the Creator himself. The experience of suchness is the experience of God's presence. In Christian terms we could say that all of creation is contingence. It is as it factually is, held and inhabited by the Creator.
>
> (p. 134)

Finally Ott suggests the beginning of a "melting of horizons" of Buddhism and Christianity, which is very encouraging for future Buddhist-Christian dialogue.

> Substantialism is gradually abandoned. Perhaps it is the beginning of a melting of horizons taking place between Buddhist and Christian language, between two ways of thinking that intend to learn to understand themselves and one another better and better. The Christian experience of God also knows the process of Emptying—of surrendering oneself to Emptiness, of transcending our daily reality, which at first we had thought to be graspable—and this experience is therefore moving in the direction of Emptiness.
>
> (p. 134)

I am strongly inspired by Heinrich Ott through this dialogue, for which I am deeply grateful.

GOD AND HISTORY

In the present dialogue we are fortunate to have not one but two voices from the side of Judaism. In her response, Sandra Lubarsky raises two questions: (1) How does the Buddhist emphasis on Emptiness and no-self modify the Jewish emphasis on particular historical events? (2) How does the Jewish emphasis on history and relationships modify the Buddhist emphasis on Emptiness?

Lubarsky's answer to the first question is affirmative. Recognizing the tendency in Judaism to hypostatize the individual self, especially in terms of the community (e.g., "The State of Israel," "Am Segula") or history (most recently, the Holocaust), Lubarsky points out that the Jewish perspective can benefit from insights deriving from such Buddhist notions as Emptiness and no-self.

> What Sunyata reminds us is that idolatry—attachment to any thing (other than God, in the case of Judaism), whether a historical event (positive or negative) or a community—is a commitment that ends in suffering and sin.
>
> (pp. 117–18)

With regard to the second question of how the Jewish emphasis on history and relationships might modify the Buddhist emphasis on Emptiness, Lubarsky's perspective is once again affirmative.

In my essay I suggested that to cope properly with the issues humanity is now facing, we must recognize the following three different dimensions and that all issues are properly and legitimately understood from the vantage point of the third dimension:

> 1. A nonhuman, natural dimension represented by pure natural science.
>
> 2. A transnatural, human dimension represented by individual morality, and collective social and historical ethics.
>
> 3. A transhuman, fundamental dimension represented by religious faith or awakening.
>
> (p. 71)

Referring to this view Lubarsky argues that

> Abe seems to be proposing a kind of cosmic dualism with two sets of metaphysical principles governing two different dimensions of experience.
>
> (p. 118)

I am afraid that Lubarsky does not sufficiently understand my point. I have never proposed such "cosmic dualism." I am arguing not for a "cosmic dualism" of the horizontal, sociohistorical dimension and the vertical, religious dimension of human existence, but for the inseparability and dialectical unity of these two dimensions, which should not be confused or interfused with one another without clear realization of their *qualitative* difference. This is why I have argued that both of these poles are indispensable for human existence and that the latter—the religious dimension—is *more fundamental* than the former.

Lubarsky pursues her criticism a step further: "Although Abe seems to be drawing a deeply dualistic picture of human experience, he also seems to be arguing for an overcoming of the historical realm and its qualities—the very realm that is, for the Jew, 'sacred' because it is the 'ongoing illustration of religious truth,' that is, the covenantal story" (pp. 119).

This criticism brings us to a crucial point of Jewish-Buddhist dialogue—the problem of "God and History." This problem derives from different understandings of the absolute and history. Judaism construes the absolute as God, who is creator, lawgiver, and judge, working in history, especially in a covenantal relationship with Jews as the chosen people in history as a valued realm of divine activity. Buddhism construes the absolute not as a personal God but as Sunyata and the law of dependent co-origination. Sunyata connotes nonsubstantiality, and the law of dependent co-origination connotes the complete interdependency of everything in the universe. Thus history is regarded not as a valued realm of divine activity but as the beginningless and endless process in which the sacred and the secular are dynamically one. This is because Buddhism, especially Mahayana Buddhism, emphasizes that "Samsara, the endless process of transmigration, just as it is is nirvana, the blissful freedom from transmigration."

In this regard, I find something ambivalent in Judaism. In Lubarsky's words, "God-in-relation is a partner with humanity, but God-in-Godself is independent" (p. 120). I well understand that these two aspects of God are inseparable and working together in the *faith* of Jews. I also appreciate "the infusion of holiness into dailiness" (p. 119) and the mutuality between God and history in Judaism. However, the dynamic structure of "mutuality" between God and history is not clear to me, and this issue cannot be resolved by saying that it is a matter of faith. With antireligious ideologies prevailing in the contemporary world, some sort of theological dialectic is necessary.

God is quite able to go beyond the sacred realm and work in history at will. But how do Jewish people go beyond the realm of history and enter into the realm of God? The realm of history is limited by time and space and is defiled by human sinfulness and ignorance. There is no continuous path from the realm of history to the realm of God. There is an essential rupture between these two realms, which can be overcome only from the side of God. Accordingly, how is divine-human *mutuality* in a covenantal relationship possible?

We may find a Jewish answer to this question in the following statement by Lubarsky: "The foundation of Jewish belief is the ability of humans to 'be holy' because they are made in the image of God who 'is holy.' Humans can 'imitate' God (though they often mock God, instead), who is wholly good" (p. 120).

But if humans can "imitate" God and become "holy," there is a continuous path from the human to the divine, and the limitation or finitude (sinfulness, ignorance, death) of humans is not clearly realized. In my view, humans can enter the religious realm only by overcoming — by negating — the ethical, sociohistorical dimension, that is, by realizing the limitation of the ethical dimension. In this regard, the realization of sinfulness and a spiritual death are a springboard from the human realm into the divine realm.

Buddhism, especially Mahayana Buddhism, emphasizes that "Samsara just as it is is nirvana; nirvana just as it is is samsara." This is a Buddhist version of "the infusion of holiness into dailiness." Samsara is the sociohistorical realm in which distinctions and ethical judgments prevail and in which we are transmigrating from birth to death without final rest. Buddhism teaches us to overcome samsara by awakening to wisdom and attaining nirvana. In order to awaken to wisdom one must clearly realize the endlessness of samsara, and there one attains nirvana through a realization of human finitude and the negation of value judgment. Nirvana thus attained is the realm of blissful freedom from transmigration. This freedom is transspatial and transtemporal, and in it one realizes nondiscrimination or equality. In this nirvana, however, one may enjoy his or her own emancipation while forgetting the suffering of fellow beings who are still caught up in transmigration. Strictly speaking, however, this nirvana is not completely free from discrimination, for "nondiscrimination" is distinguished from discrimination. In order to attain true nondiscrimination or true equality, this discrimination between discrimination and nondiscrimination must be overcome.

On the basis of the idea of the Bodhisattva, Mahayana Buddhism rejects nirvana as a mere transcendence of samsara and teaches true nirvana as a return to samsara through the negating or transcending of the first nirvana. Therefore, nirvana in the Mahayana sense, while transcending samsara, is nothing but the realization of samsara as samsara — no more, no less — through a complete return to samsara itself. This is why Mahayana Buddhism claims that in true nirvana "samsara as it is is nirvana." This paradoxical statement is based on the dialectical character of true nirvana, which is, logically speaking, the negation of negation (that is, absolute affirmation) or the transcendence of transcendence (that is, absolute immanence). According to Mahayana Buddhism, true nirvana is the real source of both *prajna* (wisdom) and *karuna* (compassion). It is the source of *prajna* because it is entirely free from the discriminating mind and thus is able to see everything in its uniqueness and distinctiveness without any sense of attachment. It is the source of *karuna* because as expressed through one's own returning to samsara, it is unselfishly concerned with the salvation of all others in samsara. Again, this is the Buddhist version of "the infusion of holiness into dailiness." In Judaism, however, I do not see such a dynamic structure of this infusion. Judaism does not appear to negate the holiness understood as the negation of dailiness; nor does it appear to set forth a mutuality between God and history that is realized through a negation of negation.

At the end of her response, Lubarsky raises a question concerning the status of evil on the horizontal dimension: "If distinction is overcome on the more fundamental level, then what is the point of maintaining a valuative system on the historical level?" (p. 123). When we transcend the sociohistorical dimension on which ethical judgment of good and evil predominates and enter the most fundamental religious dimension in which evil as well as good people are saved, the distinction between good and evil is overcome. This does not mean, however, that the distinction between good and evil on the sociohistorical dimension becomes unreal or ambiguous. Instead, as far as the sociohistorical dimension is concerned, the distinction between good and evil is still real and clear, not in an absolute, substantial, and enduring sense, but rather in a relative and temporal sense. The tendency to absolutize, substantialize, or reify the distinction between good and evil is done away with by entering the religious dimension, but the distinction between good and evil is now regrasped and reestablished in the light of divine will and compassion.

Moreover, one no longer gets caught up in idolatry or falls into despair, for one can now function fully and appropriately on the sociohistorical dimension. If I am not mistaken, this understanding is not different from the "transvaluation" for which Lubarsky argues in the Jewish tradition when she writes: "In the development of Jewish thought, the rabbis often transvalued the past" and "the Torah itself should be vastly reinterpreted" (pp. 123–24).

Finally, realizing the affinity and difference between Judaism and Buddhism more deeply than before, I am grateful to Professor Lubarsky for her insightful and stimulating response to my essay.

SUNYATA, TRINITY, AND COMMUNITY

In the opening page of her response, "Sunyata, Trinity, and Community," Marjorie Suchocki writes that my essay enters "the heart" of the doctrine of the Trinity and that "Sunyata, emptied into Christianity, becomes a new way of expressing Christianity's central doctrine of the Trinity" (p. 136). However, she does not fail to detect a risk in my approach. She continues:

Abe's article, like many Christian attempts to read another religion through Christian symbols, reverses the process by reading Christianity through Buddhist symbols. Even if we succeed in transforming ourselves through our understanding of ourselves seen through the other, we are appropriating that other in terms of our own categories. Do we not risk remaining monological rather than dialogical?

(p. 144)

However, I did not interpret the Christian notion of the Trinity in terms of the Buddhist category of Sunyata, but suggested that the one God is to be understood to have the character of Zero, *Nichts* or *Ungrund*, because I believe this interpretation deepens the dynamic structure of the Trinity. For when the One God has the characteristic of Zero (*Nichts*), three distinctive beings—Father, Son, and Spirit—are then clearly and thoroughly realized in their distinctiveness without any possibility of being reduced to one Godhead, and at the same time the oneness of the one God is completely preserved from the haunting presence of the fourth being. With the notion of great Zero (*Nichts*) I reject the understanding of the one God as *substantia* or *essentia* as distinguished from the three persons as *hypostasis*, and regard the one God as *nonsubstantial* and dialectically identical with three persons: Father, Son, and Spirit. Only through a clear realization of the *nonsubstantiality*—the characteristic of Zero—of the one God, can one follow David Tracy's claim that "the divine essence *is* intrinsically self-manifesting and thereby dynamic, relational, and dialectical; and necessarily Father, Son, and Spirit."[6] In short, in my interpretation of the Trinity, I do not impose the Buddhist category of Sunyata on the Christian notion of the Trinity from outside but try to grasp it from within as deeply and as dynamically as possible.

My usage of Zero or Great Zero in the context of the Trinity, I am afraid, may be misleading, because "one" and "three" in the trinitarian doctrine are not numerical but transcendental categories. I was not unaware of this point, and I intended to indicate the nonsubstantiality and the unfixed, dynamic character of the Trinity by the term Zero or Great Zero, which can imply the freedom from any numbers, including one and three. Zero can also imply the creative source from which all possible numbers are generated and into which all possible numbers return. Further, I am suggesting that the notion of God, or Godhead, as the Great Zero can indicate *perichoresis*, which is community in the mutual interdependence and interpenetration of three persons and One God. Accordingly, I am encouraged when Suchocki writes:

From within my own Christian tradition, I can affirm otherness through that very trinitarian symbol that Abe interpreted through Sunyata, for the

Christian understanding of the Trinity requires a unity through irreducible diversity. The Christian story is that the internal perichoretic relations of what is called the immanent trinity yield the external perichoretic work of the economic trinity.

(p. 145)

But, with regard to the inner trinitarian relations, Suchocki emphasizes the irreducible otherness within the trinitarian structure, in contrast to my stress on the unity realized through the radical self-emptying of Sunyata: "Were there no *relata*, there would be no relation. Hence in the traditional language, the Father is always the Father and never the Son or Spirit; the Son is always the Son and never the Father or Spirit; the Spirit is always the Spirit and never the Father or Son" (p. 145). In the self-emptying of Sunyata, the irreducible diversity of everything is dynamically united through the nonsubstantial, empty character of Sunyata. The complete self-emptying of each and everything is sine qua non for this unity. Along these lines, how can the Father, the Son, and the Spirit be united if there also is irreducible otherness within the trinitarian structure? It is nothing but perichoresis or a perichoretical relationship that makes possible the community in mutual interdependence of irreducible diversity. However, in order for perichoresis to become the principle of community in mutual interdependence and interpenetration, the essential surrendering to and love of other persons is necessary. That is, the realization of nonsubstantiality or emptiness is necessary. Perichoresis becomes truly and fully perichoresis through the realization of the nonsubstantiality or emptiness of the one God. On the other hand, nonsubstantiality or emptiness (Sunyata) in the Buddhist sense becomes more explicit and concrete in its suchness or as-it-is-ness in terms of interdependence and interpenetration by taking perichoresis into account. Our dialogue, when deepened, will lead us to this mutual realization—the deeper realization of perichoresis through Sunyata and the deeper realization of Sunyata through perichoresis.

Finally, I fully agree with Suchocki when she argues in her concluding remark:

If I read Abe correctly, Sunyata as well as trinity suggests an affirmation of difference, metaphysical as well as religious. Without the affirmation of differences, the ground for peace is tenuous. . . . We must begin with the wisdom of appreciative understanding through conversation and compassionate solidarity in furthering well-being. Having affirmed differences in religions among ourselves, perhaps we can broaden and share this affirmation toward the deeper realization of community in this troubled world.

(p. 148)

KARL RAHNER IN DIALOGUE

In response to the questions I raise about Rahner in my essay (pp. 37–40), Waldenfels offers an extensive clarification of Karl Rahner's theological position. Like Waldenfels, I recognize that Karl Rahner is not a merely speculative theologian but one of the most profound theologians of our time, whose thought is deeply grounded in the God-experience. Accordingly, I quoted three paragraphs from Rahner's major writings: *The Foundations of Christian Faith: An Introduction to the Idea of Christianity* and *Sacramentum Mundi*, vol. 2. But I do not think these quotations are, as Waldenfels says, "nothing but certain abbreviations and summaries of what Rahner has learned by contemplating the life of Christ" (p. 158).

Unlike most theologians, Karl Rahner clearly recognizes "the self-emptying of God" and "kenosis and genesis of God himself," and he emphasizes the death of Jesus as the death of God. To me this is the quintessence of the Christian faith. But I disagree with Rahner's view of incarnation. Rahner states:

> God can become something. He who is not subject to change in himself can *himself* be subject to change in *something else*. . . . The absolute One [God] in the pure freedom of his infinite unrelatedness, which he always preserves, possesses the possibility of himself becoming the other, the finite. He possesses the possibility of *establishing* the other as his own reality by dispossessing *himself*, by giving himself away. . . . God goes out of himself, he himself, he as the self-giving fullness. Because he can do this, because this is the free and primary possibility, for this reason he is defined in scripture as love.[7]

With regard to this quotation from *The Foundations of Christian Faith*, I argue that "although these statements emphasize the self-emptying of God, they still leave behind traces of dualism, a dualism of God and the other, the infinite and the finite, immutability and change, within and without, and so forth" (p. 38). I am well aware that language presents problems in our attempt to convey ultimate reality. However, in contemporary interfaith dialogue, the use of language is inevitable in the attempt to conceptualize the transconceptual ultimate reality as precisely as possible. I pointed out "traces of dualism" in Karl Rahner's statement quoted above because, in the light of Buddhism, "traces of dualism" do stand out. In this regard Buddhists cannot help but ask, "Are these 'traces of dualism' absolutely necessary for Christian faith in God? Do these 'traces of dualism' have a positive rather than negative significance in Christianity?" In response to these questions I contend that "God's self-emptying must be understood not as partial but as total to the extent that God's infinite unrelatedness has no priority over relatedness with the other and that God's self-emptying is dynamically identical with God's abiding and infinite fullness" (p. 38). I expected Hans Waldenfels, who is a follower of Karl Rahner, to offer responses to these questions and remarks of mine, but unfortunately he does not do so in his essay.

At the end of his essay, Waldenfels does present a direct response to other facets of my essay. First, emphasizing the importance of the consideration of the problem of the modern world situation in the context of our interfaith dialogue, Waldenfels criticizes my approach, stating, "Abe often uses basic Buddhist statements in a rather dogmatic way, such that he is prevented from the elaboration of a more sober and convincing analysis of the modern world situation" (p. 161).

I cannot agree with his criticism, for I began my Buddhist-Christian dialogue not merely as interfaith dialogue but as an inseparable part of the wider, sociocultural problem of religion versus irreligion. I clearly argue this point in my essay:

> [I]deologies that negate religion prevail in our society. Scientism, Marxism, traditional Freudian psychoanalytic thought, and nihilism in the Nietzschean sense all deny the *raison d'être* of religion, not merely on emotional grounds but on various rational or theoretical grounds. Not stopping with criticism of particular religions, these ideologies negate the very being of religion itself.
>
> The most crucial task of any religion in our time is to respond to these antireligious forces by elucidating the authentic meaning of religious faith.
>
> (pp. 25–26)

The second issue raised by Waldenfels concerns my view of the three dimensions of human existence. Waldenfels argues:

> The main objection is to be raised against a restriction of ethics to the second dimension. Neither is it allowed—to give only one contemporary instance—after Hiroshima and other bloody experiences with murderous weapons—to exempt the realm of natural sciences from ethical norms and standards; nor do we do justice to most of the world religions if we separate faith from ethics.
>
> (p. 161)

Here again, similar to the case of Lubarsky, I face an insufficient understanding of my view. As I stated in my rejoinder to Lubarsky, these three divisions can be made for the sake of clarification of human issues; but in our living reality they are inseparably connected with one another, and all issues should be grasped ultimately from the vantage point of the third dimension in order to be understood properly and legitimately. Accordingly, although the atomic bomb on Hiroshima has a purely scientific dimension, it includes a moral or ethical dimension. But in order to understand legitimately the meaning of atrocious events like Hiroshima, we must go beyond the ethical dimension and return to the religious dimension and base ourselves in enlightenment or faith. On this religious basis ethical norms and standards are reestablished and natural science and technology can be legitimately utilized.

At the end of his response Waldenfels raises the following question:

> Is "dialogue" the final word we have to offer, or is not the "self-emptying of the self-emptying" demanding not that we look so much at each other but that we turn our eyes away from us and fix them *together* on the suffering people in the world of today?
>
> (p. 162)

In my view, "dialogue" is not the final word, but it is always the new beginning for unity and cooperation. If we fully realize the kenotic or self-emptying God, and dynamic Sunyata as the self-emptying of the self-emptying, we will realize blessings and compassion in the realm of human suffering.

SUNYATA AND ETHICS

In his response, "The Return to the Relative: Sunyata and the Realm of Ethics," Christopher Ives poses penetrating questions about Sunyata and ethics, especially the ethical realization and action resulting from the awakening to Sunyata. His questions constitute a serious challenge to Buddhists, and they call for a serious response. Some of his questions overlap with the issues raised by Lubarsky, and my rejoinder to her may answer some of them. Nevertheless, given the challenge of his questions, I feel a need to discuss the issues again from the most fundamental standpoint, even though, in doing so, I may risk some repetition.

Referring to my statement "In and through self-emptying, Sunyata always ceaselessly turns itself into a vow and into acts" (p. 84), ives argues:

> Abe's assertions here are ambiguous. He claims that Sunyata "must" empty itself and thereby give rise to vows and acts, but does "must" mean that it *necessarily* will do so, or that *if* Sunyata is to generate active religious and/or ethical engagement in the world it *will have to* empty itself? Judging from his statement at the end of the above quotation that "Sunyata always ceaselessly turns itself into a vow and into acts," the former appears to be his stance.
>
> (pp. 168–69)

Facing this criticism, I would like to make the following t
First, I feel that when Ives understands my phrase "Si
empty itself" to mean "it *necessarily* will do so," he objec.
emptying of Sunyata somewhat from the outside and is concerned wɪu.
"logical following" without committing himself to the self-emptying of
Sunyata. However, the issue is legitimately understood only existentially, that is, from within through one's own commitment to the self-
emptying of Sunyata. Then "must" indicates a spontaneous resolution.

Second, precisely because this existential commitment is necessary,
the issue becomes more serious when Ives asks:

> How might Abe square this claim [Sunyata's self-emptying into vow and
> act] with the fact that many supposedly awakened Zen Buddhists histor-
> ically have been socially passive, which might indicate the lack of a neces-
> sary connection between Sunyata and action (unless one restricts "vow"
> and "act" to the soteriological arena)?
>
> (p. 169)

This question is directly connected with his following question, which
is the chief issue calling for consideration.

> Does a realization of collective karmic responsibility constitute a sufficient
> ethical response to such a radically evil historical event as the Holocaust?
> Does the Buddhist recognition of such responsibility also lead to respon-
> siveness or to an active "response ability"? And if so, does the realization
> of Sunyata equip one sufficiently to discern and formulate adequate,
> effective responses, or is something else needed as well, such as a serious
> encounter with and sustained study of concrete, historical "facts" and pro-
> cesses, however nonsubstantial they may be?
>
> (p. 166)

In order to answer these questions properly, I must return to my basic
understanding of human existence. As I argued earlier, in my understanding, human existence consists of two dimensions: the horizontal
and the vertical. The horizontal dimension refers to the sociohistorical
aspect of human existence that is conditioned by time and space,
whereas the vertical dimension indicates the metaphysical or religious
aspect that is transspatial and transtemporal. The former is the realm of
immanence, whereas the latter is the realm of transcendence. These
two dimensions are essentially and qualitatively different from one
another and yet are inseparably connected in the living reality of human
existence, in that the human "self" is always *living at the intersection* of
the horizontal and the vertical dimensions.[8]

It is precisely at this intersection that our "self" realizes collective
karma and the accompanying responsibility. In the vertical dimension,

the self existentially and subjectively realizes *avidya*, the fundamental ignorance innate in human existence, and recognizes responsibility for, say, the Holocaust. At the same time, in the horizontal dimension the self that is knowingly rooted in the vertical depth tries to extend its "response ability" to the world.

In this regard we must recognize three points: (1) The extension of "response ability" to the world is the process in which Sunyata, awakened through the realization of the collective karma of *avidya*, empties itself and turns into vow and act to save all sentient beings. (2) The compassionate activity of the Bodhisattva on the horizontal dimension does not directly issue forth from the vertical dimension as an unmediated extension of that dimension, but dialectically in sociohistorical time through the negation (self-emptying) of the vertical, subjective realization of Sunyata. This dialectical operation is necessary because the compassionate activities performed on the horizontal dimension must be done under the limitations of time and space and formulated in light of concrete historical facts. Although the realization of Sunyata is the ground or source of one's activity, it must be conditioned or occasioned by concrete sociohistorical situations. In other words, realization of the vertical dimension of human existence is a necessary, but not sufficient, condition for the generation of an active, engaged response to specific social evils. (3) In Buddhism, this compassionate activity does not necessarily entail social reformation movements as in Christianity.

Paul Tillich regards *agape* and *compassion* respectively as the Christian and the Buddhist ethical principles of human relations in society, and he discusses the *revolutionary* nature of Christianity and the *detached* character of Buddhism in their attitudes toward history.[9] The revolutionary nature of the Christian attitude toward history is oriented by the prophetic quest for justice and eschatological fulfillment. (One might ask whether this prophetic quest is absolutely necessary in a religion's attitude toward humanity, toward society, and toward history.) In contrast, the Buddhist attitude is not oriented in this manner. The Buddhist attitude toward history and secularism is not to resist attacks and challenges directly on the level of secularism. In dissolving and regenerating individual and collective karma, Sunyata functions as a stabilizing element running beneath all social and historical levels. And on these levels the Buddhist attitude is not *detached*, as Tillich thinks, but *tolerant* of social and historical events, cultivating culture and the arts. However, precisely because of this tolerant character Buddhism often becomes indifferent to social and historical evils.[10]

Thus it is inevitable that instances where tolerance has drifted into indifference should elicit the response from Ives with regard to the realization of Sunyata and its ethical formation.

The realization of Sunyata does not necessarily transform the personal ethical stance that one has transcended in moving to the absolute, religious dimension, but may simply reaffirm it in one's return to the relative, ethical dimension. In short, where is the empirical, historical evidence that the realization of Sunyata leads to the kind of transformation of ethical being implied in Mahayana Buddhist talk of the awakened individual (a Bodhisattva, as it were) returning from the absolute dimension to serve others with wisdom and compassion? And, if such a transformation can be demonstrated to occur necessarily as opposed to occasionally, is there any specific pattern to it, or is it simply haphazard with a range of newly taken ethical stances (as appears to be the case historically)?

(pp. 167–68)

As a "specific pattern" of this sort, the following "The Four Major Vows" of a Bodhisattva can be cited from the Buddhist tradition.

However innumerable sentient beings are,
I vow to save them;
However inexhaustible the passions are,
I vow to extinguish them;
However immeasurable the Dharma teachings are,
I vow to master them;
However incomparable the Buddha-truth is,
I vow to attain it.

The first vow, directed toward innumerable sentient beings, concerns the salvation of others. The second, third, and fourth vows—which pertain to the extinction of passion, to Dharma teachings, and to the Buddha-truth—point to one's own awakening. This formulation of the Bodhisattva expressed in the Four Major Vows gives first priority to the salvation of others as the necessary prerequisite for one's own awakening. One can attain true enlightenment only through helping others to attain enlightenment. For the Bodhisattva, self-benefit and benefitting others are dynamically nondual. In Japanese this is called *jiri-rita-enman*, the perfect fulfillment of self-benefit and benefitting others. In this regard I made the following remarks some years ago.

The vow of the Bodhisattva to save all beings and to attain Buddhahood himself is a single process involving both self and others, and provides the basis for the transformation of society in Buddhism. Mahayana scriptures often talk about the construction of the Buddha Land. But when Buddhism emphasizes the perfect fulfillment of self-benefit and benefitting others, the term "other" actually indicates other persons and not necessarily society at large. Traditional Buddhism lacks a concrete program of social transformation. This is partly because Buddhism is more concerned with the ground or religious basis for social transformation rather than a practical program, and partly because in Buddhism the ground or religious basis for social transformation is not limited to human beings but includes all beings, human and natural. It is an urgent task for Buddhism to actualize the Bodhisattva ideal in a concrete plan for social transformation in the contemporary human predicament.[11]

As another and more recent example of a "specific pattern" of Buddhist transformation for which Ives is asking, Shin'ichi Hisamatsu's notion of FAS can be considered. Hisamatsu, an outstanding Zen philosopher of modern Japan and reformer of Zen Buddhism, advances the notion of FAS as the basic principle of transformation. "F" stands for "Awakening for the Formless Self," referring to the depth dimension of human existence; "A" stands for "Standing in the standpoint of All mankind," referring to the dimension of the breadth of human existence; and "S" stands for "creating history Suprahistorically," referring to the dimension of the chronological length of human existence.

Traditionally, Zen Buddhism almost exclusively emphasizes the "Investigation of Self" (What is the true Self?), but Hisamatsu emphasizes the inseparability of this and the "Investigation of the World" (What is the true World?) and the "Investigation of History" (What is the true History?). His emphasis on the inseparability of the problems of Self, World, and History is not essentially different from my emphasis on the intersection of the vertical and horizontal dimensions of human existence, because Hisamatsu's notion of "A" and "S" is an explanation in detail of my notion of the horizontal dimension.

Ives recognizes my notion of the "ultimate criterion of value judgment" ("whether or not a thing or action in question does accord with the vow and act to make one's self and all others awakened" [p. 84]) as constituting "a Zen formulation of a way to discriminate good from evil." But he argues that "actions that lead oneself or others to awakening are not necessarily ethically acceptable at the relative level."

> For this reason, Abe's "ultimate criterion for value judgment" does not pertain to value judgments in general but to *religious* value judgments and hence might actually be an unacceptable criterion for *ethical* value judgments.
>
> (p. 168)

He continues:

Abe indicates that the ultimate goal is to lead all others to awakening while paradoxically realizing that people will continually and endlessly be born with the karma and ignorance Buddhism works to overcome. Though not explicitly outlined by Abe, this also implies an ethical telos as well; but as indicated above Abe seems to put forth a religious criterion for ethical action and thereby commit a category mistake and conflate two dimensions he works hard to distinguish in other parts of his essay. Regardless of the extent to which his essay implies an ethical teleology, his discussion of time throws a major obstacle in the way of his efforts to delineate and develop ethical dimensions of Sunyata.

(pp. 169)

My reaction to these statements is threefold. First, when Ives argues that "Abe's 'ultimate criterion for value judgment' does not pertain to value judgments in general but to *religious* value judgments and hence might actually be an unacceptable criterion for *ethical* value judgment," I am afraid that Ives belittles religious value judgment. Religious value judgment transcends ethical value judgment. Religious value does not necessarily carry the meaning of value in the normal sense. Religious value judgment takes for its goal the transcendence of ethical value. In this respect there is no difference between Christianity and Buddhism. Jesus said, "God makes his sun rise on the evil and on the good, and sends rain on the just and on the unjust" (Matt. 5:45, RSV), and "I came not to call the righteous, but sinners" (Mark 2:17, RSV). These words indicate that religious value judgment (nondifferentiating divine love) completely transcends ethical value judgment and even inverts moral value. The same idea can be found in Buddhism. Shinran, the founder of Pure Land Shin Buddhism, says, "Even a good person is saved in the Pure Land; how much more so an evil person." Zen also says, "The immaculate practitioner takes three *kalpas* (eons) to enter nirvana, whereas the apostate *bhikkhu* (monk) does not fall into hell." The essence of religion is found in such religious value judgments, which are based in nondiscriminating divine love or all-embracing compassion that is paradoxically beyond ethical value judgment. However, this religious value judgment rooted in the vertical depth of reality is not directly transferred onto the horizontal sociohistorical dimension as ethical value judgment, but ethical value judgment is embraced and reappraised by nondiscriminating love or compassion. And in this connection we should notice that people like Shinran issue such warnings as, "Even if medicine is available, do not choose poison [evil]."

Second, when Ives argues, "Abe's 'ultimate criterion for value judgment' does not pertain to value judgment in general but to *religious* value judgments and hence might actually be an unacceptable criterion for *ethical* value judgments," he seems to assume that ethical value judgment exists independently or separately from religious value judgment. I am afraid that in his argument he misses the dynamic nature of our existence, which is always working at the *intersection* between the horizontal ethical dimension and vertical religious dimension. The same dynamic nature is also missed when he says, "Abe seems to put forth a religious criterion for ethical action and thereby commit a category mistake and conflate two dimensions he works hard to distinguish in other parts of his essay" (p. 169).

Although the issue of whether religious value judgment is an acceptable criterion for ethical value judgment is important on the horizontal, ethical dimension, it is not the only or final criterion of value judgment for human existence. This is because, as discussed earlier, ethical principles based on the distinction between good and evil inevitably fall into a dilemma when they are carried to their final conclusion. We see an example of this dilemma in Paul's confession: "I do not do the good I want, but the evil I do not want is what I do. . . . Wretched man that I am! Who will deliver me from this body of death?" (Rom. 7:19, 24, RSV). Because of the realization of death (or Great Death in Buddhism) we move from the horizontal, ethical dimension to the vertical, religious dimension. Because our self is always working at the intersection of the ethical and religious dimensions, ethical value judgment is always reappraised in light of religious love or compassion. Even when the criterion of religious value judgment is unacceptable for ethical value judgments, it has a soteriological function. In this reappraisal of ethical value judgment in the light of religious love or compassion, the good-evil distinction becomes clearer; yet one is not confined by that distinction, and one does not fall into the dilemma innate in the ethical value judgment. This reappraisal of ethical judgment in the light of religious love or compassion is not, as Ives misunderstands, "to put forth a religious criterion for ethical action and thereby commit a category mistake and conflate two dimensions" (p. 169), for nondiscriminating religious love and compassion transcend while subsuming ethical judgment.

THE REVERSIBILITY OF TIME

A further issue is the reversibility of time. Ives argues:

Regardless of the extent to which his [Abe's] essay implies an ethical teleology, his discussion of time throws a major obstacle in the way of his efforts to delineate and develop ethical dimensions of Sunyata.

(p. 169)

He also writes:

> Given the reference to emancipation from karma, one might suppose
> that it points to a religious recontextualization or reevaluation of past
> events in a liberating manner not unlike the effects of repentance as con-
> strued by certain Christian theologians. If Abe indeed is ultimately refer-
> ring to such a discovery of a new interpretation of or meaning in past
> events, the appropriateness of "reversibility" needs to be questioned.
> Whatever his intent, the sense in which "past and future can be re-
> versed" is in need of clarification.
>
> (pp. 169–70)

As I have explained in the "Time and History" section of my rejoinder in *The Emptying God*,[12] the Buddhist notion of the reversibility of
time is neither mechanistic (like the reversibility of time demonstrated
by scientific experiment in the laboratory), nor mythological (in the primordial night of eternal return), but thoroughly existential through the
realization of the Great Death, the death of the beginningless and endless process of living-dying. Through the clear realization of the beginning*ness* and endless*ness* of the process of living-dying (samsara) *at
this moment* in samsara, one transcends samsara into nirvana; yet this
nirvana is realized in the midst of samsara, not at the end of samsara.
Through this realization at this moment in time one transcends time
into eternity; yet this eternity is realized in the midst of time, not at the
end of time.

This transcendence, or "transdescendence," is possible by cutting
off the spatio-temporal process of living-dying and opening up the bottomless depth of the transtemporal, eternal dimension. This is the
"absolute present," which is the fountainhead of all possibilities – past,
present, future. This cutting off is possible not by our speculation but by
our religious practice and the "death" of the ego-self. It is this realization of the death of the ego-self (Great Death) that opens up the princi-
pal, vertical dimension of the absolute present directly below the
present moment – "now." This is the aspect of wisdom in which the limitations of time are overcome. From this depth of eternity one can grasp
or embrace the entire process of beginningless and endless living-dying
and thus can reverse the serial-order process of time; that is, reverse
past, present, and future on the basis of the absolute present.

Through the cutting off of time and the opening up of eternity, one
rises up from the bottomless depth of eternity to the dimension of temporality and moves forward toward the endless end along the process
of living-dying. But now, coming from the bottomless depth of eternity,
one is not confined by living-dying as one works for others in the midst

of living-dying. This is the aspect of compassion in which one tries endlessly to save others.

The usual understanding of time as a continuity or a unidirectional forward movement represents only one aspect of time, neglecting the other aspect of discontinuity or transdescending movement. When one understands time as a unidirectional continuity and a forward movement from the past, through the present, and into the future, does not one stand somewhat *outside* time and objectify or conceptualize it? If we grasp time not from outside, but existentially from within, we realize the discontinuity of time at each moment, the depth of time rather than the expanse of time. The continuity of time without the realization of its discontinuity is an abstraction. Real continuity of time is realized only through the realization of discontinuity. Discontinuous continuity is real continuity. In this regard, an unrepeatable, unidirectional forward movement is not a real forward movement. Real forward movement must include its self-negation; that is, the repeatability and reversibility of time.

The absolute present understood as the transtemporal depth of eternity is the source of temporality to which the descending movement from the dimension of temporality returns and from which the ascending movement to the dimension of temporality springs. Time dies and is reborn at each and every moment. Accordingly, Buddhism is not closed to the possibility of a forward-moving and irreversible historical time; further, it affirms anew every possible identity of time on the basis of the transtemporal depth of eternity.

To a Buddhist, in any moment of the beginningless and endless process of history, an advance toward the future is not merely a forward movement on the horizontal dimension, but an advance that is at once a return to the root-source of time and history in the vertical dimension. Likewise, the return to the eternal root-source of time and history in the vertical dimension is not simply a "downward" movement but a return that is simultaneously an advance toward the endless future on the horizontal dimension. The advance is a return, and the return is an advance. This dynamic movement is possible through each and every moment, which as awakened time is the intersection of the horizontal and the vertical dimensions of human existence. It is on this basis that the salvation of all sentient beings and the salvation of the individual person are pursued in Buddhism.

As quoted earlier, Ives argues:

> Regardless of the extent to which his [Abe's] essay implies an ethical teleology, his discussion of time [especially the reversibility of time] throws a

major obstacle in the way of his efforts to delineate and develop ethical dimensions of Sunyata.

(p. 169)

My impression of his arguments is that (1) in his understanding of the reversibility of time the realization of the Great Death is lacking, and (2) he absolutizes ethical judgment somewhat apart from the dialectical character of the human self working at the intersection of the horizontal, ethical dimension and the vertical, religious dimension.

As I stated in the previous section, the reversibility of time is realized on the basis of the absolute present opened up through the realization of the Great Death. On the basis of the absolute present, the forward movement of past-present-future and the backward movement of future-present-past are equally realized. Accordingly, even when past karma is emancipated through the realization of Sunyata in the absolute present, the ethical value judgment implied in the past karma is not simply eliminated but reappraised toward the future. However, this reappraisal is not a mere reevaluation of past events but a reevaluation through the realization of the Great Death and the Great Life. At the same time the forward movement toward the future is not merely teleological but is revived through the realization of the Great Death at each and every moment from the bottomless depth of absolute present. Just as time dies and is reborn at each and every moment, ethics dies and is reborn at each and every moment. Otherwise, nondiscriminating divine love and all-embracing compassion are inconceivable. Although ethics cannot stand by itself due to its innate dilemma (see Paul's words), it comes alive through the support of religion.

At the end of his response, Ives raises three more concerns: first, the problem of justice; second, the question of whether Amida Buddha is a transcendent savior; and third, the connection between Sunyata and a personal deity. All of these are important issues that I would like to address in detail here, but because of length restrictions I will have to discuss them on another occasion.

NOTES

1. Richard L. Rubenstein, *After Auschwitz: History, Theology, and Contemporary Judaism*, 2d ed. (Baltimore: Johns Hopkins University Press, 1992), p. 47.
2. Ibid.
3. Ibid., p. 174.
4. Ibid., p. 332.
5. Richard L. Rubenstein, *Morality and Eros* (New York: McGraw Hill, 1970), pp. 185–86.

6. David Tracy, "Kenosis, Sunyata, and Trinity: A Dialogue with Masao Abe," in John B. Cobb, Jr., and Christopher Ives, eds., *The Emptying God: A Buddhist-Jewish-Christian Conversation* (Maryknoll, N.Y.: Orbis Books, 1990), p. 152.

7. Karl Rahner, *The Foundations of Christian Faith: An Introduction to the Idea of Christianity*, trans. William V. Dych (New York: Seabury Press, 1978), p. 222.

8. Cobb and Ives, eds., *The Emptying God*, p. 174.

9. Paul Tillich, *Christianity and the Encounter of World Religions* (New York: Columbia University Press, 1963), pp. 72–73.

10. Masao Abe, *Zen and Western Thought* (London and Honolulu: Macmillan and University of Hawaii Press, 1985), pp. 175–85.

11. Masao Abe, "Transformation in Buddhism," *Buddhist Christian Studies*, vol. 7 (1987), p. 13.

12. Cobb and Ives, eds., *The Emptying God*, pp. 189–95.

PART IV

FURTHER DIALOGUE WITH HANS KÜNG AND WOLFHART PANNENBERG

7

God's Self-Renunciation and Buddhist Emptiness: A Christian Response to Masao Abe

HANS KÜNG

Since the beginning of the profound crisis of contemporary European society around World War I, the "postmodern" world order which has developed is no longer Eurocentric, but postcolonial, post-imperialistic. Speaking more positively: we find ourselves moving into a multicentered, transcultural, multireligious paradigm. Outwardly, the European powers have lost the domination of the world which they achieved earlier and, more profoundly, the sociocultural driving forces of modernity which were released in the seventeenth century—science, technology, industry, and democracy—have met with difficulty and have lost their godlike status, together with the most honored of the gods, Progress. They are ensnared in a crisis.

Religion, which because of its senseless opposition to modern science, technology, industry, and democracy is increasingly oppressed and often severely persecuted, seems to have a new chance in postmodernity. Religious movements, together with other, alternative movements—civil rights, women's, peace, and environmentalist—once again burst forth throughout the world. It seems to me that this chance will be well-utilized only if this movement proves itself to be not simply a restoration (of the premodern, medieval) but an innovation (of the postmodern)—if religion is renewed not, as so often in the past, as a reactionary, repressive, and regressive power of an intellectual minority, but is experienced as a future-oriented, instaurative power of individual and social liberation. As soon as liberation stands at the very center of both the Buddhist and Christian messages, a new opportunity is certainly offered Buddhism and Christianity.

The situation of this paradigm change makes it clear how important

the challenge of Masao Abe, along with John Cobb (the primary initia-
tors of a Christian-Buddhist dialogue upon a new, scholarly base) is: the
interreligious dialogue is to be led in the sociocultural context of the
exchange between traditional religion and modern irreligiousness and,
given that, a fundamental, new understanding of the religious message
of Buddhism and Christianity must stand at the center of our efforts; so
also must the other side of the horizon of contemporary history not
escape our notice – including, indeed, the still virulent, modern religious criticism of a Feuerbach or Marx, a Nietzsche or Freud. Masao
Abe in an impressive and original manner has made clear the entanglement of the problematic from the Buddhist standpoint, and I, as a Christian theologian, am pleased by the frequent concurrence: regarding the
affirmation of rational science (which is fully consonant with religion)
and the rejection of any antireligious ideology of science – of modern
scientism – but also regarding the epochal import of the contemporary
criticism of Nietzsche and the necessity of overcoming the meaninglessness of life and history, of nihilism. To be sure, here is where our discussion opens, and, being challenged to respond from the Christian
standpoint, I gladly face this astute and learned Buddhist discussion
partner.

NIHILISM AS THE RESULT OF MODERN ATHEISM

We agree: Nietzsche, without a doubt, skillfully analyzed European
modernity. As Abe emphasizes in connection with Martin Heidegger,
nihilism is the inner consequence of Western history – but by all means
is not, I should qualify, the consequence of European antiquity, of the
Middle Ages, or of the time of the Reformation. It is, instead, the consequence of the modernity which began in the seventeenth and eigh-
teenth centuries, and which in the nineteenth and twentieth centuries
subsequently fell into an utter crisis with the notorious "Dialectic of the
Age of Enlightenment" (Adorno/Horkheimer). The crisis of modernity
was noted by Nietzsche long before the First World War, together with
a few other clear-sighted persons (above all, Kierkegaard and Dostoev-
sky) and he recognized his time, when European enthusiasm over progress was still at its zenith, as a time of decadence, of inner deterioration.
Why? "The most important recent occurrence – that 'God is dead,' that
the belief in the Christian God has become incredible – already begins
to cast its first shadows over Europe": so begins Friedrich Nietzsche in
the fifth book, "We, the Fearless," of his *A Gay Science.* Casting a
shadow over Europe, but not only Europe! Like a warning to the countries of Asia, who find themselves, more than anyone else today, in the

frenzy of modernization—it speaks to us today when Nietzsche adds, "The decline of belief in the Christian God is an incident which concerns all of Europe, in which all peoples shall have their share of benefit and honor."[1]

So what are the consequences of modern atheism? The result in the near future is—we recall the oppressive and repressive form of religion during the Ancien Régime—an inexpressible brightening, unburdening, invigoration, encouragement, a new dawn, a broader horizon, the open sea; however, the consequences of this enormous occurrence in the more distant future are, according to Nietzsche, gloomier, though the nationalistic optimists of progress do not want this to be true. The "insane man" describes, according to him, something which only scarcely allows itself to be rendered in terms: "How were we able to drink the sea? Who gave us the sponge to erase the horizon? What did we do when we unchained this earth from its sun? Whither does it now move?" God's death signifies, then, the great collapse! Wretched vacuity: a drained sea. A hopeless environment: the erased horizon. Abysmal nothingness: the earth unchained from the sun. For the individual, a deadly plunge without orientation in any direction, which necessarily ruptures him: "Where are we going? Away from all suns? Are we not dashing perpetually onward? Backwards, sideways, forwards, in all directions?" Here is chaos unfolding, yes, the deadly cold and night of nihilism: "Is there still an above and below? Are we not lost as in an unending nothingness? Does the void not breathe its breath upon us? Has it not become colder? Does night and more night approach unceasingly?"[2]

Thereby it is made clear: modern nihilism is not, as Abe says, the consequence of religion, at least not directly. It is the consequence of religious deficiency, of irreligiousness, of atheism. And modern humanity has indeed "offered God as a sacrifice to Nothingness," but has also paid a great price therefor with the hell of world wars, of concentration camps, and of Solzhenitsyn's Gulag, with the desolation or meaninglessness of life. The Buddhist cannot be pleased with this, for a Buddhist—inasmuch as he participates in modernity—is also affected. And Masao Abe is correct when he sees an absence of Christianity and Buddhism in nihilism. Not only in modern Europe, but also in modern Japan, religion has been replaced by a pseudoreligion (nationalism and militarism)—with catastrophic consequences for Japan's neighbors and ultimately for Japan itself. Nietzsche was of the opinion that not only belief in God itself, but also all the consequences of belief in God must be overcome. God is dead, but His shadow is long: "After the Buddha was dead, people displayed his shadow for centuries afterwards in a cave—a ghastly shadow. God is dead: but such is the nature of humanity that perhaps for millennia there will be caves in which his shadow will be displayed. And we—we, too, still have to conquer his shadow."[3]

Yet, Friedrich Nietzsche—patient, critic, and therapist of the fatal illness: nihilism—was not truly able to conquer nihilism—neither with his message of the superperson and of the reevaluation of all values nor with the idea of the conquest of the eternal return of the shadow of God's likeness. Certainly, to the extent that Nietzsche exposed nihilism as a consequence of modern atheism, he proved himself a precise analyst of the end of modernity. However, insofar as he proclaimed the death of God without the possibility of resurrection, he proved himself a false predicter, who, demented from 1889, was not even able to witness postmodernity.

Nietzsche's criticism of religion sought also to strike at Buddhism, which he understood as "passive Nihilism" (*Der Fall Wagner*).[4] It must be supplanted with active nihilism, a nihilism of strength.

The "most extreme form of nihilism" is, according to him, "the insight . . . that *every* belief, everything held to be true is necessarily false: because there is no *real world*" (*Ecce homo*).[5]

But is there actually no "real world"; is there no "God"? Certainly there is no longer "God" according to Nietzsche in the "traditional form" of another world (here Masao Abe is correct): no longer in the sense of a Platonic, and also often Christian dualism, where God and world are separated. But is this the only alternative? Is it impossible and spurious to conceive of God's being *in* the world and the world *in* God? Even Nietzsche's philosophy uses unproved hypotheses and constructions, and his structure of history from the end of modernity to atheism and nihilism—at the current threshold of postmodernity—allows itself to be turned around. How? I would like to illustrate this in a manner similar to Abe's in connection with an earlier work[6] by using a text from Nietzsche which opposes the Platonic "real world," and which is yet more aggressive than that advanced by Abe.

FROM MODERN NIHILISM
TO POSTMODERN BELIEF IN GOD

In Nietzsche's *Twilight of the Idols*, which appeared after his collapse, he briefly describes the history of the disintegration of the "real world," as it was established by Plato and passed on to the future by Christianity, was afterward deflated by Kant and left behind by positivism as an unknown quantity, and was finally fully abolished by nihilism, and creatively overcome through the Dionysian "Yes" to all uncertainties—this all under the title of "How the 'Real World' Finally Became a Fable: The History of an Error":

1. The real world, attainable to the wise, the pious, the virtuous man — he dwells in it, *he is it.*
   (Oldest form of the idea, relatively sensible, simple, convincing. Transcription of the proposition 'I, Plato *am* the truth'.)

2. The real world, unattainable for the moment, but promised to the wise, the pious, the virtuous man ('to the sinner who repents').
   (Progress of the idea: it grows more refined, more enticing, more incomprehensible — *it becomes a woman,* it becomes Christian.)

3. The real world, unattainable, undemonstrable, cannot be promised, but even when merely thought of, a consolation, a duty, an imperative.
   (Fundamentally the same old sun, but shining through mist and skepticism; the idea grown sublime, pale, motherly, Konigsbergian.)

4. The real world — unattainable? Unattained, at any rate. And if unattained also *unknown.* Consequently also no consolation, no redemption, no duty: how could we have a duty toward something unknown?
   (The grey of dawn. First yawnings of reason. Cockcrow of positivism.)

5. The 'real world' — an idea no longer of any use, not even a duty any longer — an idea grown useless, superfluous, *consequently* a refuted idea: let us abolish it!
   (Broad daylight; breakfast; return of cheerfulness and *bon sens;* Plato blushes for shame; all free spirits run riot.)

6. We have abolished the real world: what world is left? The apparent world perhaps? . . . But no! *with the real world we have also abolished the apparent world!*
   (Mid-day; moment of the shortest shadow; end of the longest error; zenith of mankind; INCIPIT ZARATHUSTRA.)

Is this an end . . . or a turning point? A succession of scenes sparkling and scintillating with wit, irony, and malice, provoking us to reverse the series? Might it not be possible to turn Nietzsche's "history of an error" back to front — so to speak — into a new future? The new title might be "*The* (future) *history of a* (newly discovered) *truth*":

6. The idea of God — it cannot be abolished. Humanity never reached that peak. Zarathustra turned out to be a myth.
   (Twilight of the superperson — end of the briefest error; no replacement of religion by science.)

5. The idea of God, of no further use, no longer binding, even superfluous, shows signs of new life.
   (Nihilism — particularly for the *bon sens* of the truly liberated spirits — an unproved idea. Joy among the angels. Red faces among the devils.)

4. The idea of God, certainly unattainable by pure reason and unknown in its reality, nevertheless begins again to be consoling, redeeming, binding.

(The gray of dawn. The last yawnings of reason as it becomes aware of itself; positivism awakes from its illusions.)

3. The idea of God not only as imperative à la Konigsberg or as feeble consolation for the weak.

(Fundamentally the same old sun, but shining fresh through mist and skepticism as reality and great promise: no remythicization.)

2. The idea of God now attainable, not only for the virtuous, the pious, the wise, but also for the culpable, the irreligious, the "sinners."

(Progress of the idea; bright day; enlightenment of the world by faith; return of the Christian reality. The idea of God becomes more comprehensible, more straightforward, more concrete, more human.)

1. The idea of God perceptible, relatively simple and convincing: the God of Israel. Oldest form of the idea. He, Jesus, dwells in it, *he is it*. Transcription of the proposition: "I *am* the way, the truth, and the life."

(Noon; moment of the briefest shade; beginning of eternal truth; peak of humanity. INCIPIT REGNUM DEI.)

Hence: not only the God of philosophers and scholars in the pallor of thought (Descartes), but the living God as the "Not-other" (Nicholas of Cusa) and yet "wholly Other" (Barth, Horkheimer), as the truly "more divine God" (Heidegger). Not only a *causa sui* (Spinoza) but "the God of Abraham, Isaac, and Jacob, the God of Jesus Christ" (Pascal).

Thus in the end truth could become fable and fable truth. A turning away from the atheistic antithesis to a new "theistic," Judeo-Christian synthesis. A vision? A projection? An illusion? A suggestion? A hope— not more, but also not less?

As always: these reflections upon Nietzsche and nihilism now allow me passage to a deeper level, to reflections about the kenosis of God, the humiliation, renunciation, the emptying of God, which is linked by Masao Abe in an illuminating manner with the Emptiness of Buddhism. But the question poses itself to the Christian theologian as follows.

THE KENOSIS OF GOD HIMSELF?

Masao Abe gives, it is quite clear, his own Buddhist interpretation of the hymn found in the Epistle to the Philippians (Phil. 2:5–8, possibly pre-Paul and later recast by Paul)—a Bible passage especially impressive and moving for Abe. If I might immediately get to the decisive point of his detailed interpretation: the kenosis, humiliation, renunciation, emptying of Jesus Christ by the crucifixion is to be understood, according to Abe, as the kenosis, renunciation, emptying *of God himself*, completely and radically, which accords in a nondualist sense with the renunciation of ourselves in the unity of nonduality.

That is, emptying is the basic nature of God himself. Not only the Son of God, no, God empties himself completely of his divinity. And this is to be understood not objectively like a temporal-historical occurrence, but religiously and empirically as an essential-eternal state of affairs. So can the kenotic God of the Christians ultimately be replaced by the all-inclusive (dynamic) Emptiness (Sunyata) of the Buddhists? Indeed, the absoluteness of God can be equated with its relativity, the nature of God with every individual thing, and, similarly, the unending abundance with its unending emptiness! From this respect, the outcome of Masao Abe's paradox is in accord: God is not God; and exactly because he is not God, he is truly God. A God and Father who has not fully renounced himself in his self-sacrifice is not the true God.

But of course the question suggests itself: Can this ingenious Buddhist interpretation also be the Christian interpretation? Does it faithfully render the text? In my book *The Incarnation of God*, I grappled with this difficulty in the context of Hegelian philosophy.[7] I must, however, limit myself here. Masao Abe himself draws attention to decisive points, which can only be acknowledged and clarified here:

1. In the New Testament, the term "God" (*ho theos* = God, purely and simply) for all practical purposes always means the one God and Father and never a divine nature consisting of several persons.

2. The man, Jesus of Nazareth, is the likeness or Son of God's Word rather than a likeness of Christ or of God's Messiah.

3. In the entire New Testament (and in principle also in the later doctrine of the Trinity) the distinction of God's Son from God the Father, and the subordination of the Son under him who is "greater" than he, is steadfastly maintained.

4. Consequently, nowhere is there mentioned an incarnation or a renunciation (kenosis) of God himself; the Philippian hymn only speaks of a kenosis of Jesus Christ, the Son of God. Furthermore, this kenosis is not understood as a permanent status, position, relationship, but as a humiliation occurring in a unique, historical life and death on the cross. Even the Hellenistic congregation of Philippi (more interested in the divinity of Jesus than was the original Jewish congregation) was less interested in a divine Christ than in the event of the humiliation and renunciation initiated by God.

5. Certainly, the self-sacrifice of the Son does not occur against the will of the Father. God desires the redemption of humanity and so also the self-sacrifice of Jesus. Still, God the Father does not give himself up, but his Son (the church condemns the monophysitic "patripassianism"),

and so God the Father (*ho theos*) does not die upon the cross, but the man, Jesus of Nazareth, the Son of God. Only he, not God himself, is (according to the dying words of Jesus quoting Psalm 22:1 [Vulgate 21:1]) forsaken by God! Jesus being forsaken by God is, according to the New Testament, no divine "paradox," but human agony crying to heaven.

6. Given this, it seems to me – and Abe appropriately quotes my criticism of Jürgen Moltmann's Christology – that the discussion about the "crucified God" and that of a "killed" or "dead" God is unbiblical. The Buddhist appropriately places the question before those Christian theologians (also Karl Rahner) who in an unbiblical (in fact monophysitic or Hegelian) manner speak of the kenosis of God himself: must not they themselves, given God's truly successful emptying of himself (his death), consequently have to confess the Emptiness of Buddhism?

7. The stumbling block of a (Buddhist or Christian) Christology (and trinitarian doctrine) which completely identifies Jesus with God and brazenly declares Jesus' death to be the death of God is made strikingly clear in the case of the resurrection: such a Christology cannot explain who brought this supposedly dead God back to life.

8. According to the hymn in Philippians, it is (as in the entire New Testament) quite unequivocally God himself, the Father, who awakened the man, Jesus of Nazareth, his Son and Messiah, to eternal life, and exalted him. This is the significant flaw in Masao Abe's interpretation: he indeed makes reference to the resurrection, but practically speaking neglects it – has to neglect it. Why? In order to be able to abide by his interpretation: the renunciation of God himself in Buddhist Sunyata. A very basic question arises here: the question of the effective hermeneutic for this interreligious dialogue.

THE TRUE DIALOGICAL HERMENEUTIC?

There is no question: Masao Abe's basic intention is dialogic. He isolates key concepts from Christian texts, which he then transplants into a Buddhist context, where the concept of kenosis is understood not simply as ethical, exemplary humiliation, but is recast as ontological emptying, an emptying of God himself, yes, ultimately as Emptiness in general, Sunyata. In this manner, as a Buddhist, he discovers his own world – even on foreign, Christian soil. Just as the Christian authors earlier gave a Christian exegesis of Greek or Buddhist texts, so also Abe gives a Buddhist exegesis of the Christian texts. He wants in this manner to overcome the cultural and religious gap. Both of these religious traditions seem closer than hitherto had been assumed.

But is this an adequate hermeneutic for the interreligious dialogue?

Basically nothing personal is at stake because, even in foreign raiment, one finds only one's own world again. Is such a dialogical hermeneutic not truly selective and reductive? It becomes clear with the example of the Epistle to the Philippians: one chooses from the context of the Christian Scriptures only a few welcome passages and ignores the rest (it is selective), then interprets these passages according to one's personal interest (it is reductive). Indeed, such a hermeneutic — whether Buddhist or Christian — compels one to warp the meaning of other traditions' texts so that they will fit one's own tradition. Exegesis becomes eisegesis. . . .

And what is the alternative? It seems to me that the true dialogical hermeneutic must encompass whenever possible both speaking one's personal vision with reference to one's own sources and allowing the vision of others to gain expression based on the sources or their own tradition, beginning with objective information from both sides, moving on to a reciprocal, productive challenge, and culminating in a mutual transformation (John Cobb); more concretely, proceeding from the obvious divergences between Christianity and Buddhism *in the context of their respective traditions* and looking for points of convergence, for openings, for possibilities of expansion and enrichment.

Masao Abe is of the opinion that this kenotic God, who disintegrates himself in the Absolute Nothingness, not only overcomes Christian monotheism, but also the nihilism of Nietzsche, which he aligns with Relative Nothingness. Why? Because, for Abe, Absolute Nothingness is Absolute Being. And here, by looking at Masao Abe's interpretation of his own Buddhist position, is where new possibilities of understanding are uncovered.

SUNYATA—BEING—GOD

Masao Abe brings to his own attention the relationship of Sunyata, "Emptiness," and "Being": Being, which is indeed as meagerly objectifiable as it is conceptually graspable, which is not simply a Something, not simply outside of ourselves, but is dynamically identical to our self. Only that "Being" is a primarily positive concept, and Sunyata, primarily negative. Yet the dialectic, which is characteristic of these "transcendental" concepts (beyond and including all individual things, classifications of being, and categories) may not be overlooked.

The dialectic of Being in Western philosophy: the reader might recall that Hegel already has redefined "Being, pure Being — without any further designation" as "pure indeterminateness and vacuity": "There is nothing in it to intuit, if we can speak here of intuiting: or it is only this pure, vacuous intuiting itself. There is little in it to think, or it is equally only this empty thinking. Being, the indeterminate immediate, is indeed nothing, and neither more nor less than nothing." Hegel's subtle dialectic aims at the unity of Being and Nothing: *"pure Being and pure nothing are, then, the same."*[8]

The reverse of the dialectic of Nothingness in Eastern-Buddhist thought! Masao Abe brings attention to this; the "Absolute Nothingness" in a Buddhist sense is not the nihilistic Nothingness. Abe acknowledges the Mahayana teaching that Sunyata is non-Sunyata and is, therefore, highest Sunyata. Although the term Sunyata, or Emptiness, at first sounds negative, it has, according to Abe, a decidedly positive, even religious and soteriological significance: universal and encompassing everything—human, natural, divine—and, precisely so, limitlessly open without any particularly fixed center; dynamically spontaneous and including all opposites (interdependent and reciprocal) within itself: that is Emptiness.

Similarly, Martin Heidegger tried in our time to conceive and express Being in its fullness—not taken to be static and Greek, but, more in the direction of Hegel, dynamic and modern—without being able to put it into a formula. Ever starting anew, he tried to paraphrase Being, to evoke it by allusion: no longer understanding being as isolated from time, as a static condition, but as an occurrence in time, that which is not motionless, abstract, or a mere empty formula, but a happening, establishing, controlling, unhinderedly ordaining, uncovering and concealing, enduring and elusive fullness and liveliness. Being as the all-encompassing and luminating basic happening, which is not effectual by the grace of humanity, but through itself, and carries its meaning in itself. Briefly, Being understood as "Being in becoming."

Are Eastern Buddhism and modern Western philosophy of Being thereby reconciled at the highest philosophical or even religious level? Here, I believe, is where the question must be theologically sharpened: if one can speak in this manner about Being—as something which again and again reveals itself anew through the Nothingness; if, as in Heidegger, Being can be testified to only by means of almost mystical words and images, divine attributes, and metaphors—what distinguishes it from God? More precisely: if *Nothingness, through which Being* reveals itself throughout, is *the veil of Being*, is then the Being which belongs to humans, for whose truth we are set upon the path as wanderers and whose human history fate determines, not indeed *the veil of God*?

Just as the question of *differentiation* poses itself within the framework of the concept of Being for Western philosophy, so in Buddhism the same question poses itself in the context of the concept of Emptiness. And Masao Abe makes it welcomely clear that the traditional Buddhist position stands in need of clarification, completion, or correction with respect to two points:

1. It is important—in spite of the mutual pervasions of past and present—to take *history* seriously: its direction with respect to each new event.

2. It is important—in spite of all dissolutions of opposites—to maintain the distinction of good and evil and to establish an *ethic*.

Given this, according to Abe, it is important for contemporary Buddhism to set out on a serious and urgent task:

1. How to connect the principle of *free will* with the understanding of Emptiness: how can Emptiness, an undetermined spontaneity, accept a personal God in its unlimited openness? Abe has recourse at this point to the aspect of compassion, which Emptiness exhibits along with an aspect of wisdom: in its emptying of self, Sunyata concentrates on this special center of compassion, which in Buddhism is called the promise or vow, which should flow out of every "act" and "deed."

2. How the directions, the linearity of time, which is essential for an understanding of history and which in Buddhism, in comparison with Christianity, Marxism, and even Leninism comes decidedly too abruptly, can be connected with the understanding of Emptiness. Here, also, Abe refers to the aspect of compassion in Emptiness: as matters stand, not all people are enlightened. It is the task of the enlightened ones to help the numerous unenlightened people to attain enlightenment—an obviously endless process which necessitates, however, the progression of history: indeed, no eschatology or teleology of history in the Christian or Western sense, yet—within the context of a completely dynamic Emptiness—a realized eschatology and an open teleology.

I cannot set forth this solution in detail here: Buddhists themselves must first of all judge whether the synthesis is successful from the Buddhist standpoint. For my part, I would like to throw out one more basic question: What is actually the highest truth, what is the ultimate Reality in Buddhism? Is it Sunyata for all schools of Buddhism?

SUNYATA—THE CENTRAL CONCEPT OF BUDDHISM?

Is it really true, historically true, that, despite significant cultural variations in world Buddhism, from the true primitive Buddhism of the first centuries Emptiness was accepted as ultimate reality, as the ultimate truth, as the Dharma? Sunyata, as it is well known, appears in only a few passages of the Pali canon. That it became the central concept for the Madhyamika, which is therefore called the Sunyavada, is a clear indication of a *major paradigm shift in Buddhism.*

Nagarjuna was the one who *conjoined Emptiness to pratitya-samutpada* and both to the Middle Path, understood now as a critical-dialectical negation of both and all conceptual extremes. For the first time, in the *Madhyamka-karika* (and this is the genius of Nagarjuna):

> What is caused and conditioned,
> That is Emptiness;
> That is *pratitya-samutpada;*
> And that is the Middle Path.

In the history of paradigm shifts in Buddhism, in this matter of continuity and discontinuity of ideas, we have here an interesting case of a continuity of ideas, but in a radically new configuration (an equation of these four items not found earlier, not even in the *Prajnaparamita*).

It is difficult to overlook the fact that in the Buddhist tradition Emptiness is used also in another sense. And this new approach finds expression already in a work formally ascribed (in the broad sense) to Madhyamika, in the *Mahayana-Uttaratantra*, composed by a philosopher named Saramati around 250 C.E. (or later). And at the center of his vision is the Supreme Being, "spotless, luminous spirit." Different terms are often used here to characterize the Absolute: "suchness" (*tathata*), "element of dharma" (*dharmadhatu*), "element of the buddhas" (*buddhadhatu*). In this way, the Yogacara doctrine (whose actual founder is Maitreyanatha, ca. 300 C.E. and Asanga, 4th century), resulted in a new kind of "Buddhology," that is, a new understanding of the true nature of the Buddhas. Their real nature is identical to the Absolute. They have, apart from their "changing body" (*nirmanakaya*), that is, the form of their earthly appearance, a heavenly mode, the "pleasure body" (*sambhogakaya*), and finally the "doctrinal body" (*dharmakaya*), which is their true essence, identical with the Highest Being.

It would be not only a different paradigm, but a different religion, if with all the discontinuities of a paradigm change we would not see some continuity, if despite all variables we would not have some constants. And what would be a Buddhism without refuge to the Buddha, refuge to the Dharma, refuge to the Sangha? Would it be more than some more or less religious philosophy à la late-Heidegger or late-Wittgenstein? Are not all sutras supposed to be "Buddha-vachana," words of the Buddha?

In short, Sunyata has also to be seen in the context of the macroparadigm changes which I tried to analyze in my book *Christianity and the World Religions.* Not only significant cultural variations, but the epochal change of an "entire constellation of beliefs, values, techniques shared by a given community,"[9] affects radically the refuge in the Buddha, in the

Dharma, and in the Sangha, and determines also the notion of Sunyata. If I am not mistaken, Masao Abe did not propose Buddhist Ultimate Reality as all Buddhists would understand the term, but as it is understood in a very specific Buddhist paradigm: in the Madhyamika as interpreted by a specific Zen philosophy.

All this leads now, after this plea for a fair hearing of all Buddhist paradigms, to more constructive elaborations in view of the Buddhist-Christian dialogue.

But there is no stifling the critical question—what is a Buddhist supposed to make of talk about an Ultimate Reality, when each and every thing is "empty" and emptiness is somehow everything. Can we talk concretely, or do we go around in circles? So we come back to what is likely the most difficult point in Buddhist-Christian dialogue, which some see as an unbridged abyss.

TWO BUDDHIST OPTIONS
WITH REGARD TO ULTIMATE REALITY

One of the main difficulties posed again and again by dialogue about the central concepts of Buddhism is that they are interpreted by Buddhists themselves in quite different, indeed diametrically opposite ways. We can see this with nirvana, and now with the concept of Emptiness, which is understood very differently even by the first two great philosophical schools of Mahayana Buddhism. Here, it seems to me, we have especially *two* options to consider, of which Masao Abe primarily considered the first.

The first option: Anyone who wishes to can understand "Emptiness" with Nagarjuna and the Madhyamikas as primarily *negative.* In that case, all the beings and facts of everyday life, seen from a distance, are "empty," because they come into being and pass away, neither exist nor do not exist, and in any case "are" not. Thus all positive statements are impossible; the question of an Ultimate Reality, which is not simply identical with this world of passing phenomena, is false and perfectly useless, a projection, a fiction, an illusion. Where does that leave us?

Well, Masao Abe will probably object: Emptiness may not be all negative. Things come into being and pass away. As such they are empty. As such they are there. Emptiness is "suchness," *tathata.* But that positive note is, it seems to me, rather weak. And it is no accident that Madhyamika is known as Sunyavada, that Hindus and even Buddhists had charged it—at least with the appearance of—nihilism. Whatever clever dialectical objection you might have, Madhyamika is tied to what we would call a "mystical philosophy." This is because *prajna* is said to be nondiscursive and Emptiness is said to be known *ultimately* through intuition—and not just by the dialectical critiques which, like Kant's or Hegel's, a diligent student can ultimately learn without necessarily intuiting Emptiness.

My question is: If, according to Abe, "Emptiness" may not be understood nihilistically as Nothing, then why is there anything at all, rather than nothing? This is the fundamental philosophical question not only for Leibniz, but also for Heidegger about "the marvel of marvels": "Why is there any Being at all—why not, far rather, Nothing?" In other words, are these beings and facts possibly empty, do they possibly have no being, precisely because they are altogether not their own source but are identical, in varying ways, to the one Absolute? This is the teaching not just of a poor "dualist" Christian theology, but also of the second (later) great Mahayana school of Yogacara, which answered some important questions which the Madhyamika did not answer (e.g., that of the origin of this world of appearances), which was a crucial factor in East Asian (and Tibetan) Buddhism and which even today governs the more "theological" Japanese understanding of the doctrines of original Buddhism.

The second option: This, too, is an authentically Buddhist position— anyone who wishes can interpret "emptiness" *positively* with the Yogacara school. In fact, its has been said that Yogacara, with its interest in the *alaya-vijnana* (storehouse consciousness), often identified with the Ultimate Reality or "suchness" (*tathata*), was precisely such a reaction to the seeming "negativism" of Madhyamika. And it is no accident that there rose a new interest in a *positive* Buddha Nature, that the Sutra of Queen Shrimala (*Shrimaladevi Sutra*) specifically identifies an *Asunya* (Not-Empty). I am not saying that *asunya* negates *sunya* necessarily. I am only saying that there is more than one way to present the Ultimate Reality, and that the best way for me is to present it dialectically. And that to say there is God or an *Adi-Buddha* may hardly contradict Emptiness or *pratitya-samutpada*. In that case, all beings and facts are forms of expression of the one ineffable Highest Being, which also is real. Now, of course, the question of the one true Ultimate Reality which is obviously more than just this world of conditioned co-arising (*pratitya-samutpada*), which is rather the spotless, luminous, pure spirit, which constitutes the facts and even the Buddhas as their "element"—stands at the center of attention.

No one will ever get an advocate of Yogacara to call this question useless or even falsely put. No wonder the fusion of the Madhyamika and Yogacara traditions was already under way during the heyday of Yogacara in India, and the "new" (but from the Indian standpoint most ancient) notion of the Absolute prevailed. Because, insofar as they did not fall victim to total skepticism, Nagarjuna's successors made one thing clear: All these negations include an affirmation. Denial is not the end but the means of discovering the hidden reality, the transcendent ground of everything and at the same time the true nature of things as the norm for true and false. Nagarjuna's great critic, the Vedanta philosopher Shankara (eighth century), who learned so much from him that he has been called a "crypto-Buddhist," thought it consistent to proceed from the "emptiness" of the world of appearances to the true being of Brahman. Shankara in turn was corrected, as we know, by Ramanuja, who defended a modified nondualism, a differentiated unity of the Absolute and the world which is very near to the classical Christian position. And even though the Buddhists themselves rejected a "Brahman," or "God," the majority in no way flatly objected to a transcendence which is immanent. I think there are Buddhists who accept the term "panentheism," and maybe they would accept also the term proposed by Masaharu Anesaki and Theodore Stcherbatsky: "cosmotheistic."[10] All these notions of Buddhist transcendence are not as far away from the Christian concept of Ultimate Reality as many imply.

AN EASTERN-WESTERN UNDERSTANDING OF GOD

Maybe also Masao Abe could agree with this vision: *Nirvana, Emptiness, Dharmakaya do, in fact, manifest qualities of an Ultimate Reality:* a different dimension within phenomena, a truly religious dimension, true reality. Nirvana, Emptiness, Dharmakaya have, in fact, brought about a twilight of the gods or idols: they have supplanted the Hindu gods as the supreme authority, yet they have not put any other gods—not even the Buddha—in their place. Nirvana, Emptiness, and Dharmakaya appear in this sense as parallel terms for the Ultimate Reality. Their function is analogous to that of the term "God." Would it, then, be wholly impermissible to conclude that what Christians call "God" is present, under very different names, in Buddhism, insofar as Buddhists do not refuse, on principle, to admit any positive statements?

What is, according to Christianity, the one infinite reality at the beginning, in the middle, and at the end of the world and humanity? Based on what I have developed in *Christianity and the World Religions,* I would like to attempt to answer in a single complex proposition:

If God is truly the "Ultimate Reality," then God is *all these things in one:*
    Nirvana, insofar as God is the goal of the way of salvation;
    Dharma, insofar as God is the law that shapes the cosmos and humanity;

Emptiness, insofar as God forever eludes all affirmative determinations; and the *Primal Buddha,* insofar as God is the origin of everything that exists.

Discourse about the Ultimate Reality that is not at the same time discourse about the ineffability of the Ultimate Reality easily turns into idle talk. Discourse about the Absolute is adequate only so long as it is conducted in the awareness of the dialectic of gripping and releasing, speech and speechlessness, language and silence, with utmost discretion in the face of what is not determined by the factitious "mysteries" of the theologians, but *is simply the secret heart of this reality.* And actually, silence before this hidden reality is often the most appropriate demeanor, a silence which comes from the negation that the East so urgently insists on and that is not continually being drowned out by the affirmations to which the West is undoubtedly inclined.

Language, to be sure, is a barrier. Yet language can break down barriers. Language limits, but it can also remove limits and open the way to the ever greater mystery, for which Nicholas of Cusa used the term *coincidentia oppositorum,* the "synthesis of opposites," *the* distinctive mark, as it were, of the Ultimate. Could it be that from this point we can make out a structural similarity between that "Emptiness" which, for Buddhists, transcends all opposites, and that "pleroma," that infinite "fullness" which embraces all opposites?

How, then, can we try to think adequately about the Ultimate? In such a way, at all events, that it simultaneously transcends and permeates the world and humanity: infinitely far and yet closer to us than we are to ourselves, intangible even though we experience its presence, present even when we experience its absence, affirmative through all negations. An Ultimate that pervades the world and still does not merge with it, that encompasses it but is not identical with it: transcendence in immanence. Every statement about Ultimate Reality would, in this approach, have to pass through the dialectic of negation and affirmation. Every experience of Ultimate Reality would have to survive the ambivalence of nonbeing and being, dark night and bright day.

NOTES

The background of this essay can be found in Hans Küng, *Christianity and the World Religions: Paths to Dialogue with Islam, Hinduism, and Buddhism* (New York: Doubleday, 1986).

1. Friedrich Nietzsche, *Werke in drei Baendan,* vol. 2, ed. Karl Schlechta (Munich: Carl Hanser, 1955), pp. 205, 227.

2. Ibid., p. 127.

3. Ibid., p. 115.

4. Ibid., pp. 901–38.

5. Ibid., p. 1141.

6. Hans Küng, *Does God Exist?*, tr. Edward Quinn (New York: Doubleday, 1980), pp. 613–15.

7. Hans Küng, *The Incarnation of God* (Edinburgh: T. & T. Clark, 1987).

8. G. W. Friedrich Hegel, *Wissenschaft der Logik*, ed. Georg Lasson (Leipzig: Felix Meiner, 1923), pp. 66f; see "Becoming," in *Science of Logic*, vol. I, tr. W. H. Johnston and L. G. Struthers (New York: The Macmillan Company, 1929).

9. Thomas S. Kuhn, *The Structure of Scientific Revolutions*, 2d ed. (Chicago: University of Chicago Press, 1970).

10. Theodore Stcherbatsky, *The Conception of Buddhist Nirvana* (Delhi: Banarsidass, 1978), p. 55.

8

Beyond Buddhism
and Christianity:
"Dazzling Darkness"

MASAO ABE

In his response, "God's Self-Renunciation and Buddhist Emptiness: A Christian Response to Masao Abe,"[1] Hans Küng raises a number of crucial issues for the Buddhist-Christian dialogue. Due to the
restriction of space, however, I would like to limit myself to answering
the following three questions that I believe to be the most essential.
First, is Abe's approach a true dialogical hermeneutic? Second, is the
idea of the kenosis of God himself truly Christian? Third, is Sunyata the
central concept of Buddhism?

In response to the first question, Hans Küng argues:

> There is no question: Masao Abe's basic intention is dialogic. He iso-
> lates key concepts from Christian texts, which he then transplants into a
> Buddhist context, where the concept of kenosis is understood not simply
> as ethical, exemplary humiliation, but is recast as ontological emptying,
> an emptying of God himself, yes, ultimately as Emptiness in general, Sun-
> yata. In this manner, as a Buddhist, he discovers his own world—even on
> foreign, Christian soil. Just as the Christian authors earlier gave a Chris-
> tian exegesis of Greek or Buddhist texts, so also Abe gives a Buddhist
> exegesis of the Christian texts.
>
> (p. 214)

Hans Küng concludes that my interpretation of the kenotic passage
in Philippians is "a Buddhist exegesis of the Christian texts" in that it isolates key concepts from Christian texts and transplants them into a Buddhist context. Is this understanding of my interpretation of the hymn in
Philippians and the subsequent discussion of the kenosis of God a fair

and pertinent one? My basic intention in this regard is not to impose Buddhist categories upon the Christian context and then to formulate a "Buddhist" exegesis of the Christian texts. Instead, I have tried to understand the Christian texts, in the present case relative to the concept of kenosis, from within a Christian framework, as much as this is possible.

Nevertheless, I have offered a new interpretation that differs from the traditional orthodoxy (1) because I cannot be completely satisfied with the traditional interpretation and (2) because, in order to cope with the challenge by contemporary antireligious ideologies, a new interpretation is urgently needed today. In this connection, I have tried to understand the Christian notion of kenosis by deepening the spirituality of Christianity without at the same time distorting Christianity. Careful readers of my interpretation (pp. 31–50), I hope, will not fail to recognize this intention.

Although I am a Buddhist, I hope my readers will dispel the presupposition that my discussion and interpretation of Christianity is a "Buddhist" exegesis. I sincerely hope that my discussion of Christianity will be judged not in terms of whether it is Buddhistic or not, but in terms of whether or not it is in accord with Christian spirituality. The interreligious dialogue may adequately and effectively take place if both sides of the dialogue try to grasp the other side's spirituality from within, without imposing its own ontological and axiological categories.

In "Kenotic God and Dynamic Sunyata," which considers the Epistle to the Philippians (2:5–8), I emphasized that "Christ's kenosis [self-emptying] signifies a transformation not only in appearance but in substance, and implies a radical and total self-negation of the Son of God" (p. 32). I also argued that in the kenosis of Christ, "it is not that the Son of God *became* a person through the process of his self-emptying, but that fundamentally [Christ] *is* true person and true God at one and the same time in his dynamic work and activity of self-emptying" (p. 33).

Taking one step further, I insisted that if Christ the Son of God empties himself, should we not consider the possibility of the self-emptying of God, that is, the kenosis of God the Father? Is it not that the kenosis of Christ—that is, the self-emptying of the Son of God—has its origin in God "the Father"—that is, the kenosis of God? Without the self-emptying of God "the Father," the self-emptying of the Son of God is inconceivable. This is why I stated:

> In the case of Christ, kenosis is realized in the fact that one who was in the form of God emptied "himself" and assumed the form of a servant. It originated in the will of God and the love of God, which is willing to forgive even the sinner who has rebelled against God. It was a deed that was

225

accomplished on the basis of God's *will*. On the other hand, in the case of God, kenosis is implied in the original *nature* of God, that is, love.

(p. 37)

Criticizing Karl Rahner's understanding of the self-emptying of God as still leaving behind traces of dualism, I argued:

> If God is really unconditional love, the self-emptying must be total, not partial. It must not be that God *becomes something else* [Rahner's words] by partial self-giving, but that in and through total self-emptying God *is* something—or more precisely, God *is* each and every thing. This emphasis, however, should not be taken to signify pantheism. . . . On the contrary, only through this total kenosis and God's self-sacrificial identification with everything in the world is God truly God. Here we fully realize the reality and actuality of God, which is entirely beyond conception and objectification. This kenotic God is the ground of the kenotic Christ. The God who does not cease to be God even in the self-emptying of the Son of God, that is, the kenosis of Christ, is not the true God.

> (pp. 38–39)

This is the point of my understanding of the kenotic God. Does this understanding indicate, as Hans Küng suggests, that I take the concept of kenosis "not simply as ethical, exemplary humiliation, but is recast as ontological emptying, an emptying of God himself, yes, ultimately as Emptiness in general, Sunyata" (p. 214)? Because the *nature* of God is *love*, an emphasis on the self-emptying of God as his dynamic nature does not necessarily indicate an "ontological" interpretation at the expense of the "ethical" meaning of the Son of God's self-emptying. And, in my understanding, I am *not* trying to "replace" the kenotic God of Christianity "by the all-inclusive (dynamic) Emptiness (Sunyata) of Buddhism," as Hans Küng suggests.

Everything in my understanding and interpretation of the idea of kenosis is based on the most fundamental tenet of Christianity, namely, that "God is love" (1 John 4:8). If God is really all-loving, God does not have the Son of God emptying himself without God himself ceasing to be God the Father. Again, if God is really an all-loving God, he is not self-affirmative, but self-negating, not self-assertive, but self-emptying, and becomes *das Nichts* by completely identifying himself with everything in the universe, including the most sinful man. This understanding may not be the same as the traditional Christian understanding, but it is not correct to characterize it as a "Buddhist" interpretation, as Hans Küng suggests, because my understanding arises from reflection on this central Christian definition, "God is love."

Second, is the kenosis of God himself truly Christian?

Rejecting the notion of the kenosis of God as unbiblical, Hans Küng strongly maintains:

> In the entire New Testament . . . nowhere is there mentioned an incarnation or a renunciation (kenosis) of God himself; the Philippian hymn only speaks of a kenosis of Jesus Christ, the Son of God. Furthermore, this kenosis is not understood as a permanent status, position, relationship, but as a humiliation occurring in a unique, historical life and death on the cross.
>
> (p. 213)

It is clear that an explicit literal reference of kenosis can be found only in the Philippians passage. This does not, however, mean that the concept of kenosis is a limited or special one in the New Testament. Second Corinthians 8:9 (RSV) conveys the same idea as the Philippians passage:

> For you know the grace of our Lord Jesus Christ, that though he was rich, yet for your sake he became poor, so that by his poverty you might become rich.

This idea of kenosis or condescension can also be found in John 3:13, 16:28, 17:5, and Romans 15:3. A New Testament scholar states: "We should recognize that the *kenosis* motif is not confined to any one or two, or more passages, but is the underlying theme of the New Testament. The very incarnation assumes a condescension."[2]

The crucial issue of our present dialogue is not, however, the kenosis of the Son of God, but the kenosis of God himself. In this regard, Hans Küng argues:

> Certainly, the self-sacrifice of the Son does not occur against the will of the Father. God desires the redemption of humanity and so also the self-sacrifice of Jesus. Still, God the Father does not give himself up, but his Son (the church condemns the monophysitic "patripassianism"), and so God the Father (*ho theos*) does not die upon the cross, but the man, Jesus of Nazareth, the Son of God. Only he, not God himself, is (according to the dying words of Jesus quoting Psalm 22:1 [Vulgate 21:1]) forsaken by God! Jesus being forsaken by God is, according to the New Testament, no divine "paradox," but human agony crying to heaven.
>
> (pp. 213–14)

Thus Hans Küng's attitude toward the kenosis of God is basically the same as that of the early church. With this understanding of God who is impassible and immutable, how does Hans Küng understand the problem of evil, especially the problem of the Holocaust at Auschwitz? Because of the contemporary human predicament, the theological climate has been considerably changed. In this regard we should not overlook the following remarks by Karl Rahner, a leading Catholic theologian of our time.

> If it is said that the incarnate Logos died only in his human reality, and if this is tacitly understood to mean that this death therefore did not affect God, only half the truth has been stated. The really Christian truth has been omitted. . . . Our "possessing" God must repeatedly pass through the deathly abandonment by God (Matthew 27:46; Mark 15:4) in which alone God ultimately comes to us, because God has given himself in love and as love, and thus is realized, and manifested in his death. Jesus' death belongs to God's self-utterance.[3]

Through a uniquely trinitarian interpretation of the Christ event, Jürgen Moltmann also emphasizes the death of God's Fatherhood in the death of the Son.

> When one considers the significance of the death of Jesus for God himself, one must enter into the inner-trinitarian tensions and relationship of God and speak of the Father, the Son and the Spirit. . . . The Christ event on the cross is a God event, and conversely, the God event takes place on the cross of the risen Christ. Here God has not just acted externally in his unattainable glory and eternity. Here he has acted in Himself and has gone on to suffer in Himself. Here He Himself is love with all His being. So the new Christology which tries to think of the death of Jesus as the death of God must take up the elements of truth which are to be found in *kenoticism* (the doctrine of God's emptiness of himself). . . . In the forsakenness of the Son the Father also forsakes himself, though not in the same way. . . . The Son suffers dying, the Father suffers the death of the Son. The grief of the Father here is just as important as the death of the Son. The fatherlessness of the Son is matched by the Sonlessness of the Father, and if God has constituted himself as the Father of Jesus Christ, then he also suffers the death of his Fatherhood to the death of the Son. Unless this were so, the doctrine of the trinity would still have a monotheistic background.[4]

Although I have some disagreement with and criticisms of Karl Rahner's and Jürgen Moltmann's interpretation of the kenosis of God (pp. 37–50), I deeply sympathize with them because to me the kenosis of God as understood by them deeply accords with the spirituality of Christianity. In this regard, Hans Küng raises a very crucial question to the notion of the kenotic God, one that must be properly answered by a kenotic theologian.

> The stumbling block of a (Buddhist or Christian) Christology (and trinitarian doctrine) which completely identifies Jesus with God and brazenly

declares Jesus' death to be the death of God is made strikingly clear in the case of the resurrection: such a Christology cannot explain who brought this supposedly dead God back to life.

(p. 214)

The answer is dependent on how the notion of kenosis is to be understood. If kenosis is merely understood as a humiliation or condescension in terms of self-emptying, the question that Küng raises above is naturally inevitable and its answer must be negative; that is, there is no living God who could have brought Christ back to life. But the Philippian hymn clearly shows that kenosis includes not only the humiliation of the Son of God but also the *exaltation* of the Son of God. Precisely as a result of his humiliation, Christ was raised to a place higher than before. Thus, quoting the following words from *The Interpreter's Bible:* "The way he took was that of self-denial and entire obedience, and so acting he won his sovereignty."[5] I clearly recognized the inseparability of the state of humiliation and the state of exaltation in the event of Christ's death on the cross. Self-emptying is nothing but self-fulfillment. Thus my answer to the above question is affirmative: God the Father and God the Son glorify each other through an inverse correspondence, through an "other-self affirmation via own-self negation."

In this connection, we must not overlook the following passages in the book of Colossians, about which it is unclear how much attention Hans Küng pays in his current discussion: "For in him [Christ] all the fulness (*pleroma*) of God was pleased to dwell" (1:19, RSV); and "For in him the whole fulness (*pleroma*) of deity (*theotetos*) dwells bodily" (2:9, RSV). These passages clearly show that the fullness of God dwells in Christ, especially in bodily form. It was God's pleasure that all of his fullness should dwell in Christ in order that through Christ, God might "reconcile to himself all things, whether on earth or in heaven, making peace by the blood of his cross" (1:20, RSV).

As I said earlier, in Jesus Christ the state of humiliation and the state of exaltation are inseparable; kenosis and pleroma are inseparable. Now the most crucial question is *how* they are inseparable. Does the state of humiliation come first and then the state of exaltation follow afterwards? Is kenosis a cause and pleroma an effect or result? Such a temporal or causal understanding of the inseparability of these twin sides of the same reality is nothing but a conceptualization or an objectification of the two sides without existentially and religiously committing oneself to the midst of the event. It is an outsider view, not an insider view. For an insider, committing one's self religiously to faith in Jesus Christ, the state of humiliation and the state of exaltation are not two different states but a single, dynamic one; that is, humiliation as it is is

exaltation, and exaltation as it is is humiliation; kenosis as it is is pleroma, and pleroma as it is is kenosis. Each pair in these two sets of
biconditional terms is dynamically nondual through mutual and simultaneously reciprocal negation. How is this dynamic identity of the
"as-it-is-ness" of humiliation and exaltation, kenosis and pleroma, possible? It is possible because the dynamic identity is based on the kenotic
God the Father, who is self-emptying and unconditional love, and ultimately on the Godhead who is neither *essentia* nor *substantia,* but *Nichts*
or *Ungrund* (pp. 48–50).

Thus, in concurrence with Moltmann I stated:

> The death of Jesus on the cross is not a divine-human event, but most cer-
> tainly a trinitarian event of the Father, the Son, and the Spirit. What is
> important in this regard is the total, personal aspect of the sonship of
> Jesus. This sonship of Jesus, however, is ultimately rooted in *Nichts* or
> *Ungrund* as the Godhead in "the unity of three persons in one God." Only
> here . . . can we say with full justification – as Moltmann does – that "in
> the cross, Father and Son are most deeply separated in forsakenness and
> at the same time are most inwardly one in their surrender." Again, only
> here – when the sonship of Jesus is understood to be ultimately rooted in
> *Nichts* as Godhead – can the event of the cross of Jesus be understood
> truly as the event of an unconditioned and boundless love fully actualized
> for the Godless or the loveless in this law-oriented society.
>
> (pp. 48–49)

In this way I understand Godhead as *Nichts* or *Ungrund,* which is
exemplified by Christian mystics such as Meister Eckhart and Jakob
Böhme. Is my interpretation of God as *Nichts* "a Buddhist exegesis of the
Christian texts," or "the renunciation of God himself in Buddhist Sunyata," or a replacement of the kenotic God "by the all-inclusive (dynamic) Emptiness (Sunyata) of Buddhism," as Hans Küng suggests? (I also
came to understand God as *Nichts* through my critique of Hans Küng's
statement "God in the Bible is subject and not predicate: it is not that
love is God, but that God is love – God is one who taces me, whom I can
address" [p. 49]).

At this point we must turn to the third question, that is, is Sunyata the
central concept of Buddhism? In this connection, Hans Küng raises (a)
the question of Being and Nothingness and then (b) the problem of Sunyata as Buddhism's ultimate Reality, and finally (c) the issue of an
Eastern-Western understanding of God.

BEING AND NOTHINGNESS

Referring to Hegel and Heidegger, Hans Küng points out an affinity and difference between them and Buddhism (pp. 215–17). Unfortunately, his point of discussion is not so clear to me, so I would like to present my own view of this question. As Hans Küng correctly points out, for Hegel neither pure Being nor pure Nothing is true, and only Becoming as their unity (*Einheit*) or unseparatedness (*Ungetrenntheit*) is their truth. In his *Science of Logic*, Hegel argues:

> The truth is not their lack of distinction, but they are not the same, that they are absolutely distinct, and yet unseparated and inseparable, each disappearing immediately in its opposite. Their truth is therefore this movement, this immediate disappearance of the one into the other, in a word, Becoming: a movement wherein both are distinct, but in virtue of a distinction which has equally immediately dissolved itself.[6]

This is strikingly similar to Buddhist understanding of Being and Nothing. However, as I pointed out elsewhere:

> Despite Hegel's emphasis on the unseparatedness and material passing over (*übergehen*) of Being and Nothing, it cannot be overlooked that in his system Being is prior to Nothing. In Hegel the beginning (*Anfang*) of everything is Being as such, and his dialectical movement develops itself in terms of Being (thesis), Nothing (antithesis), and Becoming (synthesis). In this way, Being as such is the supreme principle of Hegel's metaphysical logic. In so far as Being is thus given priority over Nothing, however dialectical "Becoming" as the unity may be, it is not a genuine Becoming but a quasi-Becoming which is after all reducible to Being because in Hegel Becoming is a synthesis of Being and Nothing in which "Being" is always the thesis. In addition, by asserting that there is a final synthesis, his system cuts off all further development: it swallowed up the future and time itself. For all its dynamically fluid, dialectical character, his system is consistently formulated in an irreversible, one-directional line with Being as the beginning.[7]

By contrast, in Buddhism Being has no priority over Nothingness; Nothingness has no priority over Being. There is no irreversible relation between Being and Nothingness. Thus "Becoming"—to use this term— in Buddhism is not a *synthesis* that presupposes duality of Being and Nothingness with priority given to Being, but is instead a complete *inter*dependence and *inter*penetration among everything in the universe— that is, *pratitya-samutpada* or dependent co-origination. "Becoming" in Buddhism is grasped in terms of *pratitya-samutpada* and, as such, is completely free from irreversibility and from any sort of priority of either contrary, being or nonbeing, over the other. Dependent co-origination is not *Werden* in Hegel's sense, which is a synthesis of Being and its conceptual contrary, Nothing. Dependent co-origination is neither Being nor Nothing, nor even Becoming.

SUNYATA AS BUDDHISM'S ULTIMATE REALITY

Hans Küng raises a very basic question that any Buddhist thinker must answer: "What is actually the highest truth, what is the ultimate Reality in Buddhism? Is it Sunyata for all schools of Buddhism?" (p. 217). Then he points out various paradigm shifts in the history of Buddhism from the primitive Buddhism to Madhyamika and Yogacara schools in which such key notions as Nirvana, Sunyata, and Dharmakaya have been interpreted differently. This historical fact makes the question "What is the ultimate Reality in Buddhism?" difficult.

In this connection we must first clearly realize an essential difference between Christianity and Buddhism in understanding "Ultimate Reality." Christianity also underwent various paradigm shifts in its history, but the Ultimate Reality has always been believed to be "God." And as Paul emphasizes, "One God and Father of us all, who is above all and through all and in all" (Eph. 4:6, RSV). God is believed to be "one" absolute God. This monotheistic character of God is the underlying theme of all forms of Christianity regardless of their historical diversity. By contrast, Buddhism is fundamentally free from the monotheistic character. Rejecting the age-old Vedantic notion of Brahman as the sole reality underlying the phenomenal world, Gautama Buddha advanced the teaching of *pratitya-samutpada*, that is, dependent co-origination in which everything in and out of the universe, without exception, is interdependent, co-arising and co-ceasing; nothing exists independently. Even the ultimate does not exist by itself. Rather, this complete interdependency itself among everything in the universe is understood as "ultimate Reality" in Buddhism. It is often called "not one, not two" because it is neither monotheistic nor dualistic. The diversity within Buddhism is bigger than that in Christianity, because Buddhism has no single volume of canon like the Bible in Christianity, and instead of talking about one absolute God, Buddhism takes *pratitya-samutpada* and Sunyata, that is, Emptiness, as the ultimate Reality.

The diversity of understanding of ultimate Reality in Buddhism should not be judged by Christian standards. It is rather natural in Buddhism that even such key concepts as *pratitya-samutpada*, Nirvana, Sunyata, and *tathata* (suchness) have been grasped differently.

Buddhism, and particularly Mahayana Buddhism, based on the idea of sunyata or anatman, developed itself freely and richly according to the spiritual climate of the time and place into which it was introduced. Thus, throughout its long history in India, China, and Japan, Buddhism produced many divergent forms that are radically different from the original form of Buddhism preached by Sakyamuni. Nevertheless, they were not driven out from the Buddhist world, but became spiritual foundations from which new spirits of Buddhism emanated. In this connection it may be interesting to note that one Buddhist scholar regards the history of Buddhism as "a history of heresy," meaning by this that Buddhism has developed itself by means of heresy and by continually embracing various heresies.

In the West, where Mahayana Buddhism in China and in Japan is relatively unknown, people are apt to judge the whole of Buddhism by taking the "original" form of Buddhism preached by Sakyamuni as their standard. Such a static view fails to appreciate the dynamic development of Buddhism. The diversity and profundity of the history of Buddhism, especially of Mahayana, is no less rich than the whole history of Western philosophy and religion. It is a development coming out of the inexhaustible spring of sunyata or *tathata* (suchness). Yet this "history of heresy" in Buddhism has evolved without serious bloody inquisitions or religious wars. There is no equivalent to the European Crusades in the history of Buddhism.

Even though, as I said earlier, it is rather natural for Buddhists to employ such key concepts as *pratitya-samutpada*, Nirvana, Sunyata, and *tathata* differently at different times in the history of Buddhist thought, we must fully realize with Hans Küng that

> there is no stifling the critical question—what is a Buddhist supposed to make of talk about an Ultimate Reality, when each and every thing is "empty" and emptiness is somehow everything. Can we talk concretely, or do we go around in circles?

(p. 219)

Hans Küng correctly emphasizes that "Sunyata has also to be seen in the context of the macroparadigm changes" (p. 218) of Buddhist thought. Thus he refers to Nagarjuna's *Madhyamaka-karika* and to the Yogacara doctrine as the two main trends in the history of Mahayana Buddhism. In this connection, Hans Küng severely criticizes my approach to the issue of the Buddhist ultimate Reality.

> If I am not mistaken, Masao Abe did not propose Buddhist Ultimate Reality as all Buddhists would understand the term, but as it is understood in

233

a very specific Buddhist paradigm: in the Madhyamika as interpreted by a specific Zen philosophy.

(p. 219)

I admit the precision of his criticism and the limitation of my approach to the issue. I did not pay due attention to the Yogacara doctrine and other schools of Buddhism particularly, when I discussed Sunyata as ultimate Reality in Buddhism. This is because I thought (and still do think) that with respect to the Buddhist-Christian dialogue in which we are now engaged, what is needed is not a detailed discussion of the doctrine of, say, Sunyata within the various schools of Buddhism, but a self-critical view of Sunyata as the ultimate Reality underlying Mahayana Buddhism as a whole. What is also needed is that each participant in the Buddhist-Christian dialogue represent his or her own religion, not merely intellectually or as based on doctrine, but existentially as well. By doing so, each participant may spiritually clarify the essence of his or her religion through a personal existential commitment. Without speaking from such an existential commitment, the interfaith dialogue may be apt to be merely conceptual and superficial. A self-critical existential commitment on the part of each dialogue partner is essentially necessary because interfaith dialogue today must take place not merely between the two religions in question, but in the face of challenge by the current antireligious idealogies prevailing in our society that seriously question the *raison d'être* of religion itself. My existential, and not merely intellectual, approach to interfaith dialogue probably gives Hans Küng the impression that "Masao Abe did not propose Buddhist Ultimate Reality as all Buddhists would understand the term, but as it is understood in a very specific Buddhist paradigm: in the Madhyamika as interpreted by a specific Zen philosophy" (p. 219).

Now, we must answer Hans Küng's basic question, What is ultimate Reality in Buddhism? Hans Küng himself rightly mentions two Buddhist options with regard to ultimate Reality. According to him, the first option is to understand "Emptiness" with Nagarjuna and the Madhyamikas as primarily *negative*, whereas the second option is, with the Yogacara school, to interpret "Emptiness" *positively*. It is true that Madhyamika and Yogacara understand "Emptiness" differently, but I am afraid that it is an oversimplification to state, as Hans Küng does, that Madhyamika understands Emptiness negatively whereas Yogacara understands it positively.

In his book *Madhyamika and Yogacara*, Gadjin Nagao, a renowned Buddhologist of Japan today, states:

Presently (by modern scholars) the Madhyamika philosophy . . . is believed to be wholly inherited by Maitreyanatha, Asanga, and other Yogacaras. The Prajnaparamita sutras are equally revered as authentic by both schools, and further, the doctrine of emptiness occupies an important position in the Yogacara school.[8]

Of course, Nagao recognizes the difference between Madhyamika and Yogacara in their understanding of Sunyata:

> Is it proper to speak of the logical process involved in establishing sunyata as the same in both schools? Isn't it that, although the name sunyata is shared by both, what is intended by this name is entirely different in the two schools? For one thing, their points of departure differ: the Madhyamika starts from pratitya-samutpada, while the Yogacara starts from abhuta-parikalpa (unreal imagination). Another remarkable difference is that the Yogacara speaks of the "existence of non-existence" when defining sunyata. We must also pay attention to the fact that, although both the Madhyamikas and the Yogacaras are thought to base their idea of sunyata on the Prajnaparamita sutras, the Yogacaras also place importance on the *Culasunnata-sutta* of the Majjihima-nikaya.[9]

Before becoming involved in detailed discussion of the difference between Madhyamika and Yogacara, it is important for our purpose of answering the question, What is ultimate Reality in Buddhism? to explore the true meaning of "sunyata" underlying both schools, Madhyamika and Yogacara, in contrast to the Abhidharma view of Sunyata, which the Mahayana Buddhists tried to overcome.

In early Buddhism, the theory of dependent co-origination and the idea of emptiness were still naively undifferentiated. It was Abhidharma Buddhism that awakened to a particular philosophical understanding of emptiness and set it up in the heart of Buddhism. But the method of its process of realization was to get rid of concepts of substantiality by analyzing phenomenal things into diverse elements and thus advocating that everything is empty. Accordingly, Abhidharma Buddhism's philosophy of emptiness was based solely on *analytic* observation; hence it was later called the "analytic view of emptiness."[10] It did not have a total realization of the emptiness of phenomenal things. Thus the overcoming of the concept of substantial nature or "being" was still not thoroughly carried through. Abhidharma fails to overcome the substantiality of the analyzed elements themselves.

But beginning with the *Prajnaparamita-sutra*, Mahayana Buddhist thinkers transcended Abhidharma Buddhism's analytic view of emptiness, erecting the standpoint that was later called the "view of substantial emptiness." This was a position that did not clarify the emptiness of phenomena by analyzing them into elements; rather, it insisted that all phenomena were themselves empty in principle and that the nature of phenomenal existence itself is empty of substantial, perduring content. With respect to everything that is, the *Prajnaparamita-sutra* emphasizes "not being, and not not being." "Isness" is not to be equated with "being," nor with the negation of "being." This sutra clarified not only the negation of being, but also the position of the double negation—the negation of nonbeing as the denial of being—or the negation of the negation. It thereby disclosed "Emptiness" as free from both being and nonbeing. That is, it revealed *prajna*—wisdom.

It was Nagarjuna who gave this standpoint of Emptiness as found in the *Prajnaparamita-sutra* a thorough philosophical foundation by drawing out the implications of the mystical intuition seen therein and developing it into a complete philosophical realization. Nagarjuna criticized the proponents of substantial essence of his day who held that things really exist in a one-to-one correspondence with concepts. He said that they had lapsed into an illusory view that misconceived the real state of the phenomenal world. He insisted that with the transcendence of the illusory view of concepts, true Reality appears as *animitta* (no-form, or nondeterminate entity). But Nagarjuna rejected as illusory not only this "eternalist" view, which took the phenomena to be real just as they are, but also rejected the opposite "nihilistic" view that emptiness and nonbeing are true reality. Nagarjuna thereby took the standpoint of Mahayana Emptiness, an independent standpoint liberated from every illusory point of view connected with either affirmation or negation, being or nonbeing, and called that standpoint the *Middle Way*.[11]

Nagarjuna's idea of the Middle Path does not indicate a midpoint between the two extremes as the Aristotelian idea of *to meson* might suggest. Instead, it refers to the way that *transcends every possible duality* including that of being and nonbeing, affirmation and negation. Therefore, his idea of Emptiness is not a mere emptiness as opposed to fullness. Emptiness as Sunyata transcends and embraces both emptiness and fullness. It is really formless in the sense that it is liberated from both "form" and "formlessness." Thus, in Sunyata, Emptiness as it is is Fullness, and Fullness as it is is Emptiness; formlessness as it is is form, and form as it is is formless.[12]

Hence, the well-known passage in the Heart Sutra (*Prajnaparamita-hrdaya-sutra*):

> Form is emptiness and the very emptiness is form; emptiness does not differ from form; form does not differ from emptiness; whatever is form, that is emptiness; whatever is emptiness, that is form.

As the Heart Sutra clearly indicates, the realization that "form is emptiness," however important and necessary it may be, is not sufficient; it must be immediately accompanied with the realization that "the very emptiness is form" and those two realizations are one, not two. In later Chinese Buddhism one encounters the saying "True Emptiness is Wondrous Being." This phrase indicates not only the dynamic identity of nonbeing and being, negation and affirmation, but also the recovery and reestablishment of being out of nonbeing.

In this connection, there are two more points that are important for adequately understanding the notion of Sunyata. First, although Sunyata is an ontological or metaphysical concept established by Nagarjuna to indicate ultimate Reality, it is also unmistakably a practical and religious ideal. In Nagarjuna and Madhyamika, as in Buddhism in general, meditation is of cardinal importance, and Sunyata or Emptiness was recognized as an object of meditation. The same is the case with respect to Yogacara. As Nagao argues, "The Yogacara who, as the name suggests, was greatly concerned with yoga-praxis, inherited the Nagarjunian notion of Emptiness, and, when they elucidated features of yoga-praxis such as the six paramitas, the ten bhumis, and so on, Emptiness seems to have been the basis of their theories."[13] Second, although the realization of Emptiness is essential, one should not *cling to* Emptiness as Emptiness. This is why Mahayana Buddhism has throughout its long history rigorously rejected the attachment to Emptiness as a "confused understanding of Emptiness," a "rigid view of nothingness," or a "view of annihilatory nothingness." In order to attain true Emptiness, Emptiness must empty itself: Emptiness must become non-Emptiness (*asunyata*). Because Emptiness is non-Emptiness, it is ultimate Emptiness (*atyanta-Sunyata*).

Precisely because true Emptiness is Emptiness that "empties" even itself, true Emptiness is absolute Reality that makes all phenomena, all existents, truly *be*, and stand forth. This is a Buddhist answer to the question, Why is there anything at all, rather than nothing?

The existential realization that true Emptiness "empties" itself indicates that ultimate Reality is not a static state that is objectively observable but a dynamic activity of *emptying* in which everyone and everything is involved. Indeed, there exists nothing whatsoever outside of this dynamic whole of *emptying*. You and I are involved in this dynamic whole of *emptying*. You are Emptiness and Emptiness is you.

Although the term "Sunyata" or "Emptiness" sounds negative, the true meaning of Sunyata is positive and affirmative. So Sunyata is regarded as the synonym for *mahayama pratipad* (The Middle Path), *tathata* (Suchness), *dharmakaya* (Body of Truth), and so forth. In the

237

Prajnaparamita sutra, ultimate Reality is called *prabhasvaram cittam* (the spotless, luminous, pure mind), and, in the latter Madhyamika and Yoga-cara schools, Sunyata is compared with *prabhasvaram cittam.*[14] I myself use the term "boundless openness" (p. 53) to make the point that Sunyata is completely free from any kind of centrism — not only from egocentrism but also from anthropocentrism, cosmocentrism, and even theocentrism.

Boundless openness is unobjectifiable; "it" cannot be thought to have a center that occupies a position relative to other points on a perimeter, for there is no perimeter, and therefore no center relative to a perimeter. It is like a circle whose center is everywhere but whose circumference is nowhere, to borrow a well-known metaphor from Christian mysticism. The state of boundless openness is the state of complete emptyingness. When realized existentially, this state or standpoint is a complete emancipation from any kind of bondage resulting from discrimination based on any kind of centrism.

AN EASTERN-WESTERN UNDERSTANDING OF GOD

At the end of his response, "God's Self-Renunciation and Buddhist Emptiness," Hans Küng seeks for a structural similarity between Buddhist "Emptiness" and Christian "pleroma" under the title "An Eastern-Western Understanding of God." I highly appreciate and share his *intention,* but I cannot completely agree with his *conclusions.*

Correctly understanding that Nirvana, Emptiness, and Dharmakaya are parallel terms for the Buddhist conception of ultimate Reality, Hans Küng argues:

> Their function is analogous to that of the term "God." Would it, then, be wholly impermissible to conclude that what Christians call "God" is present, under very different names, in Buddhism, insofar as Buddhists do not refuse, on principle, to admit any positive statements?
>
> (p. 221)

I have no objection to this argument, and, because I do not refuse, on principle, to admit any positive statements, I fully admit that "what Christians call 'God' is present, under very different names, in Buddhism." But I have some reservation with respect to the remainder of his argument:

> What is, according to Christianity, *the one infinite reality* [my emphasis] at the beginning, in the middle, and at the end of the world and humanity? . . . If God is truly the "Ultimate Reality," then God is *all these things in one.*
>
> (p. 221)

Thus he mentions *Nirvana, Dharma, Emptiness,* and *the Primal Buddha* as Buddhistic parallels to the Christian notion of God. I must part from Hans Küng when he talks about God as "the one infinite reality at the beginning, in the middle, and at the end of the world and humanity," however. For it seems to me that Hans Küng believes that infinite or ultimate Reality must be *one.* (Elsewhere he talks about "the question of the one true Ultimate Reality" [p. 220].) His Judaic-Christian understanding of Ultimate Reality is monistic or monotheistic. In Buddhism, however, the ultimate does not begin with a conception of *one* infinite reality but rather with the *denial* of the conception of one infinite reality. This is clearly seen from the fact that Gautama Buddha did not accept the age-old Vedantic notion of *Brahman* as the sole reality underlying the phenomenal universe and which is identical with *Atman* as the unchangeable substantial self. Instead, the Buddha advocated *pratitya-samutpada* or dependent co-origination and *Anatman* (no-self). The Buddha's doctrines constitute a rejection of monism or monotheism and imply an epistemic awakening to the boundless openness in which everything, including the one and the many, the divine and the human, is grasped as completely interdependent and interpenetrating. Because the Buddha was dissatisfied with monotheism as an expression of the nature of ultimate Reality, it is quite natural that the realization of Sunyata or Emptiness arose from this Buddhist context as the ultimate Reality beyond a monotheistic standpoint.

Buddhism is neither monistic nor monotheistic, neither polytheistic nor pantheistic. Buddhism may be called *panentheism,* however, because immanence and transcendence are dynamically identical. The key point in this respect is that immanence and transcendence are identical through the negation of negation, that is, the negation of immanence and the negation of transcendence. Transcendence and immanence, the one as opposed to the relative many, the finite and infinite, are diametrically opposed to each other, and yet through the negation of negation, they are realized as dynamically identical. Ultimate Reality relates to itself through the bottomless ground of its own ultimacy or unconditionality by negating itself from with itself, by emptying itself of its own infinite unrelatedness and embracing the form of its own self-negation. The form of ultimate Reality's own unconditional self-negation exists or stands forth as its own mirror image and opposite, that is, as the relative many. This dynamic identity of the finite and infinite, of the transcendent and immanent, and so forth, is realized through the function of ultimate Reality's relating to itself through its own boundless openness or *Ungrund.* This function is the principle of the self-emptying of Emptiness itself, both within and through itself. This self-relating function is

239

the unobjectifiable principle of the self-negation of ultimate Reality within and through its own timeless unobjectifiability. It is this dynamic principle of the self-negation of the boundless Whole within itself that sets up an "inverse correspondence" between the two faces of this self-interrelating Whole, between, namely, the finite and infinite, or the primal one and the relative many. The dynamic identity of the finite and infinite, of the transcendent and immanent, is realized through the inverse correspondence made possible through the realization of Emptiness that is beyond and yet inclusive of all conceptual binaries.

Inverse correspondence is not in any way a pantheistic concept; rather, it is a concept belonging to a functionalist ontology and takes its full meaning only alongside of the notion of the principle of self-transcendence via internal self-negation, or self-affirmation through self-negation, of the unobjectifiable Whole itself. This is what is meant by *dynamic* Sunyata.

Quoting Nicholas of Cusa's notion of *coincidentia oppositorum*, Hans Küng suggests a structural similarity between the Buddhist "Emptiness" and the Christian "pleroma" (pp. 221–22). However, unless the Christian notion of "pleroma" is freed from the monotheistic structure, I do not see "a structural similarity" between "Emptiness" and "pleroma," even though both concepts can be said to transcend and embrace all opposites in their respective manner. As I said before, "Emptiness" as the ultimate Reality in Buddhism is not monotheistic, nor pluralistic, nor pantheistic. But the Buddhist notion of ultimate Reality is panentheistic in that immanence and transcendence are totally and dynamically identical through mutual negation. Through "trans-descendence," ultimate Reality is at once interrelational and boundlessly open in all directions. There is no single center in any sense—even in the theocentric sense—and thus "coincidentia oppositorum" is fully and completely realized. "Emptiness" is not the one infinite reality nor one absolute God but *Nichts* in the sense of the absolute No-thingness that is beyond and yet embraces both being and nothingness. It is right here that everything, including all of nature, human, nonhuman, and divine, is realized just as it is, each in its individual and relational suchness.

On the other hand, in Christianity, the real "pleroma" or "fullness" of God is identical with the real "kenosis" or "self-emptying" of God himself, a kenosis that is total, not partial. Only through the realization of the total kenosis of God himself is the real "pleroma" of God fully realized.

Only in the kenotic God can kenosis as-it-is be dynamically one with pleroma, and pleroma as-it-is be dynamically united with kenosis. Only in the kenotic God can humiliation as-it-is be exaltation, and exaltation as-it-is be humiliation. I believe that this dynamic identity of kenosis and pleroma indicates the ultimate Reality in Christianity. However, if the notion of kenosis is applicable only to the Son of God, but not to God himself, that is to say, if God is understood *not* to empty himself even in the self-emptying of the Son of God, then the above dynamic identity of kenosis and pleroma, humiliation and exaltation, cannot be fully realized. "Ultimate Reality" is then only realized in a limited sense, unless grasped in its essential activity of total self-abnegation or self-immolation for the sake of being "all-in-all." Otherwise, "ultimate Reality" still retains a monotheistic sense and is only one-sidedly transcendent. However, if one breaks through the monotheistic framework and realizes the kenosis of God himself, ultimate Reality as the dynamic identity of kenosis and pleroma is fully realized. It is right here that the basic tenet of Christianity, "God is love," is completely fulfilled. Once freed from its monotheistic and theocentric character, Christianity not only becomes more open to the interfaith dialogue and cooperation without the possibility of falling into exclusivism, but it also becomes compatible with the autonomous reason peculiar to modern humanity and will be able to cope with the challenge by Nietzschean nihilism and atheistic existentialism. The future task of Christianity is to open up the monotheistic framework through the full realization of the kenosis of God himself and to realize ultimate Reality as the dynamic unity of kenosis and pleroma.

The dialectic identity of kenosis and pleroma, self-emptying and self-fulfillment, may be compared with "dazzling darkness," a term employed by Pseudo-Dionysius the Areopagite.[15] It does not mean that God as the ultimate Reality is half dazzling and half dark. Instead, it indicates that God is fully dazzling and fully dark at one and the same time. That is to say, being dazzling as-it-is is darkness; being dark as-it-is is dazzling. This dialectical identity as the ultimate Reality is possible only when God is understood to be completely kenotic or self-emptying and not One as a monotheistic unity, nor one nor two nor three, but as *Nichts* or *Ungrund*.

Now with respect to Buddhism, the traditional static view of Sunyata must also be broken through and interpreted dynamically—not as the static *state* of emptiness, but as the dynamic *activity* of emptying everything, including itself. In Sunyata, form is ceaselessly emptied, turning into formless emptiness; and formless emptiness is ceaselessly emptied, and therefore forever freely taking form. For this reason the Heart Sutra emphasizes: "Form is Emptiness and the very Emptiness is form." Here we may also quote the Mahayana Buddhist expression: "Samsara as-it-is is Nirvana; Nirvana as-it-is is samsara." These statements are nothing but verbal expressions of the Buddhist ultimate Reality, which may very well be compared with "dazzling darkness." Darkness (samsara) as-it-is is dazzling (nirvana); the Dazzling (nirvana) as-it-is is darkness (samsara). Again, in order properly to understand the Buddhist ultimate Reality as "dazzling darkness," one must clearly realize "self-emptying Emptiness" by breaking through the traditional view of Sunyata. The future task of Buddhism is to realize how this self-emptying Emptiness concentrates itself into a single center in the boundless openness, a center that is the locus of the real manifestation of personal deity and the ultimate criterion of ethical judgment and value judgment in general (pp. 80–84).

As Hans Küng rightly states, "Every statement about Ultimate Reality would . . . have to pass through the dialectic of negation and affirmation. Every experience of Ultimate Reality would have to survive the ambivalence of nonbeing and being, dark night and bright day" (p. 222). In full agreement with his statement, I would like to present the idea of "dazzling darkness" as the common symbol of the ultimate Reality in Buddhism and Christianity, the meaning of which can be realized only by going beyond the traditional formulations of the doctrines and practices of both Buddhism and Christianity.

> God is "dazzling darkness"
> because in God, who is the infinite love,
> self-emptying as-it-is is self-fulfillment,
> self-fulfillment as-it-is is self-emptying.
>
> Sunyata is "dazzling darkness"
> because in Sunyata, which is boundless openness,
> samsara as-it-is is nirvana,
> nirvana as-it-is is samsara.

NOTES

1. This essay first appeared as a response to Abe's "Kenosis and Emptiness," in *Buddhist Emptiness and Christian Trinity*, ed. Roger Corless and Paul F. Knitter (Mahwah, N.J.: Paulist Press, 1990), pp. 24–43. "Kenotic God and Dynamic Sunyata" is a revised and expanded version of "Kenosis and Emptiness."

2. Jennings B. Reid, *Jesus, God's Emptiness, God's Fullness: The Christology of St. Paul* (Mahwah, N.J.: Paulist Press, 1990), p. 67.

3. Karl Rahner, *Sacramentum Mundi*, vol. 2 (London: Burns and Oates, 1969), pp. 207f.

4. Jürgen Moltmann, *The Crucified God* (New York: Harper & Row, 1974), pp. 204, 205, 243.

5. *Interpreter's Bible*, vol. 11 (New York: Abingdon Press, 1955), p. 50.

6. G. W. Friedrich Hegel, "Becoming," in *Science of Logic*, vol. 1, tr. W. H. Johnston and L. G. Struthers (London: G. Allen & Unwin, 1929), p. 95; *Wissenschaft der Logik*, ed. Georg Lasson (Leipzig: Felix Meiner, 1923), p. 67.

7. Masao Abe, *Zen and Western Thought* (London and Honolulu: Macmillan and University of Hawaii Press, 1985), p. 85.

8. Gadjin M. Nagao, *Madhyamika and Yogacara* (New York: State University of New York Press, 1991), p. 189.

9. Ibid., p. 199.

10. In the T'ien-t'ai Sect, the view of emptiness of Hinayana Buddhism is called the "analytic view of emptiness," and the view of emptiness in Mahayana Buddhism is called the "view of substantial emptiness."

11. The material in the preceding paragraphs is taken from my book *Zen and Western Thought*, pp. 83–95, with some adaptation.

12. Ibid., p. 127.

13. Nagao, *Madhyamika and Yogacara*, pp. 51–52.

14. As seen in the text *Madhyantavibhaga Bhasya*, ed. Gadjin Nagao (Tokyo: Suzuki Research Foundation, 1964), 1.22c.

15. *The Complete Works of Pseudo-Dionysius*, tr. Colm Luibheid (New York: Paulist Press, 1987), pp. 135–37. Evelyn Underhill, *Mysticism* (New York: New American Library, 1974), p. 347.

9

God's Love and
the Kenosis of the Son:
A Response to Masao Abe

WOLFHART PANNENBERG

The secularist spirit of modern culture poses a challenge not only to the Christian faith, but to all religions in that it affirms the self-sufficiency of human autonomous existence with regard to all religious claims that human life and even the world of nature are in need of both some divine ground of their existence and some form of salvation. The challenge is that, according to that secularist mentality, there is no need for any religion. Masao Abe was indeed right in stating that "the most crucial task of any religion in our time is to respond to these antireligious forces by elucidating the authentic meaning of religious faith" (p. 25).

With regard to Christianity, the challenge is not so much from autonomous reason, as Abe assumes when he says, "the conflict between divine revelation and human reason has been a persistent problem" (p. 60). In early Christian history, the alliance between the Christian message and Greek rationality was one of the main factors that contributed to the final success of the Christian message in the ancient world. The Christian claim to universality could not have been articulated without that alliance with reason. What has been called the conflict between reason and revelation was a specific phenomenon of modern Christian history, when a truncated conception of reason, which cut itself off from its metaphysical origins, came to attack a Christian supernaturalism that no longer displayed the openness to rational insight and inquiry that once belonged to the glory of Christian patristic theology. Unfortunately, an important trend in modern theology met the challenge of modern autonomous reason not on the level of rational argument, but by a retreat to some form of irrational commitment. But that was unnecessary. In the basic challenge of modernity to the Christian faith, the core issue has been the conception of a self-contained and self-sufficient human subjectivity as the ultimate basis of experience and behavior. It is this idea of a self-contained human subjectivity and of its claim to unrestricted freedom of choice that is at the heart of modern secularism. On this issue, Masao Abe made the pertinent remark that "unlike most of Western philosophy, Christianity regards human free will negatively as the root of original sin" (p. 61).[1] Actually, the Christian idea of freedom is not identical with that of unlimited individual choice. Rather, the Christian idea of freedom corresponds to what is discussed in contemporary thought under the name of authentic identity, an identity that we must seek, for it is not already possessed by nature. This is not something we create for ourselves, though choice is certainly a prerequisite for such authentic freedom. Modern Christian theology, and especially Protestant theology, has been neglecting this challenge to a large extent. I consider this the most fatal weakness of modern Christian apologetics. Most modern Protestant theologians were all too ready to consider the modern idea of freedom as part and parcel of the Christian heritage. It is at this point where, from my perspective, the encounter with Buddhism could be most helpful to the Christian theologian. Concerning the human situation of estrangement—as pointed out by Keiji Nishitani—interreligious dialogue between Christianity and Buddhism can discover large areas of common ground. That the true human self is not the self-centered ego that we know from the average reality of human behavior is an insight that the two religions can share. In an earlier dialogue with Masao Abe, I stressed that point. When it comes to the question of ultimate reality, however, the situation becomes much more difficult, and we must beware of easy solutions.

The first issue, of course, has to be whether in the Buddhist perspective there is any ultimate reality at all, distinct, if not separate, from the finite reality of human beings and animals and physical processes. In a Christian view, the ultimate reality of God is clearly different, though not separate, from the finite reality of the creatures. Certainly, God is not only transcendent, but also immanent, because he is intimately present to his creatures. But nevertheless, the divine reality surpasses the finite reality of his creatures. Now the question is whether the dynamic Sunyata Buddhists are talking about also surpasses the everyday reality of finite things and processes. It is not important, at this point, whether or not that reality is personal in character. It might have the nature of an encompassing field rather than of a personal agent. At this first step, that is not the issue. The issue is whether beyond the finite things and processes and beyond their universal interrelatedness there is an ultimate reality distinct though not separate from the fleeting world of finite phenomena.

On this issue, I felt more confident with other Buddhist authors—like Nishitani—than with Masao Abe. As soon as it is clear that ultimate reality surpasses each and every finite being or process and also the interrelated totality of them, then one can go on by turning to the question of whether or not that ultimate reality is to be understood as personal or impersonal. At this point, although the Christian will insist that there is some personal aspect of that ultimate reality, Christians should not exclude the impersonal or superpersonal aspect of it. That could develop into an interesting dialogue. But in the case of Masao Abe, I am not sure that we share the presupposition for such a dialogue in talking about ultimate reality. He says that "if Sunyata is conceived as *somewhere outside of* or *beyond* one's self-existence, it is not true Sunyata," because then it would be conceived as something in contrast to something other (p. 50). I could use the same Hegelian language in talking about God, if one expression be added: God is not only to be "conceived as somewhere outside of or beyond"; "not only," because God is not only transcendent, but also immanent. But God is not only immanent either. I did not find a statement in Abe's essay that would unequivocally clarify this point. Therefore I understand the interpretation offered by Donald Mitchell that Abe in fact "posits this world as the locus of ultimate reality." In that case, there would be no genuine transcendence to ultimate reality, however related to the world of finite existence. Thus Mitchell goes on to say that Buddhist enlightenment, according to Masao Abe, "is not a realization of something beyond this world but of the true nature of the very things in this world, including ourselves."[2] And indeed, Abe not only says, as the Christian mystic can also say, that in the act of enlightenment we are in Sunyata, but also says, "We *are* Sunyata in each and every moment of our lives" (p. 52). One might wonder, then, whether finally there is a difference of ultimate importance between enlightened existence and ignorant life.

If the quoted sentences actually expressed Masao Abe's vision, then some of his other language about Sunyata would sound somewhat mystifying. He writes, "Sunyata is not self-affirmative, but *thoroughly* self-negative" (p. 51). This statement expresses a self-reference, though a negative one. What is the self, then, that is referred to in this phrase? The next sentence continues: "emptiness not only empties everything else but also empties itself." There is again the idea of self-reference. And three sentences further down one reads that true Sunyata is "the pure activity of absolute emptying." Thus we have an activity of iterated negation that is characterized by self-reference. This sounds as if Sunyata was conceived of as an active principle. But in another place Masao Abe speaks of Sunyata as an "agentless spontaneity," and he says that there is "no agent but the act and its consequences" (p. 63). But how is it possible, then, that there is self-reference in the sense of self-emptying? If there were no such self-reference, how could the negation of the negative have positive content and make "everything exist as it is and work as it does" (p. 57)? And to what extent is Sunyata as an activity different from a mere process, say, the all-pervading process of change? If there is no self-referential agent abiding in the process of negativity, how can one possibly speak of a "compassionate aspect of Sunyata" and of "wisdom realized in Sunyata" (p. 86)?

It is important to keep in mind what Masao Abe says about Sunyata in order to appreciate his interpretation of the Christian idea of kenosis and its application to the Christian doctrine of God. For when Paul said that Jesus Christ "emptied himself" in entering into our human condition (Phil. 2:7), the self-reference expressed in that phrase is to be taken literally: there is an agent, of whom it is said that he emptied himself. Abe says this "should not be understood to mean that Christ was *originally* the Son of God and *then* emptied himself and became identical with humans." Rather, the doctrine should be understood "to mean that Christ as the Son of God is *essentially* and *fundamentally* self-emptying or self-negating" (p. 33). I agree with Masao Abe on this issue, even with regard to the trinitarian relations in the eternal life of God. The apostle, of course, was not talking about the Trinity, but about Jesus Christ. And according to the more persuasive exegesis of this difficult passage,[3] Paul did not talk about the event of incarnation in the beginning of Jesus' life history, but about the character of this history as a whole: it was characterized by emptying himself and by humbling himself in becoming obedient unto death (Phil. 2:8). This whole life history, Paul wanted to say, was at the same time in unity with the eternal life of God. Therefore, I agree with Abe that not only the later christological doctrine, but Paul himself, wanted to say that Christ as the Son of God is essentially and fundamentally self-emptying. But Paul also wanted to say that in this process of self-denial Jesus Christ continued to be the Son of God. The self-emptying does not mean that he ceased to be the Son of God, as Abe seems to imply when he demands an understanding of Christ's kenosis "as complete and thoroughgoing" (p. 32). To the contrary, Jesus manifests himself to be the Son of God by emptying himself.

We must pay attention a little more closely to what Paul meant in this passage. He started by saying of Jesus Christ that "though he was in the form of God, [he] did not count equality with God a thing to be grasped" (Phil. 2:6, RSV). This sentence was meant to evoke the contrast with the behavior of Adam in the biblical story of the Fall: Adam wanted to be like God, and he hoped to become like God by grasping for the apple. In the case of Jesus, it was the reverse: he was in fact like God, sharing in his divine life, but he did not consider this something to be grasped and to be kept for himself. Rather, he emptied himself, as the following sentence in Philippians says, by taking the form of a servant and becoming one like us. That is to say, he did not identify himself with God the Father, but accepted his own existence as a human being distinct from that of the Father, an existence in obedience to the Father even when that obedience led to his own death.

We take from this description first that it is not said that Jesus ceased to be the Son of God. Second, the self-denial does not deny everything. It does not deny obedience to the Father, but, to the contrary, that obedience is kept uncompromisingly. Third, and of most importance, the emptying activity never denies the Father, but serves him.

This leads to another issue raised by Abe. He claims that the kenosis of Christ "inevitably leads" to the idea of a kenosis of God himself (p. 36). Now it is one thing to say that the self-emptying obedience of Christ has its "origin in God" the Father (p. 37), because after all the Father commissioned the Son with his mission to the world. But it is quite another thing to speak of a self-emptying activity on the part of the Father himself. With regard to this second idea, there is not the slightest evidence in Paul's letter to the Philippians, nor in any other place in the New Testament. Nowhere is it said that the Father emptied himself, and in no way is it a logical implication of the self-emptying action of the Son. To the contrary, this kenotic action on the part of the Son is described as obedience to the Father and thus presupposes the identity of the Father and of his commission to the Son.

Now Masao Abe is not to be blamed for this unwarranted generalization of the idea of kenosis, because he could feel encouraged in this interpretation by a number of Christian theologians who suggested such a generalization before. How are we to explain this tendency when there is no scriptural evidence for such a generalized idea of kenosis? Even in connection with the Son, that idea occurs only in the one place of Paul's letter to the Philippians and nowhere else in the entire New Testament. How, then, can we account for the tendency to generalize that idea?

The answer can be found in the combination of the idea of kenosis with the Christian concept of love in the sense of agape, which is not selfish love, but other-directed benevolence. In contrast to the notion of kenosis, the concept of love is indeed pervasive in the New Testament. In contrast to kenosis, furthermore, the concept of love is explicitly applied to, even identified with, God the Father: God himself is love (John 1:4, 8, 16). That he even gave and surrendered his Son is evidence of God's love for the world (John 3:16), and Paul concurred with John in the affirmation that in the death of Christ God expressed his love for the sinner, because Christ died for us (Rom. 5:8). Here the association of the idea of self-abnegation is close at hand, and that explains how the idea of kenosis could be generalized by identifying it with love.

But some observations are appropriate here. First, on the part of kenosis, that concept in Philippians 2:7 is not connected with love for the world, but with obedience to the Father (Phil. 2:8). On the other hand, the love of the Father as mentioned in John and Paul certainly involves an element of sacrifice, but the Father does not surrender himself, for he surrenders his Son. This certainly shows that love can be costly, even for God the Father, but it does not imply his self-abnegation. If so, it would have been disastrous with regard to the Son, because the Father, if he had emptied himself, could have no longer employed his omnipotence to raise the crucified one from the dead. Thus the concept of love is not exhausted by the motif of self-abnegation. The love of the Father for the Son is elective love when in the baptism of Jesus the voice from heaven says, "This is my beloved Son, with whom I am well pleased" (Matt. 3:17, RSV). It comes to the rescue of the Son when the Father raises him from the dead. Likewise, the love of the Son for the Father is expressed in his obedience, in full accord with the sh'ma Israel where it says, "you shall love the LORD your God with all your heart, and with all your soul, and with all your might" (Deut. 6:5, RSV).

Thus the biblical concept of love is very rich and complex. It is not equivalent with self-abnegation or kenosis. The redemptive love of God includes an element of sacrifice, though the Son is sacrificed, not the Father. On the part of the Son, his kenotic self-abnegation is not directly related to the world, but to the Father in expressing his obedience to him, though by way of that obedience the Son shares in the redemptive love of the Father for the world. We have a somewhat complex structure here, and the element of kenosis is only one among others and only on the part of the Son. Therefore, with regard to the inner-trinitarian life, one should not speak of a mutual kenosis, though there is a mutual devotedness of Father, Son, and Spirit in relation to each other as well as a mutual dependence. There is also a self-differentiation on their part in relation to the other persons; but only in the case of the Son does the self-differentiation from the Father become kenotic, and it is only in the incarnation that this kenotic dynamic becomes fully apparent.

The act of creation, therefore, is not a kenotic action of self-abnegation, but an act of God's benevolent sharing of this life. Again, the action of the Holy Spirit in praising the Son and the Father so that all of creation may finally share in the glory of God is not primarily kenotic. Though both creation and glorification, by involving the Son, may also include some kenotic element, one must not blur the important distinctions by reducing the entire action of God in creation, redemption, and glorification (as well as the intertrinitarian life of the triune God) to the notion of kenosis.

My conclusion, then, is that the notion of kenosis is of limited value in Buddhist-Christian dialogue, though I recognize its merit in providing inspiration for the initial phase of that dialogue. Kenosis cannot function as a common denominator in Buddhism and Christianity. This is foreclosed by the fact that in contrast with Buddhist emptiness the Christian idea of kenosis presupposes an agent, the Son, in relation to another agent, the Father, whose action is not kenotic. We have to penetrate to a deeper level in order to find a convergence between Buddhist emptiness and the Christian faith in the trinitarian God. This is the mutuality of love between the trinitarian persons, which can be conceived of as suprapersonal though becoming manifest only in the trinitarian persons. This field of perichoretic love, of mutual indwelling, is the one divine essence that the three persons share and in which the Christian mystic participates by sharing in the sonship of Jesus and thus in his spiritual relation to the Father. The Christian could perhaps recognize in the interconnectedness of everything that there is within the Buddhist concept of Sunyata a distant adumbration of the trinitarian spirit of love, but the latter cannot be reduced to emptiness.

NOTES

1. Abe continues arguing that by contrast Christianity takes "God's free will and God's word positively as the principle of creation, redemption, and last judgment." Here he correctly notices an opposition between Christianity and Buddhism. This opposition, however, need not impair the possible convergence in the description of the human condition. Besides, the application of a notion like "will" to the divine being has been considered by classical Christian theology as merely "analogical"—whatever that means.

2. Donald Mitchell, *Spirituality and Emptiness: The Dynamics of Spiritual Life in Buddhism and Christianity* (New York: Paulist Press, 1991), pp. 55, 56.

3. See Wolfhart Pannenberg, *Systematische Theologie*, vol. 2, tr. Geoffrey W. Bromily (Grand Rapids: William B. Eerdmans, 1994); and J. D. G. Dunn, *Christology in the Making: A New Testament Inquiry into the Origins of the Doctrine of the Incarnation*, 2d ed. (London: SCM Press, 1989), pp. 114–21.

10

God's Total Kenosis and Truly Redemptive Love

MASAO ABE

All humankind is now facing the global age. The East and the West, the North and the South are encountering and intermingling with each other to an extent never experienced before. This does not, however, mean that the world is being united harmoniously. Rather, the difference, opposition, and conflict among various ideologies, value systems, and ways of thinking are becoming more and more conspicuous throughout the world. How can we find a common spiritual ground in this pluralistic world without marring the unique characteristics of each cultural, spiritual tradition? This is the urgent task humankind is now facing. In this regard interfaith dialogue among world religions is extremely important.

In interfaith dialogue the importance of mutual understanding is always emphasized. In my view, however, mutual understanding, though necessary, is not sufficient. "Mutual understanding" implies that both sides of a religious dialogue presuppose the legitimacy of their own religion while asking the other party also to understand their own legitimacy. However, we now exist in a world in which many people question the legitimacy not only of a particular religion such as Christianity, Buddhism, or Judaism, but also of religion as such. Many persons in our present secularized society ask, "Why is religion necessary?" and "What meaning does religion have for us today?" They think that they can live well enough without religion. Moreover, ideologies that *negate* religion prevail in our society. Scientism, Marxism, traditional Freudian psychoanalytical thought, and nihilism in the Nietzschean sense all deny the *raison d'être* of religion not merely on emotional grounds but on various rational or theoretical grounds. Not stopping with criticism of particular religions, these ideologies negate the very being of religion itself. The most crucial task of any religious dialogue in our time is, beyond mutual understanding, to respond to these antireligious forces by elucidating the authentic meaning of religious faith. In order to do so, each religion must break through its traditional formulation of doctrine and practice to deepen its most genuine spirituality. What is needed today is not only mutual understanding but also mutual transformation of the religions involved in dialogue. This is precisely the task of theology in the future.

I understand that thus far Wolfhart Pannenberg shares more or less this same idea with me. In his response, Pannenberg discusses the Buddhist view of ultimate reality as I understand it and criticizes it in comparison with the Christian view of ultimate reality. He also discusses my understanding of the Christian idea of kenosis and criticizes it as inadequate. To me his criticism is not only challenging, but also very crucial for Buddhist-Christian dialogue.

Let me respond to Pannenberg's criticism of my interpretation of Buddhist ultimate reality. As the first issue Pannenberg raises a question, "whether in the Buddhist perspective there is any ultimate reality at all, distinct, if not separate, from the finite reality of human beings and animals and physical process" (p. 245). My answer to this question is "yes" and "no" at the same time. The answer is "yes" because nirvana, which is ultimate reality in Buddhism, clearly transcends samsara, the impermanent, living-dying process of transmigration. The goal of Buddhist life is to attain nirvana by overcoming samsara. Nirvana is the transcendent reality that is permanent, blissfully liberated from transmigration. But the answer to the above question is simultaneously "no" because nirvana as distinct from samsara stands against impermanence and thereby is still related to and linked with impermanence. True nirvana is attained only by emancipating oneself even from nirvana as transcendence of samsara and returning to the process of transmigration. This is the reason I stated elsewhere:

> Throughout its long history, Mahayana Buddhism has always emphasized, "Do not abide in nirvana" as well as "Do not abide in samsara." If one abides in so-called nirvana by transcending samsara, it must be said that one is not yet free from attachment, attachment to nirvana. It must also be said that one is still selfishly concerned with one's own salvation, forgetting the suffering of others in samsara. On the basis of the idea of the Bodhisattva, Mahayana Buddhism thus criticizes and rejects nirvana as transcendence of samsara and teaches true nirvana to be the returning to samsara by negating or transcending "nirvana as the transcendence of samsara." Therefore, nirvana in the Mahayana sense, while transcending samsara, is nothing but the realization of samsara as samsara, no more, no less through the complete returning to samsara itself. This is why, in

Mahayana Buddhism, it is often said of true nirvana that "samsara-as-it-is is nirvana." This paradoxical statement is based on the dialectical character of true nirvana which is, logically speaking, the negation of negation (that is, absolute affirmation) or the transcendence of transcendence (that is, absolute immanence).[1]

Now it is clear that "samsara-as-it-is is nirvana" does not indicate an immediate identity of samsara and nirvana, immanence and transcendence, but a dialectical identity through the negation of negation. In Mahayana Buddhism, true nirvana is not a static state of transcendence but a dynamic movement between samsara so-called and nirvana so-called without attachment to either.

Now, Pannenberg states of Christianity:

> In a Christian view, the ultimate reality of God is clearly different, though not separate, from the finite reality of the creatures. Certainly, God is not only transcendent, but also immanent, because he is intimately present to his creatures. But nevertheless, the divine reality surpasses the finite reality of his creatures.
>
> (p. 245)

I am puzzled by these statements because it is unclear whether Pannenberg is insisting that God is transcendent and immanent at the same time (dialectical identity of transcendence and immanence) or that God is simply transcendent, surpassing finite reality though not separate from it. In this latter case, transcendence has a priority over immanence, though they are not completely separate.

It seems to me that Pannenberg's position is not the former but the latter. That is, he believes that transcendence has a priority over immanence, though they are not separate. If this is the case, a Buddhist must ask, "In Christianity, is God truly immanent in the everyday reality of finite things and process?" though not separate from it, as Pannenberg suggests. Again a Buddhist must ask, "Is it not that the *ultimate* reality of God in Christianity is oriented more by transcendence than by immanence and thus cannot be called *ultimate* reality?"

Next, Pannenberg discusses and criticizes my interpretation of the Christian idea of kenosis. In his response Pannenberg states:

> when Paul said that Jesus Christ "emptied himself" in entering into our human condition (Phil. 2:7), the self-reference expressed in that phrase is to be taken literally: there is an agent, of whom it is said that he emptied himself.
>
> (p. 247)

253

Clearly, there is a self-reference in that phrase. However, the crucial issue is how we are to understand that self-reference. Then, quoting my words Pannenberg states, "Masao Abe says this should not be understood to mean that Christ was *originally* the Son of God and *then* emptied himself and became identical with humans" (p. 247). (I said this because such a view in the temporal order, or the sequential order, is nothing but a conceptual and objectified understanding of the issue, not an experiential and religious understanding.) He continues to quote my words: "Rather, the doctrine should be understood 'to mean that Christ as the Son of God is *essentially* and *fundamentally* self-emptying or self-negating'" (p. 247). To this understanding of mine Pannenberg expresses agreement by writing, "I agree with Abe that not only the later christological doctrine, but Paul himself, wanted to say that Christ as the Son of God is essentially and fundamentally self-emptying" (p. 247). However, immediately following this statement he argues:

> But Paul also wanted to say that in this process of self-denial Jesus Christ continued to be the Son of God. The self-emptying does not mean that he ceased to be the Son of God, as Abe seems to imply when he demands an understanding of Christ's kenosis "as complete and thoroughgoing." To the contrary, Jesus manifests himself to be the Son of God by emptying himself.
>
> (p. 247)

This important point demands careful consideration. First, did Paul want to say that in this process of self-denial Jesus Christ continued to be the Son of God? In the Epistle to the Philippians Paul clearly said:

> . . . Christ Jesus who, existing in the form of God, counted not the being on an equality with God a thing to be grasped, but emptied himself, taking the form of a servant, being made in the likeness of man; and being found in fashion as a man, he humbled himself, becoming obedient even unto death, yea the death of the cross.

Is it not that this self-emptying means a renunciation of the Sonship of God and taking a human form? How is it possible that the act of self-emptying implies the continuity to be the Son of God? As I argued in my essay:

> Inasmuch as the term "form" (*morphei*) in the above passage [of the Epistle to the Philippians] signifies not mere shape or appearance, but substance or reality, so we can say that in Paul's understanding, the Son of God abandoned his divine substance and took on human substance to the extreme point of becoming a servant crucified on the cross. Accordingly, Christ's kenosis signifies a transformation not only in appearance

but in substance, and implies a radical and total self-negation of the Son of God.

(p. 32)

Accordingly, in my view the act of self-emptying must include the substantial discontinuity or the complete abandonment of the Sonship of God. And yet, I would insist together with Pannenberg that "Jesus manifests himself to be the Son of God by emptying himself." But this is not because, as Pannenberg indicates, in the process of self-emptying Jesus Christ continued to be the Son of God. Rather, it is because in his kenosis, Jesus Christ completely abandoned his Sonship. The self-emptying is brought here to self-fulfillment as the savior. Here I see the self-sacrificial love of God in the genuine sense. And this is the reason I formulated the doctrine of Christ's kenosis as follows:

> The Son of God is not the Son of God (for he is essentially and fundamentally self-emptying); precisely because he *is not* the Son of God he *is* truly the Son of God (for he originally and always works as Christ, the Messiah, in his salvational function of self-emptying).

(p. 33)

Accordingly, as Pannenberg points out, the self-reference is expressed in the above passage of the Epistle to the Philippians, but it does not indicate the self-affirmative self of Jesus Christ as an agent, but the self-emptying self of Jesus Christ as an agent. There is an agent who abandoned his Sonship of God and was resurrected as the redeemer. He is not an agent in the ordinary sense. He is an agentless agent, a self-emptying and yet self-fulfilling agent.

Now I would like to respond to Pannenberg's criticism of my understanding of the kenosis of God himself. Referring to my claim that the kenosis of Christ "inevitably leads" to the idea of the kenosis of God himself, Pannenberg argues:

> Now it is one thing to say that the self-emptying obedience of Christ has its "origin in God" the Father, because after all the Father commissioned the Son with his mission to the world. But it is quite another thing to speak of a self-emptying activity on the part of the Father himself. With regard to this second idea, there is not the slightest evidence in Paul's letter to the Philippians, nor in any other place in the New Testament. Nowhere is it said that the Father emptied himself, and in no way is it a logical implication of the self-emptying action of the Son. To the contrary, this kenotic action on the part of the Son is described as obedience to the Father and thus presupposes the identity of the Father and of his commission to the Son.

(p. 248)

255

I know that there is no literal evidence of the self-emptying of God in the New Testament and that traditionally Christian theology generally states that the Son of God became a human without God ceasing to be God. Nevertheless, I have argued for the self-emptying of God himself in addition to the self-emptying of the Son of God for the following two reasons. First, as I said earlier, in our present society religion is challenged by antireligious ideologies and is urgently required to elucidate its deepest spirituality by breaking the traditional formulation of doctrine and practice; a radical new interpretation is needed to cope with the religion-negating ideologies prevailing in our time. Second, even if reinterpretation is necessary, it should not be an arbitrary one but one deeply rooted in the authentic spirit of the religion in question. "God is love" (John 1:4, 8, 16) is the most basic tenet of Christianity. If God is really love, God does not remain God while having the Son of God empty himself. A God who empties himself and becomes completely identical with humanity, including sinful men, is the truly all-loving God. In my understanding, self-emptying or kenosis is not an *attribute* (however important it may be) of God, but the fundamental *nature* of God. The kenosis of the Son of God is based on the *will* of God. It is commissioned by God the Father. But in the case of God the Father, kenosis or self-emptying is implied in the original *nature* of God who is really love.

Pannenberg calls my application of the idea of kenosis of God an "unwarranted generalization." However, I "generalized" the notion of kenosis to God the Father beyond the Son of God simply by basing myself on the Christian fundamental tenet that "God is love." In this regard my approach is not different from Pannenberg's approach when he says "the idea of kenosis could be generalized by identifying it with love" (p. 249). Here Pannenberg himself identifies kenosis with love.

However, toward the end of his essay, Pannenberg makes a rather clear distinction between kenosis and love and states, "It [the biblical concept of love] is not equivalent with self-abnegation or kenosis." Why not equivalent? The reason Pannenberg gives us is that "the biblical concept of love is very rich and complex" (p. 249). How is it rich and complex? Pannenberg argues:

> The love of the Father as mentioned in John and Paul certainly involves an element of sacrifice, but the Father does not surrender himself, for he surrenders his Son. This certainly shows that love can be costly, even for God the Father, but it does not imply his self-abnegation. If so, it would have been disastrous with regard to the Son, because the Father, if he had emptied himself, could have no longer employed his omnipotence to raise the crucified one from the dead. Thus the concept of love is not exhausted by

the motif of self-abnegation. The love of the Father for the Son is elective love.

(p. 249)

If this is the true nature of the love of God the Father in Christianity, it is difficult for a Buddhist to understand. Why must the love of the Father for the Son be *elective* love? Why in his sacrifice does the Father surrender not himself, but only his Son? Is it that God is the truly all-loving God only when he completely abnegates himself and becomes totally identical with humans and nature? Can we not argue that his omnipotence to raise the crucified one from the dead is not lost, but paradoxically fulfilled, through complete self-negation? This is the reason I wrote concerning faith in God:

> God is not a self-affirmative God (for God is love and completely self-emptying); precisely because God is not a self-affirmative God, God is truly a God of love (for through complete self-abnegation God is totally identical with everything, including sinful humans).

(p. 39)

At the end of his essay, Pannenberg makes a distinction between kenosis and love and says, "the element of kenosis is only one among others and only on the part of the Son." Thus he concludes, "the notion of kenosis is of limited value in Buddhist-Christian dialogue. . . . Kenosis cannot function as a common denominator in Buddhism and Christianity" (pp. 249–50). I cannot agree with this negative conclusion for the following two reasons.

First, Pannenberg understands the kenosis of the Son of God as "not connected with love for the world, but with obedience to the Father" (p. 249). And on the part of God the Father, the kenosis of the Son is understood by Pannenberg to imply God's commission to the Son of God that entails his mission to the world. This understanding of kenosis on the level of obedience and commission, I am afraid, is too narrow. For me the notion of kenosis and the notion of love are inseparable. Without kenosis or self-emptying there is no love, and without love, kenosis is inconceivable. Therefore the kenotic dimension is present in the dynamism of the intertrinitarian life of the triune God.

Second, the kenosis of Christ includes not only the humiliation of Christ but also the exaltation of Christ as we see from Paul's own words immediately after the above quotation from the Epistle to the Philippians.

> Therefore also God highly exalted him, and gave unto him the name which is above every name; that in the name of Jesus every knee should bow, of *things* in heaven and *things* on the earth and *things* under earth,

257

and that every tongue should confess that Jesus Christ is Lord, to the glory of God the Father.

(Phil. 2:9–11)

Precisely as a result of his humiliation, Christ was raised to a place higher than before. "The way he took was that of self-denial and entire obedience, and by so acting he won his sovereignty."[2] This point is most impressively stated concerning the person of Christ in Colossians:

For in him all the fulness [pleroma] of God was pleased to dwell.

(Col. 1:19, RSV)

For in him [Christ] the whole fulness [pleroma] of deity [theotetos] dwells bodily.

(Col. 2:9, RSV)

In Christian faith in Christ, the kenosis of the Son of God is not exhausted with the obedience to God the Father, but includes the pleroma, the fullness of God. I am afraid that Pannenberg overlooks this important aspect of the notion of kenosis. And this is strikingly similar to the Buddhist notion of Sunyata, that is, emptiness that is dynamically identical with fullness. Mahayana Buddhism emphasizes "True emptiness is wondrous beings" and "In nothing, everything is contained; limitless – flowers, moon, pavilions . . ."

In conclusion, it is my view that God's total kenosis is neither God's self-sacrifice for something else nor God's self-negation for nihilistic nothingness. Rather, God's total kenosis is God's self-emptying for absolutely "nothing" other than God's own fulfillment as love. Only in God's total kenosis is everything – including the unjust and sinner, and natural and more evil – forgiven, redeemed, and satisfied, and the love of God completely fulfilled. By deepening the religious significance of the Christian notion of the love of God, this notion of the kenotic God can overcome Nietzsche's radicalism, which insists upon the need to "sacrifice God for nothing."

In addition, the notion of the kenotic God opens up for Christianity a common ground with Buddhism by overcoming Christianity's monotheistic character, the absolute oneness of God, and by sharing with Buddhism the realization of absolute nothingness as the essential basis for the ultimate and the self-negating, unselfish love or compassion as the ground of religious life. This can be accomplished through the notion of the kenotic God – not through losing Christianity's self-identity, but rather through deepening its spirituality. This is my humble suggestion to the future of theology from a Buddhist perspective.

NOTES

1. Masao Abe, *Zen and Western Thought* (London and Honolulu: Macmillan and University of Hawaii Press, 1985), p. 178.

2. *Interpreter's Bible*, vol. 11 (New York: Abingdon Press, 1955), p. 50.

CONTRIBUTORS

Masao Abe is Professor Emeritus of Nara University of Education. The most prominent Buddhist participant in contemporary interfaith dialogue, he has taught at various universities in Europe and North America and participated in numerous conferences, including the Theological Encounter conferences he initiated with John B. Cobb, Jr. He has published widely, with *Zen and Western Thought* (1985) standing as his most important work.

David W. Chappell, Professor of Religion at the University of Hawaii at Manoa, completed doctoral studies at Yale University on the Chinese Pure Land Buddhist, Tao-ch'o (562–645). Besides scholarship on Buddhism and Taoism, including *T'ien-t'ai Buddhism: An Outline of the Fourfold Teachings* (1983), he has been the founding editor of the journal *Buddhist-Christian Studies* (1980–) and is the current President of the Society for Buddhist-Christian Studies.

Christopher Ives is Associate Professor of Religion at the University of Puget Sound. His interests include Japanese Buddhist ethics and modern Zen thought in the context of Japanese intellectual and political history. His publications include *Zen Awakening and Society* (1992) and *The Emptying God: A Buddhist-Jewish-Christian Conversation* (coedited with John B. Cobb, Jr.; 1990).

Hans Küng is Professor of Ecumenical Theology and Director of the Institute for Ecumenical Research at the University of Tübingen. He has written numerous books, including *On Being a Christian* (1976), *Does God Exist?* (1980), and *Christianity and the World Religions* (1986). In 1993 he coedited "A Global Ethic: The Declaration of the Parliament of the World's Religions."

Sandra B. Lubarsky is Associate Professor of Religious Studies and Assistant Dean of Graduate Studies at Northern Arizona University. Her interests are in contemporary Jewish theology and dialogue between process theology and modern Judaism. She is the author of *Tolerance and Transformation: Jewish Approaches to Religious Pluralism* (1990) and coeditor of *Jewish Theology and Process Thought* (forthcoming).

Heinrich Ott is Professor of Systematic Theology at the University of Basel with special interests in problems of fundamental (philosophical) theology, hermeneutics, and interfaith dialogue. His two main works are *Die Antwort des Glaubens: Systematische Theologie in 50 Artikeln* (1983) and *Apologetik des Glaubens: Grundprobleme einer dialogischen Fundamentaltheologie* (1994).

Wolfhart Pannenberg is Professor of Systematic Theology at the University of Munich. In addition to his work in theology and interfaith dialogue, he has participated in a number of interdisciplinary conferences, especially in relation to philosophy and the natural sciences. His major works include *Jesus—God and Man* (1964), *Basic Questions in Theology* (1967), *Theology and the Philosophy of Science* (1973), *Anthropology in Theological Perspective* (1983), as well as a three-volume *Systematic Theology* (1988, 1991, 1993).

Richard L. Rubenstein is Robert O. Lawton Distinguished Professor of Religion at Florida State University. First to raise the issues that came to be known as Holocaust Theology, he has published *After Auschwitz: History, Theology, and Contemporary Judaism* (1992), *Approaches to Auschwitz* (with John K. Roth; 1985), and *The Cunning of History* (1975).

Marjorie Hewitt Suchocki is Ingraham Professor of Theology at the School of Theology at Claremont. She is also Vice President for Academic Affairs and Dean. She has written widely in feminist and process theology. Her latest book, *The Fall to Violence: Original Sin in Relational Theology*, was published by Continuum Publishing Company (1994).

Hans Waldenfels S.J. is a Professor of Fundamental Theology, Theology of Religions, and Philosophy of Religion at Bonn University. With primary interests in interreligious dialogue, the Buddhist-Christian encounter, and religion in pluralistic societies, his main works are *Absolute Nothingness* (1980), *Kontextuelle Fundamentaltheologie* (2d ed. 1988), and *Lexikon der Religionen* (2d ed. 1988).

INDEX

8804